Additional Praise fo
Your Dissertatio... Coping with the Emotional, Interpersonal, and Spiritual Struggles

In *Challenges in Writing Your Dissertation: Coping With the Emotional, Interpersonal, and Spiritual Struggles*, Noelle Sterne, PhD, demystifies the dissertation-writing process. She offers practical strategies so this often overwhelming process becomes less intimidating to doctoral candidates. Sterne addresses common fears and hurdles students face when writing and defending their dissertations and provides inspiration and encouragement during this long stressful time. This important resource is a must-read for doctoral candidates. I am recommending *Challenges in Writing Your Dissertation* to my graduate student clients.
—Barbie Carpenter, owner/editor, Carpenter Document Consulting

I am happy to very enthusiastically endorse *Challenges in Writing Your Dissertation: Coping With the Emotional, Interpersonal, and Spiritual Struggles*. My remarks below are intended for the primary audience, graduate students, as well as their families and friends. If you are preparing to advance in a career by earning a master's or doctoral degree, writing an article, or just beginning a scholarly study, you are well served by considering the practical and supportive advice of Dr. Noelle Sterne. Her advice has been honed through thirty years of providing editing assistance and mentoring of more than 900 graduate students and now chronicled in *Challenges in Writing Your Dissertation:Coping With the Emotional, Interpersonal, and Spiritual Struggles.*
Having traveled down this difficult path myself, I can attest that I know firsthand how the maze of unknowns attached to the dissertation can close in on the mind and capture you in a claustrophobic grip of fear. Add family and work pressures to the situation, and completing your goals in a timely manner can often become a life-changing struggle.
In *Challenges in Writing Your Dissertation*, Dr. Sterne addresses students still in the maze. She uses informed anecdotes (with identities protected) to share lessons that have been learned by those who came before you. These lessons will prevent you from reinventing the wheel during what will seem like endless turns as you progress toward the completion of the doctorate. The book guides you to the finish line not only quickly but conscientiously. With Dr. Sterne's guidance, you may well enjoy the process while still coping with the changes in your life that impact your work, family, and friends.
My reliance upon Dr. Sterne's keen advice did not end at the conclusion of the doctoral degree. I have repeatedly relied upon her insightful critiques in article publishing and other professional matters. As Chair of the Departments of Aviation Science at two universities and Assistant and Associate Dean at my present university, I advise junior faculty always to consider the importance of an editor and mentor in their writing and project development. I consider Dr. Sterne my copilot and have come to depend upon her unfailing guidance that has always resulted in a clear and better written document. When my doctoral major advisor once referred to me as one of his "best students," in the back of my mind I thought, and continue to acknowledge, that my copilot was on the job.
—Gregory Lee Schwab, professor and chair,department of aerospace technology, Indiana State University, Terre Haute, IN

My grandfather, the late Deacon Gene Cone, was my first mentor and role model. As I observed him mentoring young African-American men in the church and community, I knew what my calling would be: With the doctorate, a dream of my life, I wanted to focus on pastoral counseling skills for African American men. I had been around them all my life; I saw them in the community, in the church, and in the U.S. Army as a Chaplain for over twenty-two years while serving on Active and Reserve duty. I knew how much they needed support of all kinds. I found joy in affirming that I was good enough to pursue a PhD, during my formative years having known in my community of Cocoa, Florida, of only one African-American (a male) who had a PhD. Finally, as an adult I pursued the doctoral program and eventually began writing the dissertation. I literally had to withdraw from all personal and fun activities. I had to write and rewrite and finally admit that I needed an editor. I found Dr. Noelle Sterne, the author of this great book that you are reading, *Challenges in Writing Your Dissertation.*

Dr. Sterne points out in the beginning of the book, and I found out, that starting the dissertation was indeed a BIG Change. I literally had to withdraw from personal and fun activities and many times talked nonstop about my difficulties to family members, friends, and ministers in my church.

Gradually, with Dr. Sterne's help, as she counsels in the book, I trusted the process even when I thought it had failed me. I became courageous, invigorated, challenged myself, and discovered a unique power within me. I graduated in 2009, having completed my dissertation on counseling African American men, a subject that remains dear to my heart.

During my dissertation journey, I experienced all the challenges Dr. Sterne discusses. I reached the victory of graduation through her mentorship. She has distilled her wisdom in this book, especially concerning the issues very few professors and other dissertation books speak about. Writing the correct content is a challenge enough. Dr. Sterne deals with the other issues that are as challenging. Without guidance such as she supplies, these can cause many doctoral students to drop out.

Any writer of a dissertation who is at risk of failing or giving up will be blessed by reading and following this book. Thank you, Dr. Sterne.

—Patricia A. Wilson-Cone, PhD, ACPE, AAPC, BCC, manager, spiritual care and CPE supervisor, Providence Alaska Medical Center, Anchorage, AL

Many graduate students look forward to writing their dissertation. They have done their research, they have something to say, and they want to move on with their careers. In some cases they already have published scholarly articles in collaboration with their thesis advisors, and they feel confident of their writing skills.

Other students look at the prospect of writing their dissertation with dread. They may be uncertain of their research results and may be working for a thesis advisor who is busy with his or her own research and has little time to provide proper advice and support. Or they may be bogged down with family and work obligations if they have been pursuing their degree on a part-time basis. Also, in an era when formal written communication is becoming a lost art, they may be unsure of their writing skills. Some may not fear writing the dissertation as much as its final completion and the inevitable oral examination by a less than charitable thesis committee. Dr. Sterne's book offers practical advice and solace to anyone who is in the midst of or is starting the process of writing a dissertation. Some will need only to read a few chapters to get the advice that they need, and others will want to read the book from cover to cover before starting or during the creation. In either case, they will find Dr. Sterne's advice extremely valuable as they progress to dissertation completion.

—Mark H. Shapiro, PhD, retired physicist, educator, author, editor/publisher of "The Irasicible Professor" emagazine

Dr. Noelle Sterne blazes a new trail into the forest of dissertation writing. In this essential resource for dissertation writers, Dr. Sterne dares to connect research with dreams and visions. She includes the student's inner mentor and urges enrolling the Higher Self and supportive networks in the endeavor. She addresses the pitfalls of the relationship with committees, as well as essentials such as proposals, writing styles, and forms. In our doctoral program, we are using this seminal book as more than a textbook. Rather, it is a map for navigation of the territory of creativity.

—Will Taegel, PhD, dean of Wisdom School of Graduate Studies, Ubiquity University, Mill Valley, CA

My dissertation journey took nearly a decade and was fraught with many bumps and detours on the road. As the studious, committed learner that I am, I completed all program requirements in record time and read many scholarly sources, mostly prescribed guidelines to dissertation writing. They were useful, but they were also devoid of the covert underpinnings, which often impede progress for many a doctoral student.

I had unresolved spiritual and emotional issues I needed to confront before concluding my dissertation. It was only when I met and spoke with Dr. Noelle Sterne that I experienced the

epiphany that catapulted me to success. Her counsel and carefully crafted tutorial material allowed me to believe in myself in spite of many hurdles encountered along the way. Through a faith-driven process, I was able to connect all the dots sensibly and logically. When I finally defended my work, I felt as though I was wearing armor and was that ready for the battle. Supporting me, intangibly, was Dr. Sterne's invaluable guidance. It is this kind of support and guidance she brings into Challenges in Writing Your Dissertation. I recommend it unreservedly to any doctoral student wrestling with the many issues that may stand in the way of completing the dissertation.
—Ariel C. Gil, PhD, assistant director, Write-to-Learn Program, Alvah H. Chapman, Jr., Graduate School of Business, Florida International University, Miami, FL

In dissertating as in life, a holistic approach provides a deeper, more engaging, and more satisfying journey through the process. Dr. Noelle Sterne has the wisdom and experience to provide such an approach in her guidance of students, from choosing a topic to writing a dissertation on that topic. I have found that, in my work as Manager of Dissertation Editor Services and in guiding students in all walks of life and at all levels of professionality, the other-than-academic problems Dr. Sterne primarily addresses frequently surface and hamper students' progress. In this entertaining yet serious and practical book, she provides useful tools, examples, and advice to help students surmount these problems, articulate dreams and goals, and then breathe them into being.
—Martha King, manager, dissertation editor services, Walden Writing Center, Center for Student Success, Walden University, Minneapolis, MN

My dissertation journey at times was fraught with confusion, anger, self-doubt, grief in the loss of a beloved professor, financial woes, and yes, writer's block—but then I found a source of help and hope. That source was Dr. Noelle Sterne, my awe-inspiring dissertation coach. Dr. Sterne's coaching and spiritual guidance were instrumental in my successfully navigating the peaks and valleys of the dissertation journey. I am blessed beyond measure to have made this journey with her by my side. As I begin a new journey as a licensed minister I shall be eternally grateful for her guidance.
I am sure her guidance, wisdom, and understanding of the numerous issues beyond scholarly content in this book will help many other doctoral candidates complete their dissertations with less frustration and anxiety. I am happy to recommend *Challenges in Writing Your Dissertation.*
—Valmarie Ward Rhoden, PhD,author, "School Leaders' Behaviors, Climate, and Student Achievement", program director for Informed Families/The Florida Family Partnership, Miami, FL

In her user-friendly book, *Challenges in Writing Your Dissertation: Coping with the Emotional, Interpersonal, and Spiritual Struggles,* Dr. Noelle Sterne offers the doctoral student an immensely practical and affirming guide to bringing the whole being to the dissertation process. She recognizes that a student's emotional-spiritual connection to the goal provides the jet fuel that propels the project to the finish line.
Dr. Sterne addresses the familiar dissertation issues (such as topic selection, time management, outlines, and dissertation committees) with new insights. More importantly, she addresses the generally neglected spiritual aspects of listening to inner guidance, affirming the dream and one's competence in achieving it, and honoring whole-person growth along the way. The spiritual perspective and accessibility make this an important addition to the books on dissertation-writing.
With both incisive wit and wisdom, Dr. Sterne brings meaning to the process as well as sound guidance for reaching the goal. Her deep experience, cautionary tales, and solid advice ease the doctoral candidate's process of grappling with all aspects of personal and academic life in support of successful completion of the dissertation journey.
—Carolyn Atkinson, RN, PhD, dean of doctoral studies, ret., Wisdom School of Graduate Studies, Ubiquity University, Mill Valley, CA

At last—a book geared toward the myriad trials and tribulations confronting many a hapless graduate student on the pilgrimage toward the graduate degree. As I experienced myself, with family and full-time job (and dog and lawn and neighborhood watch), the "nonacademic" troubles were as testy as learning APA.

I am positive all graduate students will find *Challenges in Writing Your Dissertation: Coping With the Emotional, Interpersonal, and Spiritual Struggles* a veritable fund of valuable insights and practicalities in their quest for that degree. For those of us who are veterans, not having had this book is our loss. To those to whom we pass the torch, the book is a godsend.

I recall those wonderful conversations Dr. Sterne and I used to have as I pursued my own doctorate. She wasn't a nag—well, not really. She was most influential in helping me keep my priorities straight and my eyes on the prize. Her keen sense of humor was always welcome, and it eloquently comes across in *Challenges*. For all graduate students and all those involved with them, this book is a treasure.

—Howard Chislett, Ed.D., former dissertation editor and secretary, Teachers College, Columbia University, New York, NY

Challenges in Writing Your Dissertation: Coping with the Emotional, Interpersonal, and Spiritual Struggles, is an original, positive, witty, fun-to-read, and welcome diversion from step-by-step dissertation guides overly focused on the mechanics of the dissertation and insufficiently on the full lives of students. It is good medicine for mild anxiety to panic attacks, and uniquely useful to an often invisible but large population of mature, part-time doctoral students who have family, community, and work responsibilities, and who do not get all the help they should (or some full-time students might obtain) from their committee chairs. *Challenges* gives sensitive, compelling advice plus clear talking-points for nurturing relationships and overcoming barriers in one's family, friendships, employment, and on campus on the way to the degree. It is written from the perspective of an experienced dissertation coach who is uniquely dedicated to the student's success and sufficiently outside academe to observe the big picture and call a spade a spade. Read this book right through for an overview, tab the pages that speak most loudly to you for easy referral, browse items in the comprehensive reference list, and do not let it get buried under a pile of unread articles.

—Bruce M. Shore, PhD, professor emeritus of educational psychology, McGill University, Montreal, Quebec, Canada, Fellow of the American Educational Research Association, Author of "The Graduate Advisor Handbook: A Student-Centered Approach" (The University of Chicago Press)

Challenges in Writing Your Dissertation

Challenges in Writing Your Dissertation

Coping With the Emotional, Interpersonal, and Spiritual Struggles

Noelle Sterne

ROWMAN & LITTLEFIELD
Lanham • Boulder • New York • London

Published by Rowman & Littlefield
A wholly owned subsidiary of The Rowman & Littlefield Publishing Group, Inc.
4501 Forbes Boulevard, Suite 200, Lanham, Maryland 20706
www.rowman.com
Unit A, Whitacre Mews, 26-34 Stannary Street, London SE11 4AB

Except for the list below, all allusions to and quotations from other published materials are cited per APA and listed in the References. I acknowledge the credits below and thank the following for reprint permission (in order of appearance in book):
"The Ideal Dissertation." Public access on dissertation cartoons: https://www.google.com/search?q=pop+up+doctoral+dissertation+cartoon&tbm=isch&tbo=u&source=univ&sa=X&ei=WRiqU6fCOMqgogSmxYHIBA&ved=0CBwQsAQ&biw=1280&bih=636#facrc=_&imgdii=_&imgrc=vgIPXdS2LhZK_M%253A%3BgfN7AVmcU0LxLM%3Bhttp%253A%252F%252Fwww.peterliljedahl.com%252Fwp-content%252Fuploads%252FComic-Pop-Up.jpg%3Bhttp%253A%252F%252Fwww.peterliljedahl.com%252Fwp-content%252Fuploads%252F%3B266%3B190

Richmond, C. J. (2007). "Acknowledgments" from A study of intake and assessment in solution-focused brief therapy (Unpublished doctoral dissertation). Western Michigan University, Retrieved from ProQuest Dissertations and Theses database (ProQuest document ID: 445049571). Email September 3, 2014.

Frank, J. "In soundproofing we trust." Author Magazine, October 2014. http://www.authormagazine.org/articles/2014_10_frank.html Email October 21, 2014.

John Wiley, publisher, "Dissertation Interruptus: 7 Cautionary Tales," Noelle Sterne, Women in Higher Education, vol. 23, no. 10, pp. 16, 17, 19. Copyright 2014 Wiley Periodicals, Inc., A Wiley Company.

British Library Cataloguing in Publication Information Available
Library of Congress Cataloging-in-Publication Data

Sterne, Noelle.
Challenges in writing your dissertation : coping with the emotional, interpersonal, and spiritual struggles / Noelle Sterne.
pages cm
Includes bibliographical references and index.
ISBN 978-1-4758-1503-0 (cloth : alk. paper) -- ISBN 978-1-4758-1504-7 (pbk. : alk. paper) -- ISBN 978-1-4758-1505-4 (electronic)
1. Dissertations, Academic. I. Title.
LB2369.S695 2015
808.02--dc23
2015027130

∞ ™ The paper used in this publication meets the minimum requirements of American National Standard for Information Sciences Permanence of Paper for Printed Library Materials, ANSI/NISO Z39.48-1992.

Printed in the United States of America

Contents

Foreword xv
Acknowledgments xvii
Introduction: How I Became an Academic Nag xix
Why This Book xx
What's Here xxi
My Methods and Techniques xxiv
Why Me? xxv
I Never Left School
From Professor to Typist
To Coach and Editor
Disclosure: My Writing (Mostly Nonacademic)
A Word About the Spiritual xxviii
"Academic Nag" xxix

I: Sneaking Up on the Dissertation **1**

1 The Decision: Your Dream, Your Life 3
How Is the Degree Part of Your Life's Dream? 4
What Will the Degree Do for You? 6
Visualize Your Dream 7
Affirmations for Strengthening Your Life Dream 8
As They Say, Meditate, Don't Medicate 9

2 *Big* Changes 11
It's Not Just College Anymore 11
How Ready Are You to Change Your Lifestyle? 12
No Structure
No Leisure
It's Your Time 15
Declare and Feel Your Readiness 15

II: Really Doing It **17**

3 Priorities and Promises to Yourself 19
Your Inner Mentor: Listening for Answers 19
Rethink Your Priorities 21
Find the Holes in Your Schedule 23
Keep Your Promises to Yourself 24
Your Later List 26

Affirm Your Right Time and Timing 27

4 Enroll Your Higher Self 29
Hello, Light Being! 29
Trust the Process 30
Three Puzzling and Powerful Reinforcing Laws 32
The Law of Least Effort
The Law of Intention and Desire
The Law of Detachment
Recognize and Accept Your Power 35
A Few Higher Self Affirmations 36

5 Starting the Work: Positive Patient Persevering 37
Listen for the Topic That's Right for You 37
Topic Considerations
Right Topic Considerations
You're the Scholar in Shining Armor 41
Muster Your Courage for the Proposal 41
What's Your Problem?
Courageous Affirmations
You Don't Have to Walk a Straight (Out)Line 43
Tricks to Tease and Ease Yourself Into It 45
Writing Doesn't Have to Be Torture: Proper Style and Semipleasant Process 47
Settle In: You Deserve It 50

6 Sticking With It: Temptations and Tonics 51
Dissertation Interruptus 51
Death by Rationale 53
Resisting the Extension Siren 54
Getting Sick . . . of It All 55
Fear of Finishing 57
Discipline Is a Choice 59
Continuing the Work: Your Wayward Outline 60
If You're Concerned About Your Brain 61
Reasonable Breaks and Balance 62
Working Questions
Balanced Breaks
Affirmations for Sticking with It 65

III: Your Near, Dear, and Despairing Significant Others **67**

7 Orient the Important Others in Your Life 69
Stranger in a Strange Graduate School Culture 69
Family and Friends: Starting Off Wrong 70
Starting Off Right 70
Selfish?

Saying No
Sacrifices and Rewards: Short-Term, Mid-Term, Interminable-Term 73
Educate Them
Bribe Them

8 Family: Choruses of Complaints, Songs of Support 77
Partners: "I Didn't Bargain for This" or "I Never See You Anymore" 77
Kids: "We Never See You Anymore" 78
Involve Them: Share What You're Doing 79
Involving Partners
Involving Kids
Special Dates With Partners and Kids 80
Dates With Partners
Dates With Kids
Other Relatives: "We Never See You Anymore" 81
Educate and Bribe, Again
Sabotage, Unconscious or Not
Holiday Strategies 82
Toxic Volleys and Tough Questions 83
Your Neutralizing Responses
Hard Questions and Your Brilliant Answers
Troubled Waters: Fights, Separation, Divorce 85
See Them Whole 87
Send Love Ahead
See Them Supportive

9 Friends: Are They For You or Against You? 91
"Come On—It's Only a Quick Lunch": Just Say "Not Now" 92
Community Involvement and Volunteer Activities: Just Say "Later" 92
Handle Jealousies and Putdowns 94
Let Go of the Crazymakers 95
Those Questions Again: "Aren't You Done Yet?" 96
Assure Them You Still Love Them 97
Know and Believe They Are For and With You 97

10 Make Peace and Time With Your Employer and Work Colleagues 99
Express Your Gratitude and Explain, Explain 100
Point Out How Your Degree Benefits the Company 101
Negotiate What Works for Both of You 102
Superior Jealousies 103
Recognize Toxicity
Toxicity Antidotes
Work Colleagues' Envy 105

Affirm, Visualize, and Project Employment Peace 106

IV: Good University Cops and Bad 109

11 Your Dissertation Committee: The Best/Worst Friends You'll Ever Have 111
Are Professors Really Human? 111
Excruciating or Exceptional? 113
Who Can You Work With and How Do You Know? 114
Gather Plenty of Information
Ask Questions About the Chair
Listen Inside: Gut and Guidance 118
Ask Questions of Yourself
How Do You Feel?
Design and See Your Perfect Committee 120

12 Dancing With the Committee 123
Whose Topic? 123
Buddying Up or Keeping Too Distant 124
Chums
Strangers
The Ideal Balance
Playing Humble Student and Keeping Your Self-Respect 128
Swallow Your Pride
Raise Your Head
When You're Older Than Your Professors 129
The Infinite Loop of Revisions 131
Appealing to Higher Authorities 133
On the Ground
In Your Head
Your Higher Self and Theirs 134
Psychologically Speaking
Spiritually Speaking

13 University Support: You've Got More Friends Than You Think 137
Fellow Students as Mentors 137
What Can You Learn From Learning Centers? 139
You *Can* Speak to the Geeks in the Computer Lab 139
Add to Your Team: Statisticians and Researchers 140
Statisticians
Researchers
Librarians Love You, Secretaries Stand By You 141
Librarians
Secretaries
Consider Coaches and Editors 143
Coaches

Editors
Old Course Professors Don't Have to Fade Away 147
Picture the Perfect University Friends You Need 148

V: Graduation: It's Only a Walk Away 151

14 Am I Really Almost Done? 153
Rehearse Your Perfect Defense 153
Yet Another Faculty Review 155
Master the Red Tape 156
How to Enjoy Your Own Graduation 156
Avoid Post-Parting Depression (PPD) 158

15 Waking to Your Dream 161
The Most Dangerous Time . . . 161
Envision Your Future, Take the Steps 162
Peek at Your Long-Neglected Later List 163
Reenter Your Family's Atmosphere 164
Plan Your Payoffs 165
Positions
Publications
Celebrate Your Professional and Personal Growth With Gratitude 168

Conclusion: Why I'm Still an Academic Nag 171
References 173
Selected Resources 183
A Short Glossary of Important Acronyms 185
Index 187
About the Author 195

Foreword

Challenges in Writing Your Dissertation presents a highly engaging and readable practical and spiritual approach for doctoral students embarking on the dreaded dissertation trail.

Dr. Noelle Sterne successfully weathered the dissertation rigors and emerged with her own PhD from Columbia University. She offers a treasure chest of practical tips and suggestions on prioritizing, reprioritizing, constructing day-to-day "must-do" lists, "later lists," and time management techniques. Unusual in a dissertation manual, she also provides positive affirmations for doctoral students on every aspect of the writing process—for example, how to approach, survive, and complete a doctoral degree program while in relationship(s) with significant others.

Dr. Sterne taught for several years before establishing her academic coaching and editing practice. This book derives from her longtime practice and commitment to the students she coaches. Her background and practice make her the perfect expert for launching this much-needed book. Her recent publications attest to her passion in assisting students and others in reaching their dreams, whether they are completing a doctoral degree or pursuing a business or personal passion.

Dr. Sterne's transparency is evident in sharing with readers her own struggles as a doctoral student while at Columbia and later as an academician. Moreover, she publically and courageously discusses the terrors and politics of the "Ivory Tower," as well as revealing professors' everyday lives and their own struggles, both personally (such as family obligations) and professionally (such as the quest for the elusive tenure).

One of the many highlights of *Challenges* is its attention to some doctoral students' seemingly endless position of "all but dissertation" (ABD). Dissertation chairs may be unresponsive for whole semesters at a time, of which I unfortunately had personal experience. When I was in the ABD wasteland, my chair and the entire department were in the midst of a major move from one office to another. My dissertation draft, critiqued, did not appear in my inbox until a year later. Because of this situation, I had to keep taking extensions; I know full well the truth, as Dr. Sterne says, of universities' love for extensions.

A most welcome element of *Challenges in Writing Your Dissertation* is Dr. Sterne's illustrations with frequent personal and student stories, told with candor and wit. In addition to heeding the advice, the doctoral student reader will get at least a few good needed laughs.

Dr. Sterne hones in on pivotal questions and statements for clarification of purpose. For example, "How is the degree part of your life dream?" "What will the degree do for you?" "Visualize your dream." As a specialist in solution-focused therapy, I relate her questions to the often used "miracle question"—with the focus on where one wants to be and not on why one cannot get there.

The spiritual/metaphysical is an integral part of *Challenges*, which makes this book unique in dissertation manuals. Dr. Sterne's straightforward admission in using a major metaphysical principle—"Believing is seeing"—jumpstarts her first chapter and introduces readers to her passionate belief in metaphysics. She also challenges readers to test their "inner mentor"—the guide inside who knows all our answers. In fact, she challenges, or rather dares, readers to embark on spiritual experiments that access and test their inner mentors. I confess I did a test, asking for help in writing this foreword, and it worked!

The first half of *Challenges* deals with the actual writing of the dissertation. The second half discusses related issues that can waylay the candidate, such as the impact of significant family, friends, coworkers, colleagues, and employers; and toxic others, such as parents, relatives, and friends. Among the many topics, Dr. Sterne also deals with choosing the best chair and committee, dealing with their quirks, and finally, following through with the perfect defense, graduation, and use of the dissertation for career plans. In addition, Dr. Sterne's applications of spiritual principles gently direct the candidate to persevere with less agony and more hope.

Dr. Noelle Sterne is to be greatly applauded for writing this book and providing resources that are thorough, doable, and inspirational. *Challenges in Writing Your Dissertation* is an essential reference and guide for the dissertation-writing doctoral student to successful completion of the dissertation.

Irma M. Barron, PhD
Professor
Carlos Albizu University
Miami, Florida

Acknowledgments

As with any book, this one was not written alone. It is the result of many years of working with graduate students and learning from them and their chairs, mentors, advisors, and committees. So, with great humility, I thank all the clients who let nothing stand in their way of the dream of the doctorate and trusted me to help them achieve it. I have a special place in my heart (and files) for each of you.

I thank Dr. Irma M. Barron, the writer of the foreword, and the professionals who expressed praise for this book. They took the time to read the manuscript and write generous testimonies that indicate their conviction in the worth of a book such as this.

I most heartily thank Dr. Thomas F. Koerner, vice president and publisher of Rowman & Littlefield Education, for his astounding and immediate responsiveness to the proposal for this book, his support of its audacious spiritual perspective, and his enthusiasm throughout. I thank, too, associate editor Carlie Wall for her consistent helpfulness, clarifications, and patient answers to my sometimes dense questions.

I acknowledge the exemplary agent Rita Rosenkranz for supporting me in this work when I sorely needed it and for her unstinting time and attention in the early stages.

I thank my divinely attracted soul mate and ultimate supporter, who unfailingly reminds me of divine order, listens to my laments, and unstintingly gives me reassuring hugs whenever I ask.

Finally, I acknowledge with great gratitude the inner mentor and Source of all. It is infallible, ever-reliable, and always here.

"Well, a pop-up doctoral dissertation is certainly an original idea..."

Figure 0.1.

Introduction

How I Become an Academic Nag

Graduate school is tough, and the doctoral level is the toughest. Once in graduate school, many people wish they'd never enrolled. Maybe you're one of them, and you're reading this book instead of buckling down to your dissertation.

"They don't know what they are getting into." The director of the Ph.D. Completion Project, Council of Graduate Schools, Dr. Robert Sowell, wasn't referring to *Survivor* hopefuls or newlyweds but to doctoral candidates (Jaschik, 2008).

He was right.

You may be shocked as you start the dissertation. Like other doctoral candidates, you may have gotten all A's in your predissertation program courses and are secretly preening at your 4.0 GPA. Once you leave the shelter of structured courses and the camaraderie of other students, no matter how many papers you've whipped out and courses you've taken that supposedly taught you about dissertation writing, you're still not prepared for its trials.

Why this is so is still a mystery to me, but in my longtime academic coaching and editing practice, I hear it all the time from dismayed beginning (or stuck) dissertation students. Yes, the chair and committee are supposed to guide you, but they're teaching at eight universities each and responsible for more doctoral dissertations than they can shake a rubric at. At the same time, they must somehow try to complete their own articles for publication, look good for promotion, and politic up to the right deans for elusive tenure. And raise their kids and mow their lawns. No wonder they don't return your emails!

Nevertheless, more people are entering universities for advanced degrees, and more degrees are increasingly offered, especially online (Driscoll, 2013; National Center for Education Statistics, 2012, 2013, 2014; Parry, 2010). You can get a DArch, DBA, DCL, DD, DIBA, DLitt, DMin, DPA, DPH, DScPT, DSW, EdD, EdS, JD, JSD, PharmD, PhD, PsyD, RhD, and just about any other combination of the alphabet.

Astonishingly, though, despite these increasing opportunities, from 40 percent to 50 percent of doctoral candidates don't complete their degrees (Ampaw & Jaeger, 2012; Casanave & Li, 2008; Cassuto, 2013a; Jaschik, 2007, 2008). The attrition rate can go as high as 70 percent in some fields, especially the humanities (Cassuto, 2013a; Jaschik, 2007, 2008).

I remember my own orientation seminar entering the doctoral program. The director addressed the vast audience of eager faces and intoned, "Look around you. Three of four of you won't be here in two years." A client's chair made a similar pronouncement. He said that of the doctoral students who enroll, only 10 percent would complete and get the degree.

In a 10-year compilation of 30 institutions and 330 programs, the figures were slightly better, per Sowell (2010). For engineering, the percentage of doctoral completion was 64 percent, for life sciences 63 percent, for social sciences 56 percent, for mathematics and science 55 percent, and for humanities 49 percent. These percentages are still nothing to boast about to your grandmother.

The Council of Graduate Schools Ph.D. Completion Project will be carrying out its second seven-year study of PhD completion, attrition, and retention in the United States (Ph.D. Completion Project, 2014), and the figures may change for the better. Nevertheless, you know the dread acronym: ABD, traditionally "all but dissertation" or, "ain't barely done," or, more accurately, "all but disgusted" (with thanks to Jill Dearman).

WHY THIS BOOK

Why? Both men and women candidates, campus and online, juggle family, work, and school. Their academic struggles are intensified by the intellectual, psychological, and personal stresses of such multiple responsibilities and social and emotional isolation (Rockinson-Szapkiw, 2011). They face not only the dissertation challenges in content and conventions but also personal sacrifices, progress that's slower than freeway repairs, lack or withdrawal of support from those who mean the most, and sudden inabilities to cope with the morass of problems (Spaulding & Rockinson-Szapkiw, 2012).

When I recently told a friend about this book, she confided that her husband had been wrestling with the dissertation for four years. "Of course, he's been held up by the nonacademic part." In fact, one study found that the "human factors" were overwhelmingly more important to candidates' success than the academic (Stallone, 2004, p. 18). The costs of dropout are high to the candidates, their families, the institutions, and society (Grasso, Barry, & Valentine, 2009; Smallwood, 2004). "Failure to complete can leave individuals with psychological and family turbulence, massive debt and limited career potential" (Grasso et al., 2009, p. 6).

These glum scenarios lead to one conclusion: Doctoral candidates, whether enrolled in traditional, online, or blended programs, need a lot of help in many more than academic skills.

Challenges in Writing Your Dissertation comes to their—your—aid. In my practice, I have seen, over and over, that despite all A's and the highest GPAs in the doctoral courses, graduate students fall apart at the tentative toe-in-water of the dissertation. Having suffered similar slings and arrows with my own dissertation, I felt, and continue to feel, compassion and empathy.

My mission in this book is to share what I've learned and observed as a coach of graduate students; to bolster, hearten, and inspire all of you who are struggling with your dissertations; and to help you give it your best and succeed in less time and with less stress. My mission is also to help you gain greater pleasure in the entire process and develop your gifts and self-confidence so that you can be truly proud of your accomplishment and use it to achieve your life's dream.

As you see from the title, I focus on the underlying, often-neglected human level. If you are a bewildered and beleaguered doctoral candidate, I offer much-needed guidance in many other-than-academic areas. (If you aren't b&b, congratulations!)

WHAT'S HERE

You can get the nuts and bolts of dissertation writing in many other books, and I suggest you do. Ask your chair and colleagues which books they've found are most straightforward and helpful. At this writing, the guide by Rudestam and Newton (2014) is in its fourth edition. See also my reference list for others. It's true that a book can't replace a live mentor or even an email one, but a book can still give you a lot of help (Bible, anyone?).

For you to get the most out of *Challenges in Writing Your Dissertation,* I'm assuming you're at least acquainted with the content and process of dissertation writing. By the way, as I refer throughout to the various chapters of the dissertation, I know that different universities may require somewhat different titles. For example:

- Chapter 1: Introduction/Introduction to the Study/The Problem
- Chapter 2: Literature Review/Review of the Literature
- Chapter 3: Methods/Research Methods/Methodology
- Chapter 4: Results/Findings/Data Collection and Analysis
- Chapter 5: Discussion and Conclusions/Summary, Discussion, and Implications/Conclusion, Discussion, and Recommendations

Your university likely requires some variant of these. In any case, I assume you are familiar enough with these titles to relate when I refer to a chapter in the dissertation.

If you're reading this book, puzzling over the required chapter titles may not the reason you're stuck. So, here's what's here.

Challenges in Writing Your Dissertation offers my perspectives on some issues previously addressed, like choosing the topic and getting started. This book also speaks to hardly handled or largely overlooked aspects of the dissertation-living process.

Other books on the dissertation process talk about the relationship of the candidate's dreamed-of lifework to the degree. Many of the books deal with the writing process but not with lifestyle changes that must take place or candidates getting to know their work and writing rhythms. Some of the books deal superficially with the psychological and emotional upheavals. Some look at relationships with committee members but rarely at the many other interpersonal relationships and problems that arise. Some of the books discuss life after the degree but not in depth.

None that I know of, though, takes the leap into the spiritual perspective of doctoral students' lives and how they can apply the spiritual to help them get through faster, better, and less dented. In these and other ways, *Challenges in Writing Your Dissertation* complements the current mostly practical-oriented books.

The fifteen chapters of *Challenges in Writing Your Dissertation* mirror students' mental journeys and physical demands. I am not a psychologist or minister, but with my doctorate from Columbia University (and my own stories of angst), for thirty years I have been an academic coach, editor, empathizer, listener, professional friend, thought facilitator, cerebral consultant, stressed-student solution-supplier, and gentle (or not so) "academic nag," as one client affectionately dubbed me. *Challenges in Writing Your Dissertation* reflects what I have lived through with clients and continue to learn with each one.

Like a good little essay, the book follows the prescribed sequence of beginning-middle-end and beyond, as do many practical books on the dissertation. First, we explore the beginning of the doctoral journey, then the l-o-n-g middle of *writingwritingwriting*, and finally the end of graduation and beyond. This is not only a logical progression but also makes the book easier for you at whatever stage you're at. The chapter titles and sections describe each subject I deal with, and you can turn to the specific topics you may need at any given point in your progress.

In part I, Sneaking Up on the Dissertation (chapters 1–2), I ask you to explore how the degree honors your best dreams, and I implore you to keep these dreams in front of you. I caution you to be prepared for the dissertation's demands and for changing your lifestyle—radically.

Once these demands have been identified, in part II, Really Doing It (chapters 3—6), I guide you in tackling the actual work. Feelings of inadequacy can overwhelm you, with the expected book-length document seemingly impossible. You sit alone, bewildered, surrounded by masses of unorganized materials. You've just heard that a friend you started the program with defends her dissertation next week, and you feel yourself plunging into free-fall depression. In these chapters, I help you shut out all such devastating news, set your priorities, and access practical and spiritual support from sources rarely mentioned in other books.

In part III, Your Near, Dear, and Despairing Significant Others (chapters 7–10), as you wade deeper into the work, I help you recognize and grapple with the many personal obstacles you will likely face (or have already) in writing the dissertation. The needs and demands of family, friends, and work don't disappear or even lessen. Apparently, supportive family and friends may clamor for even more attention or (incomprehensibly) attempt to sabotage your concentration and writing.

The conflicts can escalate, and you find yourself battling for the time, energy, attention, and focus necessary for survival in graduate school. I boost you with strategies that won't forever alienate everyone else in your life.

In part IV, Good University Cops and Bad (chapters 11–13), I offer insights and perspectives on the perils of working with, and in spite of, dissertation committees, and the political realities of chairs' and professors' egos. For support, I suggest that you acquaint and reacquaint with many others in the university galaxy, such as tech supporters, librarians, and former professors.

In part V, Graduation: It's Only a Walk Away (chapters 14–15)—believe it!—I help you envision actually completing the dissertation and taking the steps to graduation, from defense to ceremonial march to final deposit of the finally bound volume in the university library. I encourage you to look ahead to new goals and academic conquering—articles, conference presentations, teaching positions, and that business you've dreamt of starting since puberty.

I provide you with cushioning in your dealings with that unfathomable sense of emptiness you may feel without the albatross dissertation. I support you in gradually reentering a relatively normal life, and together we re-envision and act on life ABD—after and beyond the dissertation.

The book ends with my apologia (*dissertationese*) of why I'm still an academic nag. For your added information and exploration, references and selected resources are at the back of the book. For your enjoyment, I hope, you'll also find there a slightly tongue-in-cheek short glossary of important acronyms.

In summary, in *Challenges in Writing Your Dissertation,* you'll be helped to do the following:

- Integrate the degree with your career plans and life dreams
- Change your basic lifestyle

- Learn your own work and writing rhythms
- Gain confidence and develop intuitive direction in your writing
- Develop your inner spiritual resources and power
- Recognize and handle difficulties with family members, relatives, friends, and employers
- Manage the politics of relationships with professors and doctoral committees
- Apply spiritual tools and resources at any point in the process
- Get help and support from expected and surprising sources
- Finalize the process almost with enjoyment
- Reenter the atmosphere of normalcy
- Plan the payoffs of the degree
- Consolidate career and life lessons of your graduate experience.

Throughout, I'm your academic nag, like an aunt who slightly carps but with your best interests in mind. I prompt, prod, push, and pull it out of you and goad you to greater scholarly glory. Please consider me your confidante and professional friend, with the use of many approaches.

MY METHODS AND TECHNIQUES

Like some other authors, my methods include discussions, anecdotes, questions, and checklists. I also offer role-play scripts for knotty interpersonal dialogues and, for your inner life, affirmative, supportive, and spiritual statements.

My style is straightforward and friendly, and, as you've already seen, I cannot resist jokes, possibly lame ones.

I share squirming anecdotes of my own PhD chase and those of the many clients I've helped who have finally completed their dissertations. (In examples of clients, friends, family, and personal acquaintances, names have been changed to protect identities. The names of individuals who are publically well known are retained.)

I instruct you with remedies, many getting-through techniques, and occasional exercises (you're warned with the symbol seen below)

that I've devised and written about through my dissertation coaching and mainstream writing.

I boldly criticize established and supposedly sacrosanct university conventions and outrageous deficiencies (I didn't want to be a university professor again, anyway). For example, these include dissertation chairs who are unresponsive for whole semesters at a time, for which the registrar gladly accepts students' payments ad mountainitum.

I stand on the side of the student/reader—you. Well-meaning, sincere, and obliging university professors and staff members do exist, but for many reasons they don't or can't help sufficiently. I've heard enough sad tales to confirm this statement and know that students, in their enormous effort, need a real friend, partner, and cheerleader.

WHY ME?

My drive, background, and eventual career choices prepared me perfectly for writing this book. And there's more—a client kept asking, "Well, did you write a book about your work yet?" Happily, I can now get him off my back.

I Never Left School

From Barnard College, majoring in English, I immediately took the long trek across the street to Columbia, with only a locker change, and earned a master's in English. Then, without a lunch break, I continued to the doctorate. My dissertation topic, which I'd thought about during my doctoral seminar, was on the poems of the eighteenth-century author Jonathan Swift (an Irish clergyman, visionary, and wise guy, among other accomplishments).

Laboring over his satiric poems in a rare book library, I discovered an error—to my amazed unbelief—by a world-renowned scholar in the authoritative Oxford University Press edition of Swift's poems. When I reported this find to my chair, he became very excited—the mighty had fallen, at least in quartos. He helped me publish my discovery in a prestigious London scholarly journal, an unusual accomplishment for a doctoral candidate.

Publication didn't excuse me from writing the dissertation, though. As I plodded along, commiserating with fellow candidates, they asked me for explanations and advice (I was always a good little student). Even in that elite Columbia "academic ghetto," few resources (read: professors) were available for solid guidance.

I finally received the PhD in English and comparative literature from Columbia and taught college for several years. Then, retiring from teaching (or getting fired, depending on your position and point of view), I recognized a need, but I wasn't quite ready to plunge into actual professional advising.

From Professor to Typist

However, I knew the dissertation ropes, needed to earn money, and lived in the university community, so I advertised typing services (some of the following is related in my book *Trust Your Life*, Sterne, 2011). Clients appeared quickly, and as I typed I engaged in their content. When they next visited to pick up the work, I couldn't help but ask questions: "Do you think Keats was heavily influenced by *Paradise Regained*?" "How did Heidegger reconcile his sense of Being and his Nazism?" "Does Drucker believe managers can really become leaders?"

My clients, nascent academic doctors, began suspecting I wasn't your average word processing drone. They questioned me about their drafts: "Does this follow logically?" "Does that make sense?" "Am I stretching it?" "Do I have enough substantiation?" "Too many citations?" "Am I holding to a scholarly tone?"

From these exchanges and my outspoken replies, clients spilled their troubles. Impossible deadlines, menopausal committee members, spouses furious at them for always choosing library and computer over family, and drafts of chapters either unnoticed by their dissertation chairs for months or endlessly thrown back, dripping with blood-red tracked changes every other line. Just before clients left my office, most of them wailed, "I'll never get this degree!"

Remembering my own window staring instead of writing, I'd often felt this way too. Like a lost sheep, I sat shocked, dismayed, and paralyzed at many points during the dissertation. A mother at heart, I was unable to ignore friends' and clients' draft troubles and outbursts. I gave tentative opinions, suggested little changes, scribbled cautious sample stuffy scholarly phrases, and encouraged them.

Clients' faces relaxed and their small smiles of hope showed me I'd reached them. I felt wonderful. As I continued this informal advising, my knowledge and critical abilities grew—exponentially (sad to say) more than from the years of courses and seminars of formal graduate school training. Clients welcomed my feedback and interest like they would ice cream after Chinese food. Gradually, I phased out of typing and into academic coaching, consulting, and editing.

To Coach and Editor

For many years now, I've acted as coach, editor, motivator, cheerleader, professional friend, hand holder, ego soother, and solution-supplier to over 900 doctoral students across the nation and abroad. We communicate in person, by phone, email, postal mail, and FedEx (I am allergic to texting).

The majority of clients are in their forties and fifties and pursuing doctorates in education, business, leadership, healthcare, the humanities, and the social sciences. Like most doctoral students, they are working professionals who must juggle personal relationships, family care, and professional responsibilities, all while trying to write their dissertations.

Clients range in age from twenty-five to eighty (and beyond!). They are of many backgrounds and nationalities, from working-class employees to high-ranking executives and professionals, Americans and transplants from a range of countries. For all, the doctorate is their life's dream. They're often the first in their families to attend graduate school, much less achieve a doctorate.

Through the choices of dissertation topics and award of their degrees, my clients are strongly motivated and passionate about contributing. Their goals have included the following: to guide a developing native country to prosperity and democracy, help disadvantaged elementary school children read better, special needs kids to adjust better, at-risk adolescents to stay out of jail and graduate from high school, college students to learn and think better, teachers to teach better, and administrators to lead better.

Clients have also dedicated their doctorates to helping abused women gain courage to remake their lives, career women to balance work and family, seniors to live more active lives, and nurses to reach more community members. And there are so many more. I feel honored to help all of these doctoral candidates reach their life and career goals.

Whatever clients' topics and passions, their dissertation-completion problems are similar. I help them through despondency over their apparent writing paralysis and lack of progress; rage at chairs, committees, universities, departments, personnel, and the system; separations, divorces, and deaths of family members; alienation from children, parents, and friends; and loss of resilience, spiritual center, and faith.

As my profession evolved, I cofounded the New York City Academic Network, a service organization of editorial professionals assisting graduate students to fulfill their written degree requirements. This organization also provided seminars and guest lecturers to enhance professionalism, publicized the latest technical information, and trained new members in the highest academic standards.

I also coedited the dissertation style manual of the Office of Doctoral Studies, Teachers College, Columbia University, as well as a handbook answering doctoral students' most FAQs. With the dissertation editor, I regularly updated the style manual with plentiful examples for students. I've delivered speeches on scholarly and related subjects and have led informal workshops with graduate students at different stages in their dissertations.

With all this background, *Challenges in Writing Your Dissertation* evolved from my own doctoral struggles and victories and from my long practice bailing out doctoral students at every stage, from choosing a topic that won't take them fifty years of research to their final defense revisions of exhausting and niggling corrections.

Disclosure: My Writing (Mostly Nonacademic)

My writing by choice has been primarily mainstream oriented. Aside from that lone scholarly article (more like a paragraph) I described above, my first self-help book, *Trust Your Life* (Sterne, 2011), draws on examples from my academic coaching practice, writing, and the rest of life. I continue to publish articles and essays in online and print publications, with frequent guest blogs and interviews, and have contributed several columns.

A high point in my writing life was the publication of my children's book of original riddles, *Tyrannosaurus Wrecks: A Book of Dinosaur Riddles* (Sterne, 1983). The book was in print for eighteen years, excerpted in many children's magazines and texts for English education graduate programs, and featured in the first dinosaur show of *Reading Rainbow.* This *was* educational.

Specific to *Challenges in Writing Your Dissertation*, an essay on my practice, "My Life (Not Quite) in Academia," appeared in 2012 in *The Irascible Professor* (Sterne, 2012). "Dissertation Interruptus: 7 Cautionary Tales," an essay on the perils of tenderhearted women candidates quitting their dissertations to help family or friends, appeared in 2014 in *Women in Higher Education* (Sterne, 2014). A piece on choosing the all-important dissertation chair was published in *GradShare,* the ProQuest blog (Sterne, 2015a), and another on choosing the equally all-important dissertation topic in *Graduate Schools Magazine* (Sterne, 2015b). And I have been invited to contribute a guest blog and interview in *gradPsych,* the graduate student association magazine of the American Psychological Association.

A WORD ABOUT THE SPIRITUAL

One of the different features of this book—and maybe the one that got you interested, or at least curious about—is its spiritual component. This may have been a major reason the publisher (courageously) took it—a different, unusual take on the usual finish-your-dissertation books.

I realize that not everyone wants, needs, or admits to this aspect. You may welcome it or disdain it. You may applaud it or scorn it. You may cheer or harrumph.

Whatever your feelings, I respect them. I'll be delighted if you take them to heart. I won't be offended if you skip over or skim these parts. In fact, I've made it easy to spot them, especially the affirmations that pepper the text. Affirmations may appear in clumps or sneakily single.

AFFIRMATIONS

Hello, God. It's me, Mindy.
Please help.

Obviously, I'm biased—the spiritual is an integral and treasured part of my life. I continue to learn, practice, and use it in (almost) any and every circumstance and curve, including the writing of this book. I recommend it for all that ails you. If you've so inclined, you will learn how to use your spiritual resources and apply them to all phases of your dissertation struggles and your life.

You'd be surprised how many doctoral candidates mention God (or equivalent) in their dedications and acknowledgments. Here's one dedication: "I dedicate this work to Almighty God for His constant support, mercy, compassion, provisions, and health. To Your Glory."

Here's another, the most extensive and beautiful I've come across, and that's why I quote it at length:

> During this journey of my dissertation I have experienced several significant accomplishments and frustrations. At those times I turned to my relationship with God to offer thanksgiving for the accomplishments and ask for wisdom and understanding during the frustrations. . . .
>
> In examining myself through this journey, I found that I turn to faith and prayer as a strength and resource. Following accomplishments and frustrations I have reflected upon the following passage from Psalms:
>
> O Lord, you have searched me and you know me. You know when I sit and when I rise, you perceive my thoughts from afar. You discern my going out and my lying down; you are familiar with all my ways. Before a word is on my tongue you know it completely, O Lord. You hem me in behind and before; you have laid your hand upon me (Ps. 139: 1–5, New International Version). (Richmond, 2007)

I could cite many more. I've discovered too at least one emotional and spiritual support site for graduate students: Grad Resources (see selected resources for the web address). A nonprofit, faith-based organization in Dallas, Texas, Grad Resources "serves the practical and emotional needs of graduate students." The site maintains a policy of making available spiritual resources only to students who specifically ask for them.

I offer you the same. But I won't be insulted if you choose to close your eyes—or roll them—when you smell a spiritual section coming.

"ACADEMIC NAG"

Quite a few years ago, as I said above, a client crowned me with the dubious honorary title of "academic nag." He was no doubt exasperated by my insistence on not letting him get away with anything shoddy, a standard I, too, demand for myself (if you see any typos here, tell me *immediately*). I wear this hat proudly and may have a matching t-shirt made. Now, though, I'm wearing that hat for you throughout this book.

This commitment means that here, as in my academic coaching practice, I combine compassion, firmness, and forthrightness. I insist on the highest standards for clients so they can be proud of their dissertations, which are, after all, full-length books (most are longer than this handbook). With all the time, money, and ruffled relationships candidates weather, I am ever mindful that their dissertations can, and should, be used for later career moves, professional presentations, articles, and even subsequent books. I want to help them create the very best dissertation possible—I want to help you create the very best dissertation experience possible.

Enough stalling. Time to face the music and sneak up on the dissertation with some nervous-making questions in part I, chapter 1.

I

Sneaking Up on the Dissertation

ONE

The Decision

Your Dream, Your Life

The hardest part is over—you've made the decision to go for the doctorate. Before we continue, though, I assume you have made that decision thoughtfully and willingly, and that you really do want to complete the dissertation and get your doctorate.

If you've had more than the normal misgivings and too many pit-of-the-stomach doom feelings, you may not have made the right decision. Yes, you've invested much time and money and sacrificed a great deal to get to this point. Yet you still have the choice of dropping out. You may end up being "all but dissertation" (ABD), but you also may end up feeling happier devoting your life to other things you consider more important. Academic credentials aren't the only goals in life. In fact, the author of one study of doctoral candidates' motives and aspirations suggested that universities offer workshops for potential candidates to explore their motives (Brailsford, 2010).

If, though, you are convinced you want to continue, read on. I'll begin again: *One* of the hardest parts is over. But as the sculptor said to the block of stone, "Now the work begins."

Despite your convictions, once in the throes of graduate school, you may wish you'd never enrolled, or you've forgotten why you started. The road ahead is a little less bumpy when you think hard about and fully answer the following question.

HOW IS THE DEGREE PART OF YOUR LIFE'S DREAM?

In my years as a coach to doctoral students, I've been frequently amazed at the reasons they pursue the degree. More candidates than you'd think—and you may be one of them—desire the degree for "personal satisfaction." Somewhere, somehow, they've come to value the degree as a life goal, a career culmination (whatever their career), a fitting capstone before retirement.

In my own case, when I was still in high school, I "knew" I had to get the doctorate even before I could recite what the letters stood for. Why? Neither of my parents had gone to college, although my mother fervently wanted to. Both somehow transcended the upbringing of their less-than-well-to-do families (not that I mean to sound snobbish) and became self-made intellectuals.

I grew up in a house filled with classical music, bookshelves of literary classics (with a few Micheners and Fasts and Wouks thrown in), and regular infusions of *The Saturday Review, The Atlantic,* and *The New Yorker.* College and graduate school were assumed, and in fact, I took no breaks after undergraduate years to see the world, become a hippy, gain expertise in fast food slinging, or "find myself." All I wanted to find was the university library.

Getting the doctorate was an unquestioningly accepted life dream for me, almost programmed. What I'd do with the degree was another story. Teach, I vaguely thought. Teach English. One thing I did know was this: I was a lifelong writer (first productions at around age eleven, although nothing to write home about). English was my major, without question or guidance counselor. Thus, my doctorate was in English, and to fulfill the university requirement, I elected a minor in comparative literature.

As amorphous as my own doctoral dreams were, clients have shared much more specific and direct connections between their doctorates and life dreams. Here are some:

- Katharine was a grandmother about to retire from her administrative position in a retail company. She looked forward to spending more time with her grandchildren and sharing with them the satisfactions of an advanced education. She felt it was important to inspire them as they watched (and "helped") her develop her dissertation.
- From an immigrant family, Carlos was the first to go to college—*and* get an advanced degree. He had his eye on a steady, challenging position in upper management in business.
- Amy was born into an accomplished professional family and was the last to get an advanced degree. With it, she could finally hold her head up at Thanksgiving dinner with her doctor father, doctor

mother, Yale-doctorate brother, professor uncle, attorney aunt, and astro-bio-enviro-nuclear physicist cousin.

- Mike had grown up in a tough neighborhood and got into a gang, became dependent on drugs, and eventually served juvenile time in jail. A caring and savvy mentor in one of the institutional programs helped him get clean and steered him toward education. Completely (and miraculously) turning around his previous lifestyle, Mike pursued the doctorate to teach and counsel young people like himself and guide them on productive paths as he had been guided.
- With a brother who had intellectual disabilities, Trenton always wanted to start his own school for special-needs children. His advanced degree would give him the credentials to seek the necessary licenses and funding.
- At her university, Sonia had risen rapidly through administrative posts and was nominated for a deanship. The big obstacle was her lack of a PhD. So, middle-aged and highly motivated, she enrolled in a doctoral program.
- Marilyn had built two successful businesses, came through a successful divorce, had had four homes, and five country club memberships. With her six children and eight grandchildren, she could spend the rest of her life taking them to Disneyland, playing tennis, entering mahjong tournaments, and drinking chain lunch cocktails at her current country club. Instead, she said, she wanted to be a better model for her granddaughters, *do something,* and make a difference somewhere in the world. Marilyn became a late-middle-aged doctoral student.
- Before immigrating to the United States, Philippe had been a secretary to a government cabinet member in his native Caribbean country. He daily witnessed the poverty, illiteracy, and lack of jobs of so many of the people. His knew his advanced degree would give him entrance into a government position in education to institute national literacy and job training programs on a large scale.

Your turn. How is the degree part of *your* life dream?

Take fifteen minutes and write out your dream and the place of the degree in it. Then let your paragraph or list sit. Return a day later, and again, another day later. Add and change until you're satisfied that your description accurately represents how you really feel.

Read your statement over once a day, preferably at the same time. You may find after a few weeks that you want to change it again, add or delete. Do so. The more you refine the connection between your life dream and your doctorate, the more fuel you'll have for the tough journey and the more strength and persistence you'll have to keep going.

WHAT WILL THE DEGREE DO FOR YOU?

Think back to the first time you dared think about getting a doctorate. Excited? Surprised at your audacity? Adrenalined? Scared? What did you dream about? How did you see yourself feeling, thinking, acting, and talking (and I don't just mean making restaurant reservations for "Dr. ___")?

Be very specific. What *will* the degree do for you? Not only the basics (money, title, no more father nagging or uncle's bad jokes at every family gathering about your being a loser). List also bonuses you really want. Go ahead, go wild.

Here are some perks of all kinds my clients have shared:

- Help me get a better job.
- Help me get a promotion.
- Help me get higher pay.
- Help me change fields to a more satisfying one.
- Help me establish the credentials and credibility to develop and grow my own business.
- Help me gain the clout to help my home country.
- Help me model the value and perseverance of education for my children and grandchildren.
- Help me fulfill the personal dream of a doctorate.
- Help me earn money from what I've always wanted to do.
- Help me develop the talents I know I have.
- Help me prove my potential to myself.

One student, Russell, was particularly eloquent. When I asked why he was pursuing the doctorate, he replied passionately, "For the most important reason of all—because of my innate love of learning, which I value above all."

So, what will the degree do for *you?*

Make another little list. I'm sure several things have occurred to you already. If your answers overlap with some of those above, fine. As with any question that probes your inner desires and feelings, you may not reach all the answers in one sitting. Come back later, or better yet, don't even think consciously about your reasons. Your subconscious will do its work. When it does, and another response bubbles up, jot it down.

VISUALIZE YOUR DREAM

With all this ammunition, you can now envision your dream. What will it and you look like once the degree is awarded? What do you see yourself doing now that you have the degree? In other words, "What do you want to be when you grow up?"

For example, see yourself in your office (in a suit or jeans; your choice), degree mounted on the wall, and title on the door. This is using one of Covey's (2013) habits of highly effective people: "Begin with the end in mind" (p. 102). Imagine the movie. You're helping orphans, special-needs kids, abused women, communities, or countries. You're sagely addressing an eager college class, or you're meeting at a big, shiny table with funders for your new consulting business. You notice their eyebrows raised in admiration of your presentation (your mastery of PowerPoint from those agonizing dissertation defenses finally paid off).

Again, if you like, write out a paragraph or two describing yourself all grown up with the doctorate. A little help:

- Where are you? In an office in a high-rise? A modest three- or four-story building? Clinic? School or university? Suite of practitioners? Cozy but efficient home office?
- Who are you with? A partner working with equal concentration nearby, colleagues busily buzzing around? Assistants surrounding you? Your dog at your feet?
- What equipment, devices, and supplies are within reach? Computer, printer, cell phone, iPad, iPod, a few pieces of paper and pen, trail mix, Mozart mix?
- What are you wearing? (Don't scorn this question. As kids, we were very good at dressing up to visualize and act out our dreams.)
- How do you feel getting up to go to work?
- How do you feel leaving at night or closing the home office door?
- How do you feel telling important others about your day and work? Your partner, mother, father, great aunt who always believed in you, older brother who thought you wouldn't amount to much?

Shortly after graduation, my client Lydia reminisced about our first meeting. She reminded me that I'd asked her what her future plans were, and she replied she wanted to leave elementary school teaching and become a supervisor for student teachers at a nearby state university. A day after her graduation, she was informed she got the job. She said, "The fabulous thing was the fact that I told you my desire *before* it actually happened! The scripture tells us God will give us the desires of our heart . . . and He did!"

If you're dubious, think of this. One of the most powerful spiritual principles is "Believing is seeing." Before you snort or raise a skeptical eyebrow, I hear you. I recognize that this statement is contrary to our usual reasoning and realistic, logical, senses-based evidence. But it's a time-honored principle, promoted throughout the centuries from ancient philosophies to religious leaders to spiritual teachers to contemporary motivational pumpers and life coaches. See, for example, Wayne Dyer's (2001b) *You'll See It When You Believe It*.

If some of us didn't believe it before we saw it, we wouldn't have explored space, created great art, built great buildings, made astounding scientific breakthroughs, found the God particle . . . or finished our dissertations.

Not that you just sit there in the library worshipping your laptop and chanting. We must always move our feet. With your goal simmering below the surface, in this mind-set of seeing and believing, you know the wished-for outcome is inevitable. You're expectant, energized, and grateful. You've undoubtedly heard this often-quoted declaration by that high school dropout Walt Disney: "If you can dream it, you can do it."

Practice your picture of your dream with as much details as you can stuff in. Add new ones, outrageous as they may seem (original art on the walls, a $5,000 sound system to soothe your soul, a twenty-four-hour assistant who makes perfect Starbucks vanilla-caramel lattés). The more you "see" your dream realized, the sooner it will materialize. And the more vigor and perseverance you'll have for taking *all* the necessary steps to complete your dissertation.

AFFIRMATIONS FOR STRENGTHENING YOUR LIFE DREAM

We all need help in visualizing and sticking to our goals. Of course, you also need to do the dissertation writing required and work your way through the administrative maze. When you complete the exercises above and repeat the affirmations below, you'll not only stick with it but actually (or almost) enjoy the process.

Affirmations are positive statements for what you desire, dream of, and don't quite see in your present perspective. They should be stated in the present tense, with fervor, and encapsulate what you really want, as ridiculous or impossible as it may seem right now. If you'd like more explanation and some prepackaged affirmations, see Hay (2011) and Murphy (1982, 1987).

Here, though, are some doctoral-related affirmations to incorporate into your dream visualizations.

AFFIRMATIONS

I deserve my dream of the doctorate.
Everyone benefits from my achieving this dream.
Everyone around me helps me achieve this dream.

As I believe, I visualize and gratefully receive.
I don't need to know how it will all happen; I just need to believe and feel it will.
I expect to succeed!

Some of these affirmations may raise your anxiety and push your doubt meter into the red zone, and you may be tempted to swallow a few shots or a calming pill. Instead, let me deliver a commercial on meditation.

AS THEY SAY, MEDITATE, DON'T MEDICATE

If you don't like the term *meditation*, call it *My quiet time* or *Resting without snoring*. Whatever you call it, please consider it. Why?

Today regular features on the Internet, popular articles in magazines from *O, The Oprah Magazine* to *Playboy*, and scientific publications are full of reasons backed by studies that attest the benefits of meditation. They're physiological, psychological, emotional, social, and spiritual (Barbor, 2001; Mayo Clinic, 2014; Melnick, 2013; National Center for Complementary and Alternative Medicine, 2013; Sclamberg, 2014; Seppala, 2013; Trafton, 2011).

In the 1970s, meditation was sanitized for the West by the courageous Harvard MD Herbert Benson (1975) with his groundbreaking book *The Relaxation Response*. He documented empirically with laboratory techniques that meditation can lower blood pressure and the tendency to hardening of the arteries and stroke.

Benson virtually started mind/body medicine and demystified meditation for Westerners (Mitchell, 2013). In 1988, he founded the Mind/Body Medical Institute of Harvard Medical School and in 2006 the Benson-Henry Institute for Mind Body Medicine at Massachusetts General Hospital (Emory, 2011). He has republished the original book, many variations, and a host of other relevant publications, both scholarly and more popular.

Today, meditation is widely accepted and even prescribed by enlightened physicians. The practice doesn't need to connect to any religious movement or set of dogmatic statements. Nor does meditation have to be mysterious, and you can do it at home, in the library, at the bus stop, on the checkout line, and even in church. Books on meditation continue to proliferate, but it's really quite simple.

Sit in a quiet place (sorry, park your tech appendages out of thumbs' reach). Close your eyes and take some deep breaths. Then silently say a word, phrase, or sentence that means something to you (e.g., "Peace," "Ah," "All is in order," "Chocolate"). Or use one of your affirmations ("All answers are supplied now.") Just keep repeating your chosen words. One of the most recommended stints is for thirty minutes, but I can never last that long. At about four, my to-do lists start knocking at my head. Start with two, three, five, and ten. Set a timer if you want, and if you peek at it before it bongs, no one will know.

A caveat: If thoughts come in, and they will, you may find yourself veering off into last night's television plot, your sweetie's sudden text-messaging silence, the tuna spoiling in the fridge, or a thousand other things. As soon as you catch any of these thoughts, don't condemn yourself as a failed meditator. Just come back to your chosen words and keep repeating them. Gradually (very), those intruders will quiet down and may even cease for long periods.

Be patient with yourself. There's no right or wrong to meditating. The important thing is to keep at it, and eventually you'll experience probably unaccustomed calm and peace. Or you'll feel a lifting that is suspiciously like joy and not just a caffeine rush. Your mind will grow sharper and you will feel rested. You may even finally look forward to your next session.

What? No time? Too busy? Too stressed? You tried it and it didn't work? Too much like New Age (perceived) hooey? Take a look at Exkorn's (2014) excuses for not meditating and how she and her clients overcame all of the objections.

Here are her suggestions: No time means you haven't made time. Even three minutes works. Too busy means you don't have to add special time for the practice; just do what you do more consciously. Too stressed? Focus on doing one thing mindfully. She used eating Hershey Kisses. You can use a banana, coffee, or lunch. You tried it? For how long? Give it a fair chance, like any new habit. Too New Agey? As Exkorn pointed out, mindfulness was featured on a January 23, 2014, *Time* magazine cover, in a *New York Times* article, praised by actors and professional athletes, and has been used by staff at Google, General Mills, and Twitter.

If you need additional bolstering, buy and soak up the easy-to-read book, *Meditation for Dummies* (Bodian, 2012), or its cousin, *Mindfulness for Dummies* (Alidina, 2014). Both are legitimate excuses for not working on your dissertation.

Once you get in the habit, you'll see that meditation/mindfulness is your friend. You'll be able to turn to it for any puzzle or quandary that confronts you, as we'll see later. Right now, it will at least help you rest your eyes from that blinkin' cursor.

As you enter in earnest the lifestyle of dissertation outlanders, meditation and introspection will help you adjust to the *big* changes on the horizon. We'll look at these in chapter 2.

TWO

Big Changes

Despite intelligence, career experience, responsible titles, and worldly common sense, most adult students are little prepared for the dissertation stage of advanced graduate school. You may really have no idea of what it involves and how very different it is from previous undergraduate and graduate study. The demands and standards are different, and this phase of your higher education requires new self-discipline and dedication.

IT'S NOT JUST COLLEGE ANYMORE

As you well know by now, at the undergraduate, master's, and even the early doctoral level, the courses are structured. You know they'll last a semester or the equivalent, depending on the university and program. You attend classes a prescribed number of times a week, either in person or online. You get a syllabus that outlines with comforting specificity the course texts, additional readings, schedule of each week's assignments, and percentages of the grade for tests, papers, and class participation.

You know what you're supposed to do if you just keep to the schedule, pass the tests, respond at least minimally in classes, and turn in your assignments on time. You proudly finish each course and see it credited on your transcript. You keep knocking them off, confident that after you finish all the courses you'll have fulfilled the requirements and can go to the next stage. You feel a great sense of movement and accomplishment.

After meeting all those requirements, you're informed you can register for dissertation credits. You can now begin your dissertation! At those fateful words, you feel wonderful—for about four-and-a-half minutes. Then you realize, with a jolt, like a bucket of ice-cold Gatorade over your head, that you have no classes, no syllabus, no prescribed texts, no assignments, and no grades. *You're on your own.*

In fairness, I must say here that many universities provide resources to help you at this juncture. Some require dissertation seminars that direct you to produce progressive sections of the dissertation. Others supply outlines of the parts of the dissertation, varying from sketchy to obsessive-compulsive. These are meant to guide your production and help your chair and committee members "grade" your dissertation. The outlines have boxes and spaces for the committees' comments. In this form, the outlines are called rubrics (now you know what the word means).

Some universities during your dissertation-only semesters attempt to plug the social hole left by cessation of classes. Each term you're required to participate in online "chats" or Skype calls to report on and discuss your progress. These contacts take place with your chair and/or cohort members, who are other students lost at the same stage. Admittedly, such procedures can aid you—for a little while.

Too often, though, these contacts (a) become abhorred by doctoral students who must somehow sound to their faculty like they've produced at least some writing, or (b) degenerate into can-you-top-this competitive exchanges among students of "I'm overwhelmed" and "My chair ignores me" stories. At worst, the scheduled contacts are (c) mysteriously missed by the students who mutter via explanatory email that they mistook Central time for Pacific.

As a dissertation writer, maybe you've already realized that these planned activities, although well-meaning, generally waste your time. Maybe you develop a friendship with a colleague at the same stage and occasionally act for each other as behind-the-scenes cheerleaders. Maybe you really have been helped and can now sail into surprisingly smooth writing waters. If you are writing effortlessly, I salute you—and you don't need this book. If you're struggling with the writing, though, you may realize that you're better off on your own without all those busy-making activities. You just need to buckle down.

HOW READY ARE YOU TO CHANGE YOUR LIFESTYLE?

You soon realize something else too. With your evolution to dissertation writer, much or most about your current lifestyle must change. In my practice, I've found that beginning doctoral students, even with the greatest motivation, rarely recognize what their new life will entail.

No Structure

The lack of external structure is a terrible shock. No more neat schedules and specific tasks imposed from the outside. Complaints and commiserations with colleagues wear thin quickly. As one of my clients said, the dissertation is a "closeted journey."

You have no one to depend on except yourself. If you feel you can't, you may languish in ABD limbo for years (Blum, 2010). You must make your own schedules and stick to them, and it's not easy. If you work outside the home full-time, some structure is already imposed—consider yourself fortunate. You know what time remains for the dissertation: evenings, weekends, and an occasional call-in-sick day.

If you work at home or part-time, the lack of structure can be fierce. I've had students who think they have it made by taking a year off to do their dissertation. Can you guess what happens? They suddenly become "busy" with more nonacademic activities, events, and obligations than you can shake a dissertation handbook at.

One client proudly announced she had arranged her job and finances so that she was now "a full-time student." I cautioned her and more-than-strongly suggested she make a highly specific daily schedule for herself, and I offered to help. She politely declined. I didn't hear from her again for seven months.

When she finally did call, she was panicking. Her year was running out, she had barely defined her topic, and she was addicted to afternoon TV reruns. I calmed her down and she listened, now humbled. We worked out a sane dissertation schedule for the remaining months of her leave, including a strategy for reentry into her job.

Whatever the time or perceived lack of time you have to devote to the dissertation, face up to it. Commit to restructuring your time and sticking to your promises. In chapter 3 ("Find the Holes in Your Schedule"), I'll help you evolve reasonable plans for yourself that will give you some basic structure. If you alter, adjust, or veer from your plans—and you will—you'll at least have thought out your model and can quickly come back.

No Leisure

In this new commitment, you'll also have to change your definition of leisure—harshly. When I was working on my own dissertation, at lunch one day, several of us at similar stages were comparing how we spent Christmas. After listening to everyone else recount activities like spending time with their children, going out to a special show with their spouse, and volunteering at a local soup kitchen, Hugh told about his holiday.

"I couldn't avoid going with my family to the big dinner at the grandparents' house. I told them I'd go on one condition: I could work on my dissertation in their spare room upstairs." We all stared at him. "Sure, I wore a Christmas vest, but as soon as dinner was over, I took my pie and went upstairs with my briefcase. I spent the next four hours working.

When my family was ready to leave, they called me down, and, to my surprise, everyone was civil when we said goodbye. A cousin even wished me well with my dissertation."

Now that's commitment.

You may not dare be as radical as Hugh but recognize this: The evenings of back-to-back primetime TV and Facebook-clicking are over. Instead, after work or at your designated times, you'll be going to dissertation seminar, studying in the library, or surfing the Internet—for scholarly materials. On weekends, rather than car tinkering, sports cheering, shooting hoops with your teenager, or friendly spats with your spouse about that long-overdue yard sale, you'll still be studying, amassing too many materials, and having to confront the horrific prospect of actually writing.

Later we'll talk about how to siphon off a *few* breaks (chapter 6) and placating your family with some canny date-making strategies (chapters 7 and 8). Now, though, look your new lifestyle square in the schedule.

Your relationships will change not only with your family but with your professors. In classes, you probably had relatively cordial, relatively impersonal relationships. In any case, they only lasted for a semester or two. Now your chair is dogging you for the duration. Sitting opposite the chair in an office, whatever your title and degree of respect outside school, you can feel small and stupid while the chair spouts theories and absolute mastery of the literature. When you start getting your drafts back, marked up like a plastic surgeon's game plan or worse, with a single pronouncement like "inadequate," your self-image gets crushed into sand.

Clients have come to me after three and four rounds of image- and draft-battering, and in one case after the first proposal of 100 pages had to be jettisoned. Florence exclaimed, "What did I do to deserve this? I'm not a bad person!" Brian said he felt the conferences with his chair were "trial by torture." We'll address such torturous responses and how to lessen them in chapters 11 and 12. For now, be forewarned that this aspect of your dissertation journey, like the others, is likely a new and uncomfortable experience.

You will be facing at least two years and more likely four or six of dissertation concentration. I've had clients who have been in the trenches for ten years, with a file full of extensions (more about that later in chapter 6). As we saw earlier, large percentages drop out of doctoral programs (Cassuto, 2013a; Jaschik, 2007, 2008; Marte, 2013). You don't want to be a sad statistic.

On the required drastic changes of lifestyle and rude awakenings, get support. Talk to others at the same agonizing stage or those who received their doctorates a few years back—your cohort members, recent doctors, professors, and scholars you may know. You'll no doubt hear horror stories but should also glean some ideas about how to handle your own time and circumstances. Some clients of mine arrange periodic calls and emails with another dissertation writer to cheer each other on. Maybe they're commiseration buddies, but I like to call them "Completion Buddies." Try it; you may benefit.

IT'S YOUR TIME

Keep reminding yourself too of what it's taken to get to this point. You've undoubtedly made many sacrifices. You've worked and dreamed hard. You may have put others first until now— children, spouses, partners, parents. It's now your time to devote to this dream and complete it. A little later in this chapter, I'll suggest some declarations to keep you fueled. You'll need these as the going gets rocky(ier).

You need to know too, especially if you're a woman, that you're not being "selfish" for yearning after degree and taking all the steps to get it. This recognition may mean postponing or choosing not to have children. In a forthright essay in a collection by women professors, Warner (2008) observed that others often think "something must be *wrong* with you if you don't want to have children. You are seriously, perhaps pathologically, career driven; you are selfish" (p. 9). Conceivably (sorry for the pun), this decision can also apply to men who aspire to academia, but our social structures and conditioning , not to mention our biology, place the burden on women.

In any case, if others think or utter such accusations about selfishness, so what? Keep in mind the wise words of financier and presidential advisor Bernard M. Baruch. When arranging seating for an FDR presidential dinner, Baruch said to head off the almost inevitable criticisms, "Those who mind don't matter, and those who matter don't mind" (Josephson, 2012, originally quoted in Cerf, 1948, p. 249; this quotation is often erroneously attributed to the children's author Dr. Seuss).

So, choose *for yourself.* Remember too this principle, in relation to how you envision using your doctorate: We cannot be truly helpful to others if we don't nurture ourselves. A part of nurturing ourselves is doing what we have dreamed about and going for it.

DECLARE AND FEEL YOUR READINESS

Do you really want the degree and its rewards? Look back at those exercises you did in chapter 1 (you did, didn't you?) and review your answers. Reread them as much as you need to and feel again your initial excitement in deciding to go for the degree. Remind yourself of the noble (and other) reasons you're submitting to this self-torture.

And talk to yourself. If you don't want to think of this self-talk as affirmations, fine. Self- talk that encourages you can be extremely helpful;

Lord knows we all indulge in negative self-talk almost automatically. Here are some good self-programming declarations.

AFFIRMATIONS

I am ready!
I know I can meet the challenges of time, schedules, and self-discipline.
It's my time!
I see myself working consistently and with momentum.
I've worked long and hard to get to this point. I deserve to succeed.
I'm ready to plunge in and keep going!

Use these statements or create your own that may be closer to your particular circumstances ("I am ready to readjust my work hours to devote three days a week to research and writing"). As we continue, in part II, chapter 3, I will help you with more specifics of ways you can effectively plunge in.

II

Really Doing It

THREE

Priorities and Promises to Yourself

You've enunciated the best—your dream of the doctorate—and faced the worst—the lifestyle you've sentenced yourself to if you want to succeed. To really succeed, that is, to take the steps and keep acting, we need to plunge further. In this chapter, I'll help you lay more groundwork for effective and efficient, nay, even a little enjoyable progress.

YOUR INNER MENTOR: LISTENING FOR ANSWERS

Did you think I was finished with spirituality? Not a chance. This subject is first here because it can provide the key to everything you do in the dissertation (and life). Your Inner Mentor (IM), also called your inner guide, self, voice, spirit, higher power, soul, guidance system, intuition, even your heart or gut, has more power than your chair, the dean of your school, and even the guy who issues your annual parking sticker.

Maybe you haven't recognized or used your IM. Maybe you don't want to acknowledge it. Fine. You've already experienced it. When "something" doesn't feel right about a certain person or event, when "a little voice" tells you to turn right instead of left, when the "right words" suddenly trumpet in your brain as you greet your mother for the first time in six months. If you'd like more of my thoughts about the IM or inner voice, see the discussion in *Trust Your Life* (Sterne, 2011).

As you learn to use your IM more consciously, you'll see that it can help and guide you to many right decisions and actions. With more practice and results, you'll be less hesitant to turn to it, and you'll use it not only for dissertation quandaries but for *anything*. By the way, see Richmond's (2007) acknowledgment to his dissertation quoted in the introduction: "In examining myself through this journey, I found that I often turn to faith and prayer as a strength and resource. . . ."

Where does the IM come from? Various spiritual and New Thought teachings tell us that it is implanted, embedded in us (a sprinkling: *A Course in Miracles,* 2007; Bodian, 2012; Chopra, 2004, 2011; Harra, 2009; Hicks & Hicks, 2004, 2006, 2009; Unity, 2012; Williamson, 2000). You can subscribe to any of these teachings or not. Does it really matter? Whatever explanations or origins we choose to give the IM (admittedly not the scientific method), its efficacy remains intact.

When to access your Inner Mentor? Any time, any place, in any situation or circumstance, with any question (confession: I used it/her to start this chapter). A quiet time is preferable, such as your daily meditation session (no excuses, please). Other times can be just as effective: waiting for a traffic light, in a dentist's office, during exercise or a coffee break, just before you fall asleep, or as you're awakening. No boundaries exist of time or space.

How to access your Inner Mentor? Get quiet, take a few deep breaths (if you're not panting as you jog), and just ask what you want to know. Make the question the only thing you focus on. If you're very concerned about something—like what the hell to do with that impossible mass of articles for your literature review—it won't be hard to dump everything else from you mind and just ask.

Then—listen. This is admittedly the hard part. Resist self-talk and figuring out possible solutions. The widely known physician, author, and spiritual teacher Deepak Chopra (2011) called this tendency our feeling "compelled to force solutions" (p. 52). Suspend your skepticism and pull to logic. You'll have plenty of other chances to activate your rational mind and critical problem-solving skills. Now, humility is called for.

I've always liked Elizabeth Gilbert's (2006) account of her first encounter with her Inner Voice in her bestseller *Eat, Pray, Love.* In the middle of the night, agonizing over her terrible marriage and what to do about it, sobbing uncontrollably, she begged some admittedly amorphous god to *please* tell her what to do. An answer, startlingly, came sure and strong: "Go back to bed, Liz" (p. 16). This was as practical and correct as it gets.

What does your Inner Mentor feel like? Gilbert's (2006) description is sane and swallowable: "It was merely my own voice, speaking from within my own self. But this was my voice as I had never heard it before. This was my voice, but perfectly wise, calm and compassionate. This was what my voice would sound like if I'd only ever experienced love and certainty in my life" (p. 16).

When I hear the IM, my responses are close to Gilbert's. I feel it in my body—lightness in my chest, fear erased, a sense of well-being. I feel it in my mind—certainty and rightness of the answer, and a blissful peace. I know what to do. Gilbert (2006) realized, "Even during the worst of suffering, that calm, compassionate, affectionate and infinitely wise voice . . . is always available" (p. 53).

It gets better. The more you rely on your IM, the more you'll develop the habit of turning to it and listening. You'll come to trust its all-encompassing knowledge and peace, and you'll get stronger in asking, listening, and following.

Two affirmations about the IM:

AFFIRMATIONS

The mind of God lives in me. It is clear and full of strength and wisdom. (Unity, 2012)

My mind is a part of God's Mind, and I am always reflecting Divine Wisdom and Divine Intelligence. (Murphy, 2001, p. 117)

And one exercise (did you think I would let you escape?):

Waddaya wanna know? Pick a subject, knotty situation, quandary, or even something you're vaguely curious about. Go apart from the crowd, emails, Facebook, Twitter, Instagram, and Pinterest. Go outside, if possible, and take in some greenery. Sit there. Ask your question. Wait.

If you hear nothing except your own mental frittering, ask again. If you get impatient, still yourself once more. If you can't settle down, you may need to walk away and come back later. When you do, you may hear the answer three hours later as you're getting ready for bed, or the next hour as you're making the popcorn for a *Walking Dead* marathon. Once you get the hang of it, you'll find that your IM is nothing less than infallible. Your Inner Mentor, kind of like an academic nag, is always with you. Try it. Trust it.

RETHINK YOUR PRIORITIES

Your IM can help too as you rethink your priorities. You already have some practice in prioritizing from chapter 2, when you faced fundamental lifestyle changes you must make (you did face them, didn't you?). Hone in a little more. Now that you've reached the momentous dissertation stage, you suspect what your first priority must be.

It's totally understandable if you have to put job or career first. You may have been used to putting family first. Heartless and psychologically suspect as this may sound, rethink this priority. Remember Hugh and the Christmas dinner. In part III, I'll show you how to orient your family to your new commitment, paint the rewards, and later make it all up to them.

Right now, at this point in your graduate school life, you're *supposed* to make the dissertation a major priority. Talk to other students at or near your stage. Compare notes, choices, and concerns. Just talking about yours will strengthen you. Maybe you'll even give them a hand in reordering their own priorities toward finishing.

Liza, my client, was president of a church committee. She realized she was spending many hours a week organizing and on the phone for the meetings and events. She made the decision to cut way back and, with apologies and what she hoped was divine dispensation, resigned from the presidency.

Another client, Eric, arranged to convert his full-time job to part-time. He was also able to arrange funding to replace his full-time salary so he could cover the tuition finances. He proudly announced to me, "I'm devoting three days a week to the dissertation!"

If you're devoted to working out seven days a week, a noble devotion, examine your time. Instead of hitting the gym daily, you can still sculpt your six-pack in four days a week. If you're devoted to TV, prerecord the shows you can't live without, ration them, and reward yourself like eating chocolate truffles. If you're devoted to hourly exchanges of juicy confidences or incessant texts with a best friend, plan on once a day instead. You'll have that much more to commiserate about.

In rethinking my own priorities and the time necessary for several writing projects, this year I reluctantly gave up two columns in writing magazines. Why? To work on this book.

You may be reasoning, Oh, an hour here or there doesn't matter much. Maybe not, but I've found, as many other people have who are serious about their pursuits, that even an hour can leak into more and upset one's work momentum. I'm not talking about conscious and reasonable breaks for balance, which we'll talk about in chapter 6, but rather the spontaneous, avoidant use or misuse of your time without rethinking your priorities or keeping your new ones in mind.

Reading an article in a writing magazine (OK, I slip in a few when I should be working), I discovered a highly pertinent and too-true reply from the English master Charles Dickens to his lady love about why he could not accede to her invitation and those of others (quoted by Godwin, 2008). You may have heard similar words from relatives or friends who try to inveigle you into coming out to play:

> "It is only half an hour"—"it is only an afternoon"—"it is only an evening" people say to me over and over again—but they don't know that it is impossible to command oneself sometimes to any stipulated and set disposal of five minutes—or that the mere consciousness of an engagement will sometimes worry a whole day. These are the penalties paid for writing books. Whoever is devoted to an Art must be content to deliver himself wholly up to it, and find his recompense in it. (p. 34)

Dickens' penalties for writing are also those for finishing dissertations. As you are devoted to your work, you too will find your recompense.

FIND THE HOLES IN YOUR SCHEDULE

A little time-management music, please. Is time your enemy? Everything takes longer than you expect or plan for—waiting so many years to even get into the doctoral program, waiting for the Internet connection, waiting for librarians to locate obsolete materials, waiting for professors to send you back (much less locate) the latest draft you sent, waiting for other key people's calls or emails, waiting for the right moment to start writing (this last alone can take up to ten years).

However strongly you may feel about being time's victim, this feeling can be reversed. Time is not your taskmaster but a flexible servant. You can change your attitude about time. "Reality is an interpretation" (Chopra, 2011, p. 33). Exercise your choices.

One of the first things to do is to see how much time you really have. I'm not going to recite the usual time platitudes: "We all have the same amount of X seconds, minutes, hours." Probably meant as help, this statement has always depressed me, as if it's a reprimand, especially when I'm facing down a 114-item not-yet-done list.

Instead I'll point you to two techniques I use with clients (and myself) who (a) feel they have no time for the dissertation, and (b) go into full panic because they agonize about thinking they have too little time.

First, take a big calendar book or sheets of about letter-sized pages. I like the weekly calendar books, with a single week over two pages when the book is open and divided into hourly segments, paper or virtual. Mark in (or draw big lines through) the absolute necessities (job, kids' pick-ups, grocery-shopping, teeth-cleaning appointments). Then look at the unmarked spaces. Lo, these are the times you have for the dissertation.

The time segments may look like more or less than you'd like. Whatever they are, *use* them. Evenings after the kids are bathed or after the crucial football game? Early mornings (not my preference, for sure)? Weekends? Then fill in your dissertation-devoted time. You do have more time than you thought.

A caution: If you start off all excited and exclaim, "Wow! I have more time than I thought!" you may be tempted to fill into your schedule every single moment not devoted to your job or other necessities. Don't. You're entitled to reasonable breaks (more in chapter 6).

Listen to yourself and your body. You know you're no good at 5:00 a.m. an hour before you have to get ready for work. Or that you fade completely after 9:00 p.m. Avoid these times, and make no rash promises to yourself.

You see, though, that 7:00 p.m. could work, for two hours at least three nights a week, and Saturday and Sunday mornings. On your calendar, in these spaces write or type in big letters DISSERTATION. They are your appointments with yourself, as inviolate as your regular oil change.

As you get more into the dissertation, add specifics right in the calendar. On Wednesday night, for example, you could add "Search literature for previous studies on children overattached to their teddies." On Saturday morning, add "Write two intro paragraphs on origins of play therapy with stuffed pets."

My second technique follows from this suggestion. Make a master list of the tasks you see in front of you. This list is not meant to overwhelm you but let you schedule successive tasks in reasonable time allocations. Of course the list will change. In the example above, you could put down the following:

1. Search library databases for studies on children overattached to their teddies.
2. Make PDFs of these and put them in a file.
3. Start a reference list for them (imperative!).
4. Ask Gertie the play therapist about her experiences with children and stuffed animals and books/articles/conferences she knows about.
5. Write a *rough draft* of introduction.

This list will help you see what to do and in what sequence. You'll have the supreme pleasure, eventually, of checking off each item.

These techniques aren't only valuable for organizing yourself. When you mark off your time allotments and list the tasks, they become intentions, goals, and affirmations (I can't resist spiritual gems for too long). The techniques, rightly applied, also help you strengthen your scheduling and habits for taking action.

As you acknowledge your preferences and body clock (no 5:00 a.m., yes 7:00 p.m.) and decide on judicious scheduling, you may find too that you actually want to keep going. Absorbed in your evening 7:00 stint, you work until 9:30 and don't even feel tired. This is good. It's also known (to borrow a selling platitude) as promising less and delivering more, except that your client is yourself. With this maxim in mind, you'll make great progress.

KEEP YOUR PROMISES TO YOURSELF

Sometimes you'll promise less and deliver just about what you've promised yourself, or less. Fine. Forgive yourself. Just get back on the horse. Recognize that your promises to yourself are just as important, if not more, than those you make to others. As I said earlier, consider the promises as serious, even sacrosanct, as any other you make.

You've written your promises on your calendar to give you time to work on to your dissertation. And I hope you've staked out a special place for dissertation headquarters—study, sunroom, half the bedroom, all the dining room table. Having your special place makes it much easier to leave everything a mess and start where you last left off.

But some days, when you enter your sanctuary and sit down at your session, you just can't face analyzing another article or foraying into writing. The remedy? Do *something*, anything that has to do with your dissertation and will advance it, even if it seems trivial.

For example, start or continue your reference list or bibliography. Edit it according to the university required style manual. Draft a letter to ask permission of the originator of a survey you discovered that would be perfect for your study. Look up the template for an informed consent on your university website. *Anything.*

If you're condemning yourself for choosing rote or easy tasks during your dissertation sessions, use this perfect rationale: These things have to be done *sometime*. You'll be able to creep up later on the hard stuff (see chapter 5). What you're really doing now is keeping your promises to yourself.

This countermeasure is infinitely better than the quandary many clients come to me with. They feel blocked, don't know where to start, and can't buckle down. Florence put it graphically in her first call to me: "I'm paying the university dissertation fee every semester to sit home and watch television." I walked Florence through the calendar technique and the *Do anything* corollary. She was off.

Another client suffered from a long block that likely had its source in perfectionism. Lincoln was brilliant, had a fellowship to an Ivy League graduate program, and was studying the political ramifications of eighteenth-century French literature. At a New Year's party, he took me into the bedroom he shared with his wife and showed me the bed littered with papers, articles, scribbled notes, and books. Lincoln confided that he'd made many false starts and couldn't get over a block. Knowing what a star Lincoln was, I sensed he was feeling extraordinarily pressured by his eager chair and department members.

I said, "Linc, you don't have to write the Great American Dissertation." He looked at me startled and then relieved. A week later he called. "You freed me," he said. "I'm writing like crazy." In five months, he finished, a record time for a dissertation. He was awarded the departmental prize for the best dissertation that year.

You don't have to write the Great American Dissertation either. Just keep your promises to yourself to do a little, easy or hard, at regular times. These affirmations should help:

AFFIRMATIONS

I deserve to keep my promises to myself.
I have the mental fortitude and character to keep my promises to myself.
I overcome any seeming block and just *keep going.*

YOUR LATER LIST

During your promise-fulfilled stint, your mind may wander (read: obsess) to all the other promises you've made—to your wife to clean out the guest room cartons, to your kids to build the tree house, to your favorite great-aunt to take her out to a leisurely lunch, to your neighbor to join the community baseball team. Especially with your new conviction, you feel you can't afford the time now to do any of these things.

So, start your "Later List." Like other lists (see below), this one functions mainly as a storage area, pen or virtual, to get off your mind and put somewhere safe those other things that plague. I'm a great believer in lists; they not only get those pests out of my head but assure me I won't forget them. I just have to look in the file.

Your Later List can be any and all the things you not only promised to others but also to yourself (give away all your fatigued gym clothes, write your memoir, reorganize the kitchen junk drawer, put up the pegboard wall for tools in the garage, get away with the wife for a spa weekend). Just dump them all out here. We'll revisit your Later List . . . later, in chapter 15, when you really will, and should, have time to act on your entries.

While we're on lists, another time management technique, recommended by many organizational gurus, is making and keeping various types of lists (Allen, 2002; Covey, 2013; Lakein, 1989). You've already done a bit of this in entering on your calendar specific tasks for each dissertation session. As you get more into the work, all kinds of tasks will bombard you (get permission letter from research site, download Institutional Rewview Board [IRB] application, reorganize articles by subhead, call department secretary for latest dissertation handbook, look up *multicollinearity*, write the damn introduction).

To corral this stampede, make some lists. You can start by spilling out everything that crops up and head it "Master List," to be added to as you make progress. Once your first master list is done, make second-generation lists categorizing all these varmints. You can do them by short-term, mid-term, or long-term goals, by chapter, or by whatever seems most pressing. You'll need to spend some time in the beginning on these lists, but after you do and feel fairly organized, stop.

Lakein (1989) astutely observed that the "overorganized person is always making lists" (p. 14). You can stall endlessly spinning out lists and fool yourself into thinking that you're accomplishing something. Listen to yourself inside or your IM and obey (keep your promises) when you know you're avoiding the real work or at least tackling something on one of the lists. Put your lists in a folder and bring them out one at a time, for example only for this week or the chapter you're working on. Then hide the folder.

AFFIRM YOUR RIGHT TIME AND TIMING

To support you in judicious list making and all other aspects of this chapter, I offer some right-time affirmations:

AFFIRMATIONS

I am in the right place doing the right activities at the right time.
I am in charge of my time.
I deserve my time.
No one can be hurt by my choices.
I do what is mine to do in the right flow of time.
I accept perfect timing and perfect use of my time.

As you take these thoughts in, you'll be more open to the topic of chapter 4, "Enroll Your Higher Self." You won't even have to register and pay a university fee.

FOUR

Enroll Your Higher Self

A warning: This entire chapter should be subtitled "The Spiritual Chapter." As you've undoubtedly deduced, it's spiritually based. If you wish, skip the chapter; the plagues won't rain down. You may benefit, though (she sneakily points out), if you're a little open to the ideas here. As I said earlier, you may feel they aren't logical, rational, evidence-based, realistic, or provable, but they can be practical. The question to ask yourself is this: Will these ideas help me finish this blessed dissertation?

HELLO, LIGHT BEING!

Yes, you are a being of light. The Greek word *phós* means a source of light, radiance, illumination. In this view, you are a spiritual being in physical masquerade. The often-quoted and paraphrased passage, attributed to the French Jesuit priest and religious philosopher Teilhard de Chardin (1961) summarized this concept: "We are not human beings having a spiritual experience. We are spiritual beings having a human experience" (Covey, 2000, p. 47).

The Unity minister, scholar, and teacher Eric Butterworth (1992) echoed, "Man is a spiritual being with infinite possibilities within him" (p. 4). Chopra (1994) declared, "[W]e are spiritual beings that have taken on manifestation in physical form. We not human beings that have occasional spiritual experiences—it's the other way around: we're spiritual beings that have occasional human experiences" (p. 97).

Psychologist, PhD, and spiritual intuitive Carmen Harra (2009) put it this way: "We are not just physical beings living in a physical reality, but light-energy beings living in a realm of energy" (p. 13). As quantum physics and the Large Hadron Collider tell us, all is energy—and this includes us. More: We have all *chosen* to become physical beings for various purposes—to give, share, experience, rectify . . . and finish our dissertations.

Of course, we're attached to complete identification with our bodies and the physical reality before us. As I suggest here, if you get a glimpse of the reverse, even for a few moments, you will enlarge your very humanness. You'll feel, maybe inexplicably, even more alive, more astute, and more attuned to life than ever. You'll feel more powerful to attract and do whatever is before you to do in this human experience.

To brazenly paraphrase the Bible, we are the light of the world (John 8:12). *A Course in Miracles* (2007) tells us, "I am the light of the world" (Lesson 61, p. 784). You are the light of *your* world.

See yourself as a light being, as a being filled with light, able to leap over knotty problems in a single mental bound. See yourself as able to solve any trouble that crops up. And let your light shine.

TRUST THE PROCESS

As you do, you will realize you have the power, through your Inner Mentor, to access anything you need. You can trust the process of asking, listening, and receiving. In fact, as Hicks and Hicks (2004) instructed through "Abraham," these are the only steps we need to take:

- Step 1 (your work): You ask.
- Step 2 (not your work): The answer is given.
- Step 3 (your work): The answer, which has been given, must be received or allowed (you have to let it in). (p. 47)

When we trust the process in our quiet times, or even in an internal panic, we ask in all humility and openness. In the quiet, "we are inspired with fresh resolve, with new creative thought, with solutions to problems" (Guiley, 1998, p. 74). We recognize that the answer is already here (Step 2). We're guided to the best topic, colleague, scholar, mentor, journal, librarian, and babysitter.

In a workshop, Abraham (Hicks & Hicks, 2000) counseled, "Delegate it to the manager. You have this really good staff that will take care of everything for you. You just have to delegate it—and trust it" (n.p.). Abraham also enticingly draws our attention to "the enormous Non-Physical staff that responds to your vibrational requests" (Hicks & Hicks, 2004, p. 153).

If you're rebelling at this metaphysical assault, think of the process like this. It's what any artist experiences, I imagine, and many, including myself, have found true in writing. Novelist and essayist Joan Frank (2014) described it beautifully and clearly. We develop "a very special quality of trust—trust in your unconscious as it draws from memory, dreams, happenstance—and trust in your conscious will, as it works to organize, shape, and smooth . . . the results" (para. 25).

In two of my favorite lines, the American poet Richard Wilbur (1969) said it simply in "Walking to Sleep." I discovered this poem, incidentally, when I was in the library looking for material that was completely unrelated.

> Step off assuredly into the blank of your mind.
> Something will come to you. (p. 1)

When I've shared these realizations with clients, they've responded with their own experiences. Marilyn needed a nonprofit organization as a site for surveying participants. I suggested a couple that didn't work out. She was stumped. Then, she said, she "forgot" about the quandary and worked on her invitation letter, as if she already had participants. Shortly, driving to work, a song she was listening to reminded her of a friend from her past who had been an assistant administrator in a nonprofit organization.

Marilyn tracked down her friend, who was delighted to hear from her and was now head of the organization. She offered the organization for Marilyn's participants and cooperated fully throughout Marilyn's data collection.

Nate, in the pangs of his literature review, found a great quote in a novel he was reading before bed. He wanted to use the quote but had no idea how. So, he told me, he "asked" his IM (I was so proud of him). Two nights and two chapters later, the perfect place came to him as a transition from a certain subhead to the next. Much later, his chair praised the passage highly and confided to Nate that the novel was a favorite of his too.

These two examples, and many more, have several things in common; they are object lessons for us all. First, the outcomes required letting go of the "problem," something like Abraham's Step 2: not your work. The answer can come, like with Marilyn and Nate, much later than the asking. Or it can come immediately. Like with Brenda, as she quietly munched her lunch on a break from her dissertation writing, she "asked" for the best steps to take in her next chapter. After one more swallow, the sequence popped into her head.

This immediate response is the shower epiphany. We all have our own versions: You're scrubbing away, enjoying the jet stream, thinking of nothing much. Suddenly—there it is! The right word or phrase, name of author or colleague, elegant problem statement, right statistical procedure for your hypothesis, appears like magic. In Frank's (2014) terms, you've mentally asked, stepped away, and let your subconscious do its work.

This process can take place in many ways, with or without a shower: while you're meditating, getting through some repetitive activity like dish washing or wood chopping, driving, waiting, or any other solitary time. The only requirement is to stop your internal worry and nattering and mentally step away. Detach and breathe. Something will come to you.

THREE PUZZLING AND POWERFUL REINFORCING LAWS

To further support you, I want to introduce you to three spiritual laws that may at first seem paradoxical and contradictory. Once you get acquainted with them, though, they deliver even more emotional/spiritual strengthening. These laws were described simply and eloquently by Chopra (1994) in *The Seven Spiritual Laws of Success.*

The Law of Least Effort

Huh? You read it right. After all that talk in the previous chapters about deciding, committing, and buckling down, how can you be helped by a so-called Law of Least Effort?

The Law of Least Effort isn't quite what the name seems to indicate. It doesn't mean we loll on the couch with the world blocked out and our earphones plugged in and wish our dissertation into existence. Rather, this law "is based on the fact that nature's intelligence functions with effortless ease. . . . If you observe nature at work, you will see that least effort is expended. Grass doesn't try to grow, it just grows" (Chopra, 1994, p. 53). That is, the idea is not to strive and fight but recognize and yield to what is before us.

Another way of expressing this law is as the Law of Relaxation. The spiritual teacher, preacher, and author Emmet Fox (1992) described it like this: "In all mental working effort defeats itself. . . . When you try to force things mentally, when you try to hurry mentally," and we might add, when you *try* at all, "you simply stop your creative power" (p. 24).

Activating this law, we ask, listen, know, and trust that we will be led to the right materials, advisor, chair, research database. Having set our goals and targets (as in the earlier chapters here), we know and trust that the universe cooperates and conspires with us.

The Law of Least Effort has three aspects, all important for us. The first is acceptance—to accept this moment as it is rather than curse it because it isn't. You can't change it if you don't accept it first. You can still wish for it to be different ("My dissertation is finished."), keep the goal of completion in front of you ("My dissertation is finished."), and take the necessary steps.

But to rage against this moment when you can't work on your chapter because you're watching the kids or your boss loaded you down with reports for the weekend just wastes energy you could be using later to research obscure articles on your topic. Instead, make a plan for after the babysitting or arrange to hire a sitter. Talk to your boss about rescheduling the reports.

The second aspect is responsibility. This means that you don't blame anyone or anything else for where you are, "including yourself," as Chopra (1994, p. 59) reassuringly said, now you can respond creatively to the situation. Instead of blaming your chair, job, kids, seasonal allergies for keeping you from your work, open to creative response. The best response is one you may have heard before from different teachers and cultures, and Chopra reiterated: Every problem contains the seed of an opportunity for transformation into something we desire.

The third aspect is defenselessness. Granted, this is a hard one. Who doesn't want to be right? This aspect may seem contradictory as well to the goals of scholarship. In defenselessness, Chopra (1994) noted, you relinquish "the need to convince or persuade others of your point of view" (p. 60). The yielding releases or redirects energy from such attempts to other more worthwhile pursuits, like figuring out how to test your hypotheses. (In defense of scholarship, we can see defenselessness as not engaging in persuasive or bombastic rhetoric but pointing out the gaps in your topic, recapping what's been studied, and showing how you're filling those gaps.)

You may bristle at defenselessness ("I'm no doormat."), but if you open your mind to it, you won't be tempted into arguments. You'll develop openness to various points of view and not be "rigidly attached to any" (Chopra, 1994, p. 64). You'll save time in avoiding arguments and defending yourself. Besides, isn't openness what the scholarly stance cultivates?

The Law of Intention and Desire

The Law of Intention and Desire, the second that applies to us, is grounded in quantum theory. The universe is composed of energy and information, from the largest galaxy to the smallest microorganism. Through our human nervous systems, we can become aware of the energy and information of our bodies and beyond. As we do, through our attention and intention we can *consciously* change the energy and information that come to us.

These assertions form the basis of spiritual healing, creative works of all kinds, and success in every project. "Whatever you put your attention on will grow stronger in your life" (Chopra, 1994, p. 70). Following from attention, our (good) intention will "bring about the outcome intended" (p. 70).

The principle of intention is not original with Chopra. In a famous passage from his play *Faust,* the German poet-novelist-philosopher

Goethe (2000) gave forceful instructions for using the Law of Intention and Desire:

> What you can do, or dream you can, begin it!
> Boldness has genius, power and magic in it.
> *Only engage, and then the mind grows heated.*
> BEGIN, and then the work will be completed. (p. 30, emphasis in the original)

I recommend also to you Wayne Dyer's (2004) book on intention. The title announced his own intention: *The Power of Intention: Learning to Co-create Your World Your Way.* Now we're closer to what we talked about in chapter 1 on visualizing and affirming your doctoral dream—you were connecting with your desire and bolstering your intention. We're following from our conversation in chapter 3 on giving great attention to your priorities and promises.

As we introduce intention into our minds and hold our convictions, we activate the universal "cosmic computer with its infinite organizing power" (Chopra, 1994, p. 72). Chopra pointed out, as do many others, that every intention and desire contains the seeds and means for its fulfillment. Recognizing and taking in these truths of consciousness, we witness, astonished, the appearance in our lives of the phrases, understanding, information, events, databases, and expert statistician we sorely need.

The Law of Detachment

The Law of Detachment is inextricably connected to the Law of Intention and Desire, although the connection may seem illogical. It's not an easy law, especially if you've grown up in the acquisitive, grasping, striving, and trying Western culture. The Law of Detachment tells us that to acquire anything, we must give up our attachment to it. Chopra (1994) hastened to assure us we don't have to give up our intention, desire, and goals, but rather our attachment to the results.

Attachment is based on fear and worry that we won't, can't, even shouldn't have something. Attachment is based too on our assumption that more, bigger, and grander will make us feel more important and superior. Then, we fondly believe, we'll command respect. When we renounce our allegiance to such negatives, we are declaring that we trust ourselves and the universe to supply what we need.

For example, when you no longer care about recognition first but immerse yourself in the work, then acknowledgment or fame comes. When you no longer crave your mother's approval and stop trying everything get it, she bursts out with admiration for you and your accomplishment. When you stop craving the university Most Abstruse Dissertation award and you get genuinely caught up in your topic, your argument becomes brilliant and your research rationales solid.

Attachment makes us fearfully rigid, closed, frozen, unbending. We don't think of creative possibilities. If we do, we dismiss them quickly. We try to force our analytic faculties to solutions according to our limited thinking. We keep blinders on to the infinite possibilities available.

I'm not bashing our analytic mental powers; we absolutely need them in dissertations and many other aspects of life. But for true guided answers, they inhibit us. In detachment, we open ourselves to uncertainty, which admittedly makes most of us uncomfortable (hence our striving to amass security in all forms).

Uncertainty, though, "is the fertile ground of pure creativity and freedom" (Chopra, 1994, p. 86). Uncertainty, as in not knowing the outcome of your hypotheses, gives rise to fluidity, openness, and spontaneity. When you embrace and allow uncertainty, when you expect it and don't try to block it, your mind flowers. You may suddenly think of a new way of testing your hypotheses, or another participant pool, or another slant on the problem.

With the Law of Detachment, we are asked to become alert, to recognize that in any problem lies an opportunity and a solution. We are asked to trust (again) and step out into the unknown of our minds. Something, assuredly, will come to us.

RECOGNIZE AND ACCEPT YOUR POWER

When you become aware of and use these three laws and trust the process, you will experience everything taking place more smoothly. You will more easily recognize, understand, and accept your power. Possibly more radically, as many New Thought teachers tell us, we *do* have the power to create our experiences. Great dissertation creating is not excluded.

In fact, in a provocative scholarly article, Cozart (2010) examined her struggle between spirituality and academia, in addition to her marginalization as an African American female academic. "As such, I acted as if spirituality was a third kind of consciousness, rather than part of my merging double-consciousness into a better truer self" (p. 253).

She came to a reconciling definition of spirituality: "Inner submission to my God consciousness. This definition is not meant to refute other definitions, only to add location to my relationship with my God consciousness. I acknowledge that I cannot live within my own power but through the power of my God consciousness" (Cozart, 2010, p. 257).

Acknowledge, admit, and use your own wonderful God consciousness. Ask, relax, detach, and trust. Your questions will be answered, and you will be told. The answer may appear as a word, phrase, image, or a feeling of being "led" to email someone, call someone, or open a certain book or journal.

As you use your IM and accept that any answer is available to you, you will get stronger in asking. Your IM will become easier to access, more reliable and sure. The answers may even come, as they have many times with me, before I even finish the question.

A FEW HIGHER SELF AFFIRMATIONS

For a little more support, here are some powerful statements. As always, you can adapt them to your own needs and circumstances.

AFFIRMATIONS

All the answers I need are here now.
God is moving on my behalf. I listen and obey.
I am perfectly guided and led to the next thing I need.
I relax and trust. All answers are revealed.
I am a spiritual being. I am whole and free. I am confident and capable. I am the master of my life. (Butterworth, 1992, p. 50)

With this foundation of the right attitudes, assuming you haven't skipped this chapter, we're ready to move on—to the dissertation itself. Chapter 5 will help you tackle previously fearsome subjects you may have been avoiding—your topic, proposal, and (shudder) writing. With the input of your right attitudes, you can't help but produce right outcomes.

FIVE

Starting the Work

Positive Patient Persevering

What's your reaction when you think about starting the work? "It's too hard." "I can't." "Impossible." "I'll never get there."

If an of these laments sound familiar, you might as well throw this book into the corner and go out and rake the yard. See the first word of this chapter's subtitle? That's the key—*positive*. Why? What we mouth reflects what we think, and what we think reflects what we experience.

Talking about how many of us label our previous experiences as negative, Dyer (2001a) suggested we give our past "a new job description" (p. 75). Abraham (Hicks & Hicks, 2008) advised telling "a different story about your life and the people and experiences that are in it"; as you do, "you will see your life begin to transform to match the essence of the details of the new-and-improved story you are now telling" (p. 27).

Elucidating, Abraham (Hicks & Hicks, 2008) said, "[B]y beginning to tell stories that lean more in the direction you want . . . your vibration will shift, your point of attraction will shift, and you will get different results" (p. 126). So start telling a different story about your dissertation and look forward to the different results. The first step is to . . .

LISTEN FOR THE TOPIC THAT'S RIGHT FOR YOU

Sitting in the library, Dan solemnly promised himself that *today* he'd actually start writing. His laptop was open and the table was strewn with dissertation-related papers, open books, and note cards. All Dan could do was stare at the clock on the wall. He'd made the mistake of trying to leap into the dissertation without enough forethought or real passion for his topic.

It's undeniable. The dissertation engenders a love-hate relationship, with all the exasperations, frustrations, teeth-clenching, and eye-rolling, and all the affection, elation, and fulfillment (eventually) of a primary human relationship. Therefore, your topic should be one that initially excites you, during the process sustains you throughout the inevitable peaks and gullies, and eventually morphs into a satisfying career. The importance of topic choice hasn't gotten enough scholarly attention, I believe, although I did come across a dissertation on dissertation topics (Xia, 2013).

Topic Considerations

I've seen many students, in the heat of first passion, bite off a topic that would take forty monks without tablets or TV breaks sixty years to complete. It's inevitable that these candidates become demoralized at the enormity of their overreaching investigations. When I see this tendency with clients in the early stages, I gently and respectfully suggest they take a quarter of the original idea. To cushion the pain of separation, I soothe clients with the promise that they can tuck all those other thoughts and possible research questions into the final chapter when they discuss future research.

I've seen other candidates take on topics because their professors suggest them and the students don't know how to decline. Or they think the idea is "hot" and they'll have a better chance of publishing. Neither topics that are too broad nor others' ideas are the right ones.

It's almost axiomatic that many people choose concentrations and careers because of early personal experiences. A man becomes an oncologist because he couldn't save his mother from Stage 4 cancer. A woman becomes a social worker specializing in cases of battered women because in childhood, every night from a crack in the closet door, terrified she watched her father beat her mother. A man raised in poverty becomes a financial counselor to help merchants in neighborhoods like his own succeed in their businesses.

Right Topic Considerations

Such motivations generally guarantee sustained interest in the topic. But your motives may not stem from earlier suffering. Either way, here are some thoughts, questions, and examples to help you identify the perfect topic you'll be living with for a *long* time (see also Sterne, 2015b).

1. Revisit your childhood dreams. How did you see yourself? What "professions" were your favorites to play?

   Many kids like to play "doctor" (not *that* kind), and one of my clients loved to play "nurse." She showed me photographs of herself at age five with an impressive collection of play bandages, ointments, even casts, and a doll house she'd made into a "clinic." Today, with her doctorate, she's director of a regional hospital.
2. Review your favorite course papers. Which did you really like doing the work for? Which did you get A's on? What about your master's thesis? Would you get excited expanding it?

   Lynn, an elementary school reading teacher, really cared about those struggling, stuttering readers. When she shuffled through her course papers and reviewed her master's thesis, she saw that the comparisons of different reading programs were her best work. Her dissertation topic? A comprehensive comparison of two school reading programs for their relative effectiveness. Now a PhD, Lynn is a professor teaching aspiring elementary reading and literacy teachers.
3. Think about troubling experiences you've had. Would you like to help remedy their causes?

   If, like the doctor or social worker, your pull toward the topic originates from an early traumatic experience, accept it. Negatives can be powerful motivators toward positive actions and activities. And think of all the people you'll help.
4. What topic has fascinated you for a long time? What are you passionate about? What's close to your heart? What do you want to jump into and explore?

   Another nursing client was pursuing a degree in leadership. With many years experience at several hospitals, Jill observed how older nurses were discriminated against. Other than the obvious chronological reason (she was forty-two), she burned to explore the assumptions and possible myths administrators held onto in making assignments to these nurses. Jill's dissertation and the article she developed from it became valuable additions to the literature—and helped change hospital policies.
5. What especially meaningful experiences have you had that you want to explore and know will make a difference?

   During surgery, Derrick had what he swore was a near-death experience, and he yearned to share it. He delved into the research, interviewed many people who had had similar experiences, and even scored an interview with a major author on the subject. Derrick's dissertation dealt with near-death theories and testimonies. He is now revising his dissertation into a book and has a publisher interested.
6. What would you like to be known for?

In the examples above, the students' passions for their choices drove their ambitions. The answer to the question of what you'd like to be known for is likely inherent in your choice. Don't be modest. Think about what you really know you can contribute.

7. If the topic has been "done," don't be deterred or discouraged. Even if you discover that many scholarly articles have been published on your topic, your approach will be different because it is yours. You can use those articles to show how your study is better, different, and worth not only the doctorate but publication.
8. Dream: Imagine how the topic can be used in your dream job and how you look forward to devoting your professional life to your interest.

   Sandra was a counselor in a geriatric care agency advising adults on the placement of their elderly parents in appropriate facilities. She felt needed and fulfilled, knowing she was helping both generations to the best choices.

   Imagining her dissertation topic, Sandra saw how she could identify and discuss the many elements involved in placement. Exploration of this topic, she saw, would help professionally broaden her knowledge, enhance her abilities, and open her mind to new counseling techniques. After obtaining her degree, Sandra gave several presentations and published her findings in an elder care journal.
9. If you're not in your dream job or career, paint mental pictures of the one you are aiming for. Observe and talk to others in this or a related career. What topic did they write on? How did it help their careers? What pointers can they give you about topic choice? Have they successfully transitioned from the dissertation results to real-world application? Do they seem happy and enthusiastic?
10. Finally (this should really be first), *listen* inside for the topic that's right for you. If you meditate, in your sessions, silently ask the question about topics. You may be "led" to certain people, scholarly literature, movies, or magazines that clarify or confirm your choices. If you don't meditate, keep asking yourself the topic question and stay aware and open. As several possible topics occur to you, test them against the suggestions here and keep listening to your intuition. Let your Inner Mentor do the work of delivering. Receive. Your topic will be revealed.

AFFIRMATIONS

I listen with openness for the right answer.
I wait in dynamic patience.

Choose one or two of the recommendations above to explore each day. Don't push. Relax and let your unconscious lead you. Remember how important the choice is and how it will influence and direct your career and life. You deserve the perfect dissertation topic.

YOU'RE THE SCHOLAR IN SHINING ARMOR

The best of all dissertation topics is one that you love and hasn't been explored or studied very much. Like a good primary relationship, this is hard to find, much less continue to be attractive. There's no way around a lot of research to see if your ideas are retreads. I suggest that you look at Carter-Veale (2012), who gave excellent advice on choosing your topic and making sure it's at least somewhat new and creative.

It's true that you've got to think. As Allen (2002) and others recommended, keep jotting down your thoughts and ideas, and with "great tools" you love (p. 216), like crisp notebooks and favorite pens. In various types of writing, this technique is sometimes called free writing, just writing, or writing out the junk (Bolker, 1998; Goldberg, 2005; Rico, 2000). It's not really junk.

A mystery of the physical act of writing—and I've found this experience true of pen or mouse—is that the writing itself begets better and more thoughts and ideas. "If you stay focused on your writing, inspiration may strike at any moment" (Peters, 1997, p. 221). Keep scribbling or clacking.

See yourself too as a scholarly savior, making a real contribution. As many of my clients have shown, this is not unheard of (like Jill's nursing study that altered hospital policies). Even if many studies have been done on your topic, yours is a new perspective. The topic, type of research, and writing that filter through your brain and talents are yours and yours alone. Yes, you stand on the archives of giants. We all do. Just make sure you reference them correctly.

With your thorough research into all those giants, you have the opportunity to point out how stellar your contribution will be. You'll do so in the dissertation section, usually in chapter 1, in which you describe the need for the study or gap in the literature.

You're here to fill that gap dazzlingly. Keep this mission in mind. Combined with your love for the topic and conviction that your work really will help, as the scholar in shining armor you will carry the banner proudly into dissertation battle.

MUSTER YOUR COURAGE FOR THE PROPOSAL

If by now your hands are clammy and your breath short, take heart! The good news is that the proposal, as you may already know, becomes the first three chapters of the real dissertation. At the beginning, the proposal seems like a sky-high wall with not even a step stool in sight. Clients who come to me after their all-A's in courses or with a few ideas have said it feels like a "mountain," "weight," "endless dark," "dissertation purgatory." One student compared the process to "Sisyphus rolling the boulder up the hill every day and every night watching it roll back down" (she was a college Classics major).

This last isn't original, although common. Rudestam and Newton (2014) cited the Sisyphus metaphor as one their students often used to describe the dissertation process. Their students also compared the journey to feeling endlessly lost in a thick forest, learning a "Martian language" known only to the committee, or waiting patiently on an interminably long line until, reaching the front, they were told sternly to go back to the end (p. 3). If you've got similar delusions, you're not alone.

What's Your Problem?

Here's a good way to start the trek, though. To make the unknowns less frightening, become acquainted with the processes and the subheads for each chapter specified in your university dissertation handbook (go get it!). Once you've ferreted out your all-important topic, start with the "problem statement" or "statement of the problem."

This section really doesn't describe a problem, like where's next semester's tuition payment coming from. Rather, the problem statement (PS) section clarifies what you will be investigating, hopefully an area of study that has been neglected or little studied. The PS provides the reason for your study, or as some explain, answers the "So what?" factor.

The PS is one of the most important sections to guide you through the dissertation, and that's why I'm going a little nutsy-boltsy. Carter-Veale (2012) explained that the problem statement describes the difference between "*what is* and *what should be* (*what we think we know and what we have yet to consider*)" (p. 23, emphasis in the original). Underlying the problem statement is a question that you have raised about your topic. If the current literature can answer it, find a new question. If not, you've got the makings of your problem statement.

The PS enunciates the difference between the current knowledge that's out there in all those studies and new knowledge you will gallop in with to increase understanding about your topic. In other words, you're again relating the need for your study and the gap in existing knowledge but now with more specifics.

Look at some sample problem statements, for example in Calabrese (2012); Carter-Veale (2012); Joyner, Rouse, and Glatthorn (2012), and other dissertation content books. You'll see that in the PS candidates generally use statistics to highlight the problem and cite previous literature that falls short of their topic.

The problem statement needn't be more than a single paragraph, but it should be tight and highly specific. It will serve as your GPS to keep you on the straight road of your topic and not veer off into interesting-looking side roads. Your fully packed problem statement will also lead well (if not exactly effortlessly) to your research questions and/or hypotheses so you launch into the proposal.

Courageous Affirmations

As you progress, in addition to your research and thinking, remember to keep relaxing, breathing, and asking for inner guidance. After Tess and I had a couple of phone sessions about topic possibilities and her problem statement, she emailed this: "I've been praying a lot about the direction of this research and for wisdom. I started meditating on what I want to deal with." Then she reported her thoughts on several topics. After the last one, she wrote, "When I revisit this one, I am at peace." That's the one she began her proposal with.

Here are a few bolsterers for you:

AFFIRMATIONS

I have all the courage I need to plunge in.
The answers are here.
Divine Intelligence is working through me now. (Fox, 1992, p. 50)

YOU DON'T HAVE TO WALK A STRAIGHT (OUT)LINE

Contrary to the King's advice to the White Rabbit in *Alice in Wonderland,* you don't have to start at the beginning and keep going until you reach the end. If you attempt to follow this dictum, you may only increase your fears and tremors.

I advise clients *not* to start at the beginning, that is, with chapter 1, usually called the introduction, and with solid reasons. If you start with the first chapter, you've got to write a concise overview of your topic and its background. This requirement means you must be highly familiar with the breadth of your topic and even more familiar with the literature.

I've found—this is not a criticism but an observation of many students—that they don't get to know what they're really writing about, much less summarize the literature with authority as the introduction requires, until they've been living with their dissertation for several months. Start the proposal with something relatively straightforward or easy.

No doctoral divine lightening will strike if you start in the middle, or later. To help your sense of organization, make separate files for each chapter, with their requisite subtitles and headings, or use the templates many universities include on the dissertation section of their websites. You can keep throwing notes into each file as clever thoughts occur to you and you come upon materials that are appropriate to the different chapters.

Start in earnest with something easier, like chapter 3, Methods. In this chapter you describe who's in the study and how you will study them—your population, sample, and what you're going to put them through (usually questionnaires or interviews). The style should be straightforward and linear, with precise descriptions of the steps you'll take to gather your information and reach conclusions.

It's kind of like a recipe for dissertation brownies:

> First, I will create a flyer for recruiting students to complete my questionnaire on their most effective study habits. Then I will seek permission from the office of student affairs to post the flyer on campus bulletin boards. When students respond to my contact information, I will send them the letter of introduction to the study and the form for their informed consent to participate. Next I will . . .

Starting like this gives you great advantages. You can break into the real writing with at least a minimum of apprehension and write *something*. What you write may not be the final draft, and shouldn't be. Accept this. In the margin of the paragraph above, the student's chair asked caustically, "What's your authority for bypassing the university's institutional review board?" In the next draft, the student inserted this information.

Writing anything loosens your fear-paralyzed mind so you think more creatively about, in our example, where to recruit, who to recruit, when, and many other considerations. As you're visualizing the actual steps you will take, think about, again in our example, what your actual recruitment flyer and letter of intro to the study will say. These are great opportunities to actually draft the flyer, letter, and informed consent form—you're going to need them as appendices. Then, possibly to your elated shock, you'll have something else written!

When you see those paragraphs mounting, you feel greater confidence to keep writing. A few days after I gave my client Rod advice like this about starting with his third chapter, he emailed me with great excitement: "I finally got to a double digit page number! A miracle!" I congratulated him for reaching the milestone of page 10. Practice makes progress.

As you keep going, you'll likely find that related ideas pop up. When you decide that your specific sample will be red-headed students over six feet, you suddenly realize that another study could be done with enrolled redheads under six feet. Here's where you click to your largely empty file of chapter 5, Discussion and Conclusions, and type the new idea under the subhead for recommendations for future research.

Starting with something easy isn't a black mark on your moral fiber. It's simply a way to get moving. Tell yourself, "It's all got to get done anyway."

TRICKS TO TEASE AND EASE YOURSELF INTO IT

First, you've got to feel physically and emotionally well. If you're overly tired, hungry, angry, or worried about something other than your dissertation progress, you will defeat yourself if you start to work. Dissertation coach Rachna Jain (2014b) pointed out these drawbacks and suggested that you "do what it takes to feel better, first—and then start working. It's better to have two hours of focused work rather than four hours of so-so work" (para. 1).

Second, I'm sorry to tell you that nothing substitutes for actually writing. It can't be avoided. Graduate students aren't the only ones who abhor writing. It's likely that anyone who ever had to write anything abhors writing. As with other types of writing, especially after the original flush of enthusiasm and amazed production at the first few pages, the dissertation carries its own problems and demands unique remedies. Here I'll give you solace, support, and not ungentle goads.

To begin with what's most obvious is one trick to ease into the writing. You can lessen the pain and promote hope as you build the dissertation using the tricks and techniques below, a couple of which we've discussed already. Clients have taught me a lot of these, and I've developed a few too. If you need convincing, you'll see too some thoughts on how each method can help you.

1. As I alluded to above, for each part of your dissertation—prefatory pages, chapters, reference list, appendixes—make separate files, hard copy or computer. Create the files in the correct format (your university handbook again) for margins, headers, pagination, font style and size, spacing, chapter headings, and hierarchy of subheadings. If your university supplies a template, use it. You can still separate the different sections into your own files.

   How this method helps: Again, you feel like you're really writing something, even if it's only the chapter title. Thrilled in spite of yourself, you see the parts of the dissertation take shape. When you're in a particular chapter or section, and a fabulous idea occurs to you for another, as in the redhead example above, you can quickly click to it and make a note.
2. To begin writing, start with what's obvious or easy. (Remember "The Law of Least Effort" in chapter 4.) Decide to tackle only one chapter, or better, a section or subsection in that chapter. Again, linear outline be darned. I advised you in chapter 3 ("Find the Holes in Your Schedule") to make a schedule for the days/hours to work on your dissertation and to jot down the specifics for each session. Look at these.

   How this method helps: You're actually writing. Warming up, you'll write more and gain more confidence and comfort in the writing. After a while, to your shock, you may see three solid hypotheses emerging full-blown or feel your fingers irresistibly typing out the introduction at full speed.

3. Set a timer for 30 or 45 minutes, or 10 or 15. Promise yourself a delicious reward when the timer bongs (chocolate chip muffin, Judge Judy marathon, walk by the lake, 1997 Super Bowl replay).

   How this method helps: You're doing something, anything, and short-term rewards work.

4. Use the Diaper Method. I developed the Diaper Method (soon to be patented) when an author friend with two very small children complained that all she was doing was diapering instead of writing (for a fuller account, see Sterne, 2013b). The light dawned on both of us simultaneously: Diapering could be applied, metaphorically, to writing of all kinds.

   I thought immediately of my clients suffering through piles of higher and deeper (PhD) university instructions and rubrics, research articles, multipage handouts, endless-slide PowerPoints meant to help, nonstop lists of to-dos, and seventeen contradictory research method books. They—you—become paralyzed, not knowing where to point your pen or cursor.

   The Diaper Method can save you, especially with a dissertation. It's not complex or mysterious but almost embarrassingly simple. For example, in number 2 above, you chose an easy subhead. Whether on paper or your computer screen, isolate this subhead. If you print out your chapter subheads, cover everything else on the page, above and below, with a large scrap of paper, Post-Its, or leftover piece of flatbread. If you're on a screen, press Control + Enter so this subhead is the only thing on the page.

   Now you can concentrate only on what you see. Start writing. Your goal is to fill in text for this subhead only. When you finish, whether or not you intuit that the subhead will require more, move the diaper so it shows only your next choice. That's it.

   How this method helps: The Diaper Method is the equivalent of dissertation blinders so you focus only on the task before you. You stifle those horrible thoughts of overwhelm and endlessness (see also Jain, 2011). As a variation of the popular saying might go, "Inch by inch, you won't feel the pinch." More—you begin to feel an unaccustomed (sweet) sense of achievement and allow yourself some excitement at your progress.

5. Ignore your Inner Writing Judge. You will inevitably hear internal self-condemnation at what you've just written. To silence this tyrant and its judgment of "Drivel!" repeat to yourself: "It's only my first draft!" Luke emailed me recently: "When I looked at my draft today, I came away disgusted." Then he wrote wisely, "I know it's only part of the process."

6. To further assuage that relentless Inner Judge, jot notes to yourself as you go. When I've just written a particularly loathsome sentence, I type right after it: "FIX." When I notice heinous repetitions, like starting three consecutive sentences with the same word, I write "REP!" Or if an example is too weak or flowery, or I'm trying too hard to be literary or cute, I add "GET BETTER!" If you must know, my first draft of this chapter was littered with such notes.

   How this method helps: This technique helps you to keep going in the face of all those Judge pronouncements ("This is terrible. I don't know what I'm talking about. Must throw it all out."). You're telling yourself and your Judge that you do know and you promise to come back in the next draft to FIX, GET BETTER, or delete the REPs.
7. As bad as you think a draft is, save it. Save and back up all your drafts, electronically and printed out, whatever makes you feel most secure. I have two external backups for everything and can sleep at night. You can always delete later—a few months after graduation.
8. Keep all your literature and references, in print and PDF. This practice will save you hours of frustrated searching ("Where *did* I see that?"). My client Margie, after she handed in a research paper, rashly threw out a carton of articles she used. When we came to her dissertation, on the same topic, she had to re-find everything. When in doubt, or you think you're finished, save anyway. You can always purge later, much later.
9. Trust your Inner Mentor. Ask and listen (sound familiar?). Trust your IM to supply ideas and sequences. The description of writing by the American author E. L. Doctorow reminds me of this principle: "[I]t's like driving a car at night; you never see further than your headlights, but you can make the whole trip that way" (quoted in Plimpton, 1986, para. 20). Your IM knows. Ask, and then see and do what's in front of you. You *can* make the whole trip.

WRITING DOESN'T HAVE TO BE TORTURE: PROPER STYLE AND SEMIPLEASANT PROCESS

Some professors, editors, and coaches advise starting to write in your own words, without bothering about proper dissertation style (e.g., Joyner et al., 2012). I recommend this approach too, and it has advantages and drawbacks. The main benefit is that it gets you going, one of our goals in this chapter. The main shortcoming is that it may get you going in the wrong direction.

It's true: Academic writing is a breed unto itself. Peter, a new doctoral candidate who came from the corporate world, wrote me, "I struggle daily with identifying and understanding the shift from business and occupational writing to writing as a researcher according to certain expectations and standards."

In academic writing certain "disciplinary expectations" (Casanave, 2008, p. 15) and conventions are demanded. A few: no contractions, no colloquialisms, few or no passive voice, no "emotional" words (completely, extremely, very, utterly, fantastically), no redundancy (period of time), no jargon (with exceptions, depending on your field and topic), no euphemisms ("After ingesting licorice-flavored cyanide, the rat gave up the ghost."), no anthropomorphisms ("This book comforts you.")

See the *Publication Manual of the American Psychological Association* (APA; American Psychological Association, 2010, pp. 65–71) for a roundup. You may already know that this is the hallowed reference work for many universities and disciplines (as well as this book). I'll refer to it cozily as "APA."

You should already be acquainted with scholarly style from your research, reading of scholarly articles, and writing course papers. But reading and writing are two different animals (oops—anthropomorphism).

Good dissertation style is not that of a conversation, personal essay, or work of fiction. Neither should dissertation writing be stuffed with incessant polysyllabic words that went out of fashion with nineteenth-century classical education. Joyner et al. (2012) summarized well: "While there seems to be a trend away from the highly formal style and a reaction against turgid academic prose, there is still the expectation that the dissertation will sound scholarly. . . . scholars write in a style that is formal, not colloquial, and is objective, not subjective" (p. 7).

Yet articles in scholarly journals are notorious for incomprehensibility and obfuscation (pardon my polysyllables) and not only for scientific or medical topics. Harvard professor and chair of the usage panel of the *American Heritage Dictionary*, Steven Pinker (2014) left nothing to subtlety or prudence in his *Chronicle of Higher Education* piece, "Why Academics Stink at Writing": "Why should a profession that trades in words and dedicates itself to the transmission of knowledge so often turn out prose that is turgid, soggy, wooden, bloated, clumsy, obscure, unpleasant to read, and impossible to understand?" (para. 3).

To write good Dissertationese dialect that doesn't get you kicked out of the kingdom of Academe takes practice. Aim to achieve that balance of formality but understandability (although I do recommend words of three syllables when one will normally do). However (or But or Nevertheless), I suggest too with other advisors that you write at first in whatever style comes out. It's hard enough to get the words down without fretting about their Greek roots. With the list of APA "no's" in front of you, you can fancy up later.

You can also get the idiom of scholarly academic writing into your bones by several means. Read articles you can understand in respected journals. Read dissertations that have won awards and have been recommended by professors you trust (the quality of accepted dissertations varies *bigtime*). Do some of the exercises in Greene and Lidinsky's (2014) *From Inquiry to Academic Writing,* not only for reading and writing in academic style but also for thinking and extracting the essences of articles (this book will help too in your literature review).

Of course, I need not remind you *never* to copy passages verbatim without the proper citations, as brilliantly as they may accord with your topic. You never know when that ugly word *plagiarism* will catch up with you. Granted, definitions of plagiarism vary among faculty (Martin, 2005). Remember too that most universities subscribe to Turnitin, that devilish plagiarism hunter, even though it has received some serious criticism (Dames, 2008) and is not infallible.

Once in a client's dissertation, Turnitin tagged every use of the most generic words and phrases that were at the heart of the research and her topic! (We wrote a strong letter to her chair pointing out the deficiencies—and she passed this hurdle.) Nevertheless, your university probably requires you to put your dissertation through the Turnitin wringer. Better paraphrase than sorry.

Prices for plagiarism can be very steep. Witness only the latest scandal (at this writing) that made headlines: Seven years after Montana Senator John Walsh's award of his master's, the Army War College found out that he plagiarized his thesis. The college revoked his degree, and he dropped out of the Senate race ("Army War College Revokes," 2014; Bailey, 2014).

For your very own work, see the many helpful and frequently hilarious suggestions in the provocative booklet by Pinker, Munger, Sword, Toor, and MacPhail (2014), *Why Academic Writing Stinks and How to Fix It.* In this booklet, which reprints the Pinker (2014) article I referred to earlier and others on the art and failings of academic writing, see especially Sword's (2012) prescription for curing yourself of "jargonitis" (p.13).

Finally, the best advice I can offer for dissertation and all other writing is that of the wonderful American author Madeleine L'Engle (1971), who reprinted a poem by one of her "favorite authors, Anon":

> The written word
> Should be clean as bone,
> Clear as light,
> Firm as stone.
> Two words are not
> As good as one. (p. 149)

L'Engle noted after reprinting this poem that in her own writing she should pay more attention to these lines than she did. In our scholarly writing, so should we.

SETTLE IN: YOU DESERVE IT

As you follow L'Engle's (1971) advice and the other suggestions here, I give you one more thought. Recognize that the processes of writing, thinking, digesting, rethinking, revising, re-rethinking, and re-revising cannot be hurried. Your subconscious continues to chug along, even if you are staring out the window. Enlist your IM throughout; it's waiting to serve you.

Settling in means giving the process—and yourself—time to sit, ruminate, play with ideas, jot a few notes, write a few words, wander to the bathroom, come back, take a swig of iced tea, and write a few sentences. Maybe you label these actions as diversions or stalling. They're not; they're all part of the precious creating process. As I assured Pam that her process was working and her pages mounted, she wrote, "Received your edited draft and I will make the requested changes. I'm so excited! I feel like a child!" Pam had settled in.

A few affirmations for settling in:

AFFIRMATIONS

I open, listen, and write.

I don't need to mow it down but flow it forward. I am shown the way.

I *know* what to do, where to look, and who to ask.

This work goes smoothly, joyfully, easily, and quickly.

I am the perfect conduit. This dissertation writes itself through me (from Murphy, 1986).

Thank you, God, for perfect decisions, actions, and outcomes in this work.

These statements should hold you well as you go forward fearlessly with your dissertation. The next test is to stick with the research, thinking, and writing through many temptations that may arise, some obvious, some insidious. We'll talk about the biggest ones next in chapter 6.

SIX

Sticking With It

Temptations and Tonics

Once you've actually started writing, you can be rightfully proud and sail along. For a little while. You've conquered writer's paralysis and that sense of hopelessness, and you're using a lot of the tricks I suggested to keep going. Soon, though, another set of obstacle rears up in your path. These may not only hinder you but stop your dissertation progress entirely. They can be seductive and are all the more dangerous because they seem to be grounded in sound reasoning. Here I'll derail them, with some excruciating examples, to save you from their oh-so-rational detours and get you back on the road to successful completion.

DISSERTATION INTERRUPTUS

Barry had quickly completed his proposal and revised it into his first three real chapters. Now, when continuing with chapter 4 should have been at least manageable, if not easy, he couldn't get himself going. Night after night in his study cubicle, he sat and stared at his blinking cursor. He thought, *I just need a little time away. Then I'll return refreshed.* Finally, he decided to put in for a leave of absence from the doctoral program.

Despite his progress and love for and belief in his topic, Barry had succumbed to that hazardous time when the bloom is off the research. If you decide as he did, one leave can turn into another, and you can be at risk of quitting entirely and never finishing. What may seem like a harmless brief interlude like Barry's interrupts that little thing called "momentum."

Barry's was only one of many so-called unassailable reasons. Others can call you with their siren song. From my longtime practice guiding doctoral candidates to completion of their dissertations, I have noticed that both women and men in doctoral programs can easily become diverted by other events of life, involving partners, children, grandchildren, parents, or friends. Well-meaning decisions and actions stemming from empathy, helpfulness, or compassion may result in calamitous consequences to a dissertation.

One of the most dramatic examples I encountered of misguided judgment and compassion was the actions of Claudia. Going back to school at thirty-two for her master's, Claudia came to me feeling shaky about the academic requirements. Her goal was to leave the deadening administrative job she'd held for years so she could teach in college.

With no family responsibilities and great excitement, Claudia whipped through the master's and got her degree. She entered the doctoral program, finished the courses quickly, and began the dissertation. With my help she submitted her proposal, and her committee feedback was encouraging, with only minor suggested revisions. She promised to get back her draft to me in two weeks.

She didn't. My emails and phone messages went unanswered.

Finally, four weeks later, Claudia called. Without mentioning her dissertation, she reeled out a complicated story about having to help a friend. The friend's brother was living in their home country, a warring African nation, and his life was in great danger. They couldn't get the appropriate visa, so the only way he could enter the United States was by marriage. Claudia explained she felt she "owed" it to her friend to help.

She married the brother—I know this sounds like a supermarket novel but it's true. He came to the United States, and they worked out some way of looking like they lived together. But additional legal problems surfaced. He faced deportation, and they feared for his life. Claudia too was legally vulnerable. She told me, "I'll be embroiled in this for a long time. I've got three lawyers on it." She took a deep breath. "My friend is devastated, and I can't desert her now."

When I last I heard from Claudia she was plodding along in her dead-end job, collecting retirement credits and frustrations and probably seeing her dream career recede like low tide. She was still ABD and seemed to have lost heart. (See also my article in *Women in Higher Education*, [Sterne, 2014], for more discussion of such decisions and examples, especially pertaining to women.)

You may be tempted for other reasons to suspend your dissertation. I relate the extreme example of Claudia to help you stick to your decisions so that no major interruptions, as noble, generous, or compassionate as they may be, waylay your dreamed-of doctorate.

DEATH BY RATIONALE

Claudia and others like her have "excellent" rationales for taking a leave of absence. Overjustifying is really a signal that you know you shouldn't do whatever you're contemplating.

Here is a small embarrassing list of some of the best rationales I've heard. Don't fall for them:

- My family needs my attention.
- A good break of a few months will clear my head. Of course, I'll come back.
- I'll have a chance to get the absolutely most current materials.
- After a decent break, I'll get new insights, maybe even amazing ones.
- I'll track down that expert for his input. It will take time, but it's crucial to my work.
- I'm signing up for that six-week seminar in how to write a dissertation on the cruise ship *Nowhere*. Then I'll really have a handle on how to continue.
- I'll just clean out my study and the spare room—and the garage, attic, and storage shed. Then I'll feel organized—and I'll be able to find anything I need right away.

And the final unassailable one:

- The dissertation isn't everything, you know. You've got to live too.

Each one of these statements is immensely reasonable, logical, justifiable, understandable, even wise. Please don't misunderstand—I'm certainly not unsympathetic to the necessity to suspend work on your dissertation for real crises, severe illness, or death in the family. Some reasons are genuine.

The "reasons" on the list above, though, aren't solid walls of sense but ragged curtains that can't hide your bewilderment at having to buckle down to the dissertation. They're ways to try and avoid all your fears and misgivings. Remember—you've already made the decision that at this point in your life the dissertation *is* just about everything.

What's your rationale? Have you been tempted by any of these? Even if you're not actively thinking about quitting (just for a little while), write down five "reasons" that tempt you to stop now. This exercise will get them out of your system.

The rationales above, and others, may lead you to a first cousin of the leave of absence, an extension. For both leaves and extensions, universities require a "strong" letter justifying why you deserve the time away, with supportive documents from your chair. Most universities allow five to seven years from your entry date to finish all requirements, including the dissertation and its defense (if the school has one). They also have rules on the number of leaves or extensions.

With a leave, you drop out temporarily. For the period you don't pay tuition, and you no longer have university privileges or access to the library and other resources. With an extension, the administration grants you another block of time past your official finishing date. You pay chain-tuition and retain all privileges. Like the leave, the extension can lure irresistibly.

RESISTING THE EXTENSION SIREN

Earlier, I used the metaphor of a siren song to warn you against the temptations of a leave of absence. The metaphor referred to the story in Homer's (2006) *Odyssey* of the Greek hero Odysseus on his journey home after the Trojan War. This metaphor applies equally to extensions.

Among the many obstacles Odysseus and his crew encountered was sailing near the land of the Sirens, beautiful and dangerous women who with their irresistibly sweet songs lured sailors to the rocks, shipwreck, and death. Odysseus knew of their dangers and, ever sharp ("wily Odysseus," p. 190), as the ship neared the island, he instructed his crew to stop up their ears with wax and lash him to the mast. The crew kept rowing, and they passed safely toward home.

If you want to resist the siren call of extensions and get "home" to completion of your dissertation, you need to employ your own wits and wisdom. Otherwise, you'll crash your ship on the treacherous shoals of endless diversions and distractions, think you have so much time, get an ice-water letter from the dean informing you that you only have three months to complete everything, and miss the opportunities for which you started the doctoral program in the first place.

Universities love extensions—students just keep paying semester after semester and receive an occasional two-line email from the chair. Students also often mistakenly believe extensions will solve all their problems. You still face the same problems you did before, only now you've just put them off. So, literally or figuratively, lash yourself to the leg of your desk or arm of your computer chair and resist the subtly beckoning siren extensions.

If you need more convincing, heed the headlines about a doctoral candidate who sued her university. When she began the program in 2003, she maintained that Duquesne University did not tell her of the extension limits for her degree. After several extensions, the university refused to grant more, even though she had made substantial progress on her dissertation (Crosby, 2012; Ward, 2012). As of this writing, she had not received her degree. I admire her courage in taking on the giant, but what does one do with an orphan dissertation and a dashed dream?

Take another lesson from the saga of my client Anne. A day care center administrator for many years, she enjoyed the work but had always wanted a doctorate. She started the dissertation in her fourth year in the program, when her center was bought by a healthcare conglomerate and she was let go. She devoted her time to finding a new job. A year passed, her fifth and last official year at the university, so she applied for a year's extension.

It was granted, and Anne settled into her new job and began collecting research. She felt her apartment was too small and found a perfect small home in her price range, closer to the new office. Her house needed a lot of work, so she oversaw the necessary renovations, which took a year. Her extension expired; she applied for a second and received it.

One of Anne's new neighbors was a helpful and attractive man who became a friend. As he introduced her to the mysteries of crabgrass and weed killers, they became more than friends.

As the second extension year came to an end, Anne told her lover, who had a master's in accounting, that she wanted to get back to her dissertation. He admitted feeling threatened by her advanced degree (more about such threats in chapter 8), and Anne was shocked. But she wasn't willing to give up her goal, and they broke up.

Anne was so depressed she couldn't work on her dissertation. She applied for her third extension and received it. As this year ran out, she became ill with a stomach virus and then a urinary infection. She could hardly sit up, much less read or type. She applied for another extension, her fourth. It was now nine years since she'd started the program.

In September of her ninth year, she received a university letter approving her extension with an ultimatum. If she didn't complete by the next March, she'd receive no further extensions. Shocked, and realizing that she could lose all the money and time she'd put in, Anne went back to bed for two weeks and recovered enough to resume her dissertation. Then she called me. We worked intensely to meet the deadline, and Anne finally graduated. Whew!

GETTING SICK . . . OF IT ALL

Like Anne, some candidates get sick, literally. You could argue that they stuck their wet heads in front of air conditioned databases or that the illnesses "just happened." I maintain, though, that students "choose" their illnesses because they are literally sick of the dissertation.

For example, Walker, a dedicated student, devoted health-food addict, and runner, developed painful migraines as he began recruitment of his sample. Ellen, who gave many presentations in her work, became paralyzed on the right side of her face as she prepared for her final defense. When Jean-Paul got approval to revise his final chapters, at forty-six, he suddenly had a mild heart attack.

I'd better tell you of something here, like I did earlier about the spiritual. I believe wholeheartedly in what may still seem radical to some but has been accepted increasingly by the medical establishment and taught for centuries by spiritual teachers. Many physical illnesses, such as high blood pressure, arthritis, digestive problems, ulcers, colitis, back problems, skin disorders, and cancer, are acknowledged to be mind-related and stress-related, attested by physician/authors such as Benson (1997), Dossey (2006, 2011), Hay and Shulz (2014), Siegel (1998, 2013), and Weil (2000, 2007), among many others.

Beyond the mind-body connection of illnesses, I also believe, with metaphysical teachers Abraham (Hicks & Hicks, 2004, 2006), Louise Hay (1987, 1998) and others, that every physical ailment has a mental cause. We actually choose and create each illness we experience. Why?

We want to escape, avoid, or hide from something. We want others to wait on us. We want special sympathy and attention. We want proof others love us. We think it's "our turn." We feel things are too good and can't last. We feel things are too bad and shouldn't last. We subscribe to the "culture of suffering," in which we feel we can't be happy or enjoy anything until the dissertation is behind us (Jain, 2014a, para. 1). We just want a rest.

The illnesses of the grad students in my examples showed up at important, even critical, moments in their dissertation work. Whatever else was going on in their lives, the fact that they became sick at these particular times, to me, went way beyond coincidence (I don't believe in coincidence—but that's another book).

An embarrassing little exercise: Think back to a time during your dissertation writing when you "suddenly" became ill. Can you connect your illness to your dissertation work? What could have been some of the reasons?

I do not mean to condemn my clients, or any of us, for getting sick. Rather, this exercise and discussion are meant to show us how we can learn from such experiences and not attract them or repeat them. The very good news is that as we choose to get sick, we can also choose to stay healthy.

Here are some affirmative thoughts to keep choosing your health:

AFFIRMATIONS

I deserve to eat healthy foods and get enough rest.
I am in control; my body obeys my mind.
My body mirrors and responds to my thoughts and beliefs.
My mind and body are not subject to illness because of any common beliefs.
Illness is not "God's will." God's will for me is only for good.
I see myself as healthy and concentrate on health, success, and degree completion.
No one but myself can keep me down . . . or up. (Fox, 1992, p. 55)

Later in this chapter, we'll talk about taking good breaks and balance that help preserve your mental and physical health. First I want to alert you to a common, although often unconscious, emotion that I'm certain plays a large part in graduate students' choosing sickness.

FEAR OF FINISHING

Each of the clients I referred to above got sick just before or after a milestone in their work. On some level, even though they may have protested hotly to the contrary, these students didn't want to finish the dissertation. Why?

Much later, when their degrees were securely framed and hanging on the wall for their mothers to dust proudly, I asked these former students about their fears of completing. All were admirably open:

- I'll have to face the real world again.
- I can't be a perpetual student any more.
- I'll have to decide what I want to be when I grow up.
- I'll have to go look for a real job.
- I won't be able to escape to my study or the library to get out of babysitting.
- I'll be expected to make a lot more money.
- I'll have to start publishing immediately.

Are you blushing a little with recognition? Good. Better to dig out these rascals now. Such fears can prolong any illness or lead you to other self-sabotaging actions (for other self-sabotages, see Kearns, Gardiner, & Marshall, 2008). If you recognize any of the reasons above, do the exercise below.

1. Why am I afraid of finishing? List as many reasons as occur to you. No one else ever has to see the list. Don't resist, censor, or dismiss anything. As a self-help guru once told me, "If it's in your mind, it applies."
2. Look hard at your list: You may be shocked, startled, upset, and mortified at what's on the page since you've wished and vowed and sworn that all you want is to finish and get this weight out of your life. Face it now than have it subconsciously control you later. Otherwise, you'll add more reasons not to finish.
3. Use your powers of analysis: Do your reasons really make sense? If you think facing the "real world" is hard, what have you been doing in graduate school? The myth of the "Ivory Tower" may still exist among those outside the moat, but aren't the challenges, politics, battles, and pressures similar to those anywhere else? (Côté & Allahar, 2007; Wiener, 2012; see also Cantor & Englot, 2013, for a reminder of how academic education should be used beyond the tower). Where have you been living if not the real world? How much worse could another nonuniversity universe be? You probably already have a "real" job. It's time to grow up anyway. Look at friends or acquaintances who recently became academic "doctors." Do they immediately make a lot more money or publish?
4. Use your scheduling power: The principles still apply of choosing and scheduling your time that we talked about in chapter 3 ("Rethink Your Priorities," "Find the Holes in Your Schedule"). You can use the decisions you made to shore up your resolve to continue and finish your dissertation. What makes you think, in the distant future after the doctorate, that you're not entitled to escape time, in the library or anywhere else? You'll still be entitled to time to yourself, and it may get easier after you've practiced dissertation scheduling time.
5. Use your assertive powers: If you're worried about pressures from family and friends to earn more or publish right away, sit down with them and inform them of the realities straightforwardly, as I'll talk about in chapters 7 and 8. Tell them that reviews for promotions take time, and that writing an article, getting it accepted, and finally seeing it published take a lot more time. Now sit down with yourself and repeat what you've just told them.

Finally, for any nonfinishing reason you or anyone else can dream up, employ one more technique, your power of discipline. Whatever the seeming strength of the argument not to complete, talk to yourself like a disciplining parent:

AFFIRMATION

I am not a victim of this thought. It's only a thought, and I have the power to change it.

DISCIPLINE IS A CHOICE

As you've chosen thoughts of illness and fears of finishing, you can also choose opposite thoughts of health, completion, and discipline of your thoughts and actions. You learned of some of my convictions and suggestions on health and discipline applied to your dissertation in chapters 3 ("Keep Your Promises to Yourself") and 5 ("Muster Your Courage for the Proposal," "Tricks to Ease and Tease Yourself Into It"). If you really want to finish your dissertation, you gotta choose self-discipline.

Take the dissertation seriously, like any large, important project. It needs time, concentration, and focus. You're an athlete in training: no excessive booze, no late nights, no DIY massive projects, no offering to host a forty-guest Thanksgiving, no heady whirlwind romances or impulsive marriage proposals or acceptances (except of course if you're already married, a whole other story, for which you'll get ammunition in chapters 7 and 8).

When you're tempted to anything that will dilute your dissertation efforts, like the clients in my earlier examples, think again. Think about the extent of your involvement, the probable consequences of your actions, and the costs to you in time, effort, energy, emotional investment, depletion, and money. Think about whether anyone will be harmed by your declining, and about how much you could get done on the dissertation. Think.

Then choose self-discipline. To continue the work, choose and use any of the aids and tricks in chapter 5 and the reminders here:

- Set or review the hours you're going to work on the dissertation each day.
- Set your goals by the session, day, or week.
- Plan what you'll work on the night before and lay out your materials.
- At your session, ignore your land phone, cell phone, emails, text messages, any other smartphone dings, and doorbells (unless it's Amazon.com delivering a crucial research tome).
- Choose a small chunk (chapter section) to work on, and hide the rest in the barn.
- Warm up by doing something easy for an immediate sense of accomplishment.
- Use my "Diaper Method" (see chapter 5).
- Stop at a place where you know what you'll do next.
- Stop at a place where you don't want to stop.
- Plan a really good reward for completing this session.

- Give yourself the reward immediately. Relish and savor it.

The more you exercise your self-discipline, like any habit the easier you'll find continuing. Even though it's proverbially hard to break old habits, our brains actually construct new physical neural pathways as we repeat something (or imagine repeating it!), and our emotions get used to the satisfactions and go toward more (Duhigg, 2014; Sousa, 2011). In developing new habits, we rewire our brains (Achor, 2012). Self-discipline then becomes easier, physically, mentally, emotionally, as your new habit.

CONTINUING THE WORK: YOUR WAYWARD OUTLINE

Here we continue the idea of chapter 5 ("You Don't Have to Walk a Straight [Out]Line") for writing in the road of fewest ruts that make you spin your wheels in the slush. I gave you permission earlier to start anywhere but the beginning, and especially to avoid the dissertation introduction, until you discover what the hell you're writing about. Choose almost any order you wish—a variation of the starting easy principle above. Many writers do this for any project, and as dry as a dissertation seems, it *is* creative.

As you know by now, and I recapped in the introduction of this book, the typical dissertation has five chapters, although exceptions exist, depending on the university, department, field, and type of dissertation you choose. As you also should know, each chapter has a specific function, all written according to certain standards and conventions, always in formal academic language.

This division means that if you're stuck at a particular place, you can throw a dart at your outline and see where it lands for the next section. You can switch gears, shift the scene, change lanes, change course, let the draft sit and start another section . . . anything to keep going.

Don't be afraid of the "confusion" that may result if you start or continue somewhere other than at the beginning. One of the greatest lessons of so-called chaos theory, as leadership expert and management consultant Margaret Wheatley (2006) told us, is that *there is no chaos.* (Maybe you should be alerted again to this semi-metaphysical notion.) What appears as confusion or disorder in our limited daily perspective—or our sheaf of messy pages, random notes, and half-finished chapters—is order in the making. Wheatley's (2006) "Three-Winged Bird" (p. 106) displays the result of a chaotic system left to itself—and it looks like high art.

Continuing at a nonlinear point and turning away from your previous draft of a section or chapter has other rewards. After you do a draft of the chosen new section, you'll come back to the former one with greater clarity. No one decrees, except the King to the White Rabbit, that the work has to be done in neat, consecutive, outline order. You can work on any part and different parts as you're led to. As in the buoying principle of chaos theory, it will all finally fall into place.

IF YOU'RE CONCERNED ABOUT YOUR BRAIN

It's true that to do a dissertation, and even to entertain the idea of graduate school, you have to be quite left-brainy—that's the side that's verbal, analytic, rational, logical, sequenced, separatist, and linear. Many of us are also amply endowed with big fat right brains—the side that's nonverbal, synthetic, symbolic, metaphoric, intuitive, creative, holistic, and integrated.

We use our left brains primarily to find the library, organize our materials, and make grocery lists. We use our right brains to pick a topic that turns us on, get to know our higher self, and listen to our cravings of what to have for lunch. Whether we're an accountant or an artist, we need and use both parts, even if we live mostly from one or the other. In writing the dissertation, we can work in neat boxes, spirals, intuitive squiggles, or any combination of both.

In her wonderful book on writing, Rico (2000) quoted psychiatrist and creative researcher Albert Rothenberg from his *The Emerging Goddess* (1979) on our miraculous dual brain: "When the two halves of our brain exchange their disparate experiences, pool their viewpoints and approaches, the resulting synthesis brings to problem-solving a whole symphony of talents" (p. 69). I'm sure you'll agree that your dissertation is one gigantic mass of problem solving. Rothenberg is telling us how to master it: Use both sides of your brain.

You use both parts of your brain in the necessary recursive process of writing and rewriting, in which you review and revisit, repeat and revise. The process gradually yields clarity with your successive drafts. Admittedly disconcerting, I call the feelings of this phase "creative limbo." As we stick with it and keep going, following our inclinations and hunches, back and forth, round and round, the apparently disconnected parts gradually form into a coherent whole. When we follow our right brain and jump in as it dictates, we can be as much as or more productive than forcing ourselves to follow "The Outline." Trust yourself.

This flexibility doesn't contradict self-regulation or keeping to schedules. You can maintain an attitude of openness as you alternate between working vigorously and taking breaks from the work. Yes, they're allowed. No, I don't believe in the unrelieved torture of writing and thinking. As before, the secret is structure, self-discipline, and clear choices in how you break and balance.

REASONABLE BREAKS AND BALANCE

I offer you here more techniques for writing, but now with greater sensitivity to your best writing times and needed and appropriate breaks. Advice for completing your dissertation can be extreme: You sit there, through winter and summer, sleet, snow, sweat, and dirty socks, anything to get the monster done. I've read of people who locked themselves in a room for six months, with the only contact from the outside world a three-times-a-day tray of airplane food left at the door. Maybe they finished, but I never heard about the quality of their work or their mental states.

In academic circles, you may have noticed that many scholars self-righteously announce (and I too am guilty), "Oh, I work all the time. No, no breaks. Of course I work Saturdays and Sundays." I'm not talking here about many of you with full-time jobs who have only the nights and weekends for concentrated work sessions. Even you need to take some time off.

At the other extreme are students who take off too much time. They give you their reasons with a straight face and convincing hand gestures:

- My bar buddies help me sort out my ideas. I always get some great ones at 1:00 a.m.
- I think better at the rock concert.
- Sure, I'll get back to the dissertation after I clear my head at the double header.
- My all-morning talks with the other wives always inspire me, and I collect a lot of good recipes too.

Working Questions

So, keep working—reasonably. As you keep to your schedule of sessions and remember your goals, incentives, and rewards, refine your habits with some self-diagnosing questions:

1. Do I work better in one-hour-long or three-hour-long sessions?
2. Do I work better in the morning, evening, or silent, silken midnight?
3. Must I have total silence, or do I like music or the soft roar of other people nearby?
4. Do I feel best working in my study, the bedroom, kitchen table, a library, a restaurant, a hotel lobby, the mall center court, a bowling alley, or a car wash?
5. Must I have food, tea, coffee, or ginger-flavored water at hand, or no drops or crumbs anywhere near my workspace?

My optimal session for any writing at my trusty desktop is about an hour and a half. But sometimes my brain bubbles like a hot spring, and the rest of the world disappears. I can work for three hours straight without even hearing my stomach growl. My client Howard gets itchy after forty-five minutes and has to get up, look outside, swig some chocolate soy milk, and walk around the TV three times before settling back down.

Honor your preferences. So what if they're idiosyncratic? Your answers to the questions above will help you see your most preferred work times and settings—and those in which you'll probably be most productive and least exhausted.

When nothing seems to flow, you may be sitting and staring at the wall or your motionless knuckles on the keyboard, wishing the hour would pass so you can get up. Don't succumb to a break too soon. *Stay put.* As with so many successes in life, the breakthrough is just on the other side of not giving up.

Balanced Breaks

You do need breaks, short and long. Short breaks can siphon off your fatigue and feelings of stuckness. To take breaks from writing, I learned from Allen's (2002) "two-minute rule" (p. 132) to choose an unrelated task or two that takes no more than two minutes and preferably uses minimal brainpower. These can be straightening magazines, filing a receipt, taking out the garbage, calling a new restaurant for the Sunday brunch hours.

When we take our minds off our work for a while, paradoxically our wondrous writing and thinking processes flourish. Time between sections and drafts magically gives us distance to correct vagueness, redundancies, fudge words, obscurities, faulty logic, and gaps in thinking. In the famous example of Einstein, apocryphal as it may be, the theory of relativity burst into his mind while he was shaving.

For a slightly longer break, choose a task that's more ambitious—filing a sheaf of papers, organizing a drawer, calling a friend (but set a timer). Janet, a former client who now produces one article after another, swears by cooking. "Cooking, like writing," she said, "is very creative. My ideas simmer like my soup." She gets the added bonus of a ready meal.

We also need longer, reasonable breaks that maintain our sanity and balance. I hasten to add that these are different from the big time take-offs I gave examples of earlier. Long, nourishing breaks do refresh and feed you. Here are some suggestions you may already know. These work for many dissertation writers (for variations, see also Schaffenberg, 2014).

- Exercise. No groans, please. You've read enough about its head-clearing, endorphin-producing benefits. Several days or nights a week, exercise for an hour. My client Nick plays baseball in a league from his job. Paula jogs religiously three miles a day. Join a gym, find an exercise partner, run your cat. You'll feel *much* better and sharper for your dissertation.

- Take some TV time (*what?*). It's not evil and can be a great escape. But limit it and choose carefully. My favorites, starting usually at 9:00 p.m., are fast-paced mysteries, slick lawyer movies, and white-collar adventures in the big business jungles. Some of my brightest clients love soap operas, reality shows, *Murder, She Wrote* reruns (my other favorite), and sagas of trout fishing. Watch whatever you really enjoy.
- Go to bed an hour earlier. The world won't stop if you don't see the nightly news; you'll probably sleep better without it. People boast how they get along on four hours sleep a night. Does anyone ask them what they do in the other twenty? I'll bet they zombie through most of them. When you get enough sleep, you're more alert, renewed, clear-minded, resilient, and healthy, all of which benefit your dissertation.
- Meditate. (You knew I'd get around to this.) As I talked about in chapter 1 ("As They Say, Meditate, Don't Medicate"), it's not religious, sacrilegious, or New Age anymore. It's regularly featured in the supermarket women's magazines, a sure sign of mainstream acceptability. Meditating for ten to fifteen minutes can be as good as an hour's nap. You may find, as I do, to my astonished joy, that ideas, thoughts, phrases, and insights about the current work float in or pop up with no effort at all.
- Take an evening off with one or more family members or friends. Make it special—change into your good t-shirt. Forcing yourself to get out of the usual routine and the house gives your mind a good cleansing. When Walker, a self-confessed workaholic, took the evening off just before he started chapter 2, he reported, "Felt like I went away for a week! I came back ready to tackle the beast."
- Take an afternoon off. Combine it with some to-dos if you must, like I do. Give yourself some fun too—browse in stores, buy something impulsively, or pig out at the Cheesecake Factory. When Denise first started her proposal, she made a practice of taking off an afternoon a week. She does things she wants to, and they may even connect (obliquely) to her dissertation, like visiting the bookstore she loves that specializes in first editions and beautiful writing accessories.
- Take a whole day off (eek!). Arrange an outing that will change your environment completely. On a recent Saturday some friends and I went to the zoo (it took me two weeks to free up the time). Returning, I felt I'd been on safari, even though it wasn't the Kala-

hari but the blacktop path. Sunday, with renewed vigor, I worked for hours.

- Take a weekend off (double eek!). Tyler and his wife spent an entire weekend in Branson, Missouri. They attended successive concerts of the country music they both loved and then went white-water rafting. When he returned, he told me, "I really needed that break. Now I feel invigorated and ready to tackle my data analysis."

The secrets for successful breaks are to plan them, schedule them as you would work sessions, and stick to your schedule. Even if at first you don't feel like you're enjoying the break, you'll get into it and feel its rewards.

To return to the theme of this chapter, your breaks, short or less short, should support your resolve to stick with the dissertation and keep your momentum bubbling. Finally, here are some mantras for sticking with it so you take judicious breaks, balance your work sessions, and really finish.

AFFIRMATIONS FOR STICKING WITH IT

As I've said before, even if you don't quite believe, read and repeat these affirmations. In spite of yourself, they'll happily seep into your mind and drive your pages.

AFFIRMATIONS

I did it before (remember that first frightening undergraduate paper).
I can do it again.
"I act as if I can do it" (Hamlet, Act III, iv, 161).
I am one with infinite intelligence.
I listen to my Inner Mentor for perfect guidance.
Every idea flows to me in perfect order.
Every one of my sessions is productive.
I'm stronger than this stack of paper/notecards/journals/books/pdfs.
I stick with it, I Stick With It, I STICK WITH IT.

As you use these affirmations, and everything else in this chapter, those random notes and Post-Its, to your amazement, will take shape into a dissertation. In the process, though, you may find other obstacles than the actual production of pages looming. They're of the human kind, more insidious than writers' brain freeze. In part III, starting with chapter 7, I'll help you fearlessly face, talk back to, and appease often well-meaning but dissertation-debilitating significant others.

III

Your Near, Dear, and Despairing Significant Others

SEVEN

Orient the Important Others in Your Life

STRANGER IN A STRANGE GRADUATE SCHOOL CULTURE

The culture of graduate school is different from any others you may be a part of—those of your family, friends, workplace, original country, town, neighborhood, earlier schools. . . . Not only do you have to somehow shoehorn in the actual work but you're also plunged into a new morass of "cultural, literacy, and sociopolitical practices while under the pressure of time, financial hardship, and possibly unclear authority relationships with faculty members" (Casanave & Li, 2008, p. 3).

As you already know, graduate school has little in common with undergraduate college. It's in a different world, if not galaxy, with its own customs, traditions, and buzzwords (Stokes, 2005). Golde (1998) observed that when you're a new graduate student, you "need to accomplish four distinct but interrelated tasks: intellectual mastery, learning about the realities of life as a graduate student, learning about the profession, and integrating oneself into the department" (p. 56, as cited in Casanave & Li, 2008, p. 3). You get dunked suddenly into this culture from your first grad school courses.

As you progress, and especially once you start the dissertation, as I discussed earlier, your life changes mightily. You hole up in the library after work, eat on the run, retreat to your study all day Sunday, and always look distracted. You never really listen when a family member talks to you because you're wrestling with formulating your major hypothesis or racking your brain for the origin of the quote you forgot to make a note of that perfectly supports your position.

With the work always going so much slower than you want and all the new knowledge and tasks, your head may be spinning. You may gradually adapt, at least somewhat, but your family and friends barely comprehend what you're going through and must master. With many of my clients, both minority and so-called mainstream, their parents' education stopped at high school, their siblings or spouses got MBAs that didn't require a thesis, or their relatives couldn't understand why they just didn't go out and get a regular steady job. How could your family and friends know or imagine what you must face and conquer? It's up to you to put them in your picture.

FAMILY AND FRIENDS: STARTING OFF WRONG

Other than yourself, your family and friends are most affected by your dissertation, and they most affect your progress (West, 2014). A poignant example: Ava wailed to me, "I get calls daily from my mother, my three sisters, and my two cousins! They all say they're tired of me not coming to the family events. I *had* to go to the reunion!"

Ava had made a mistake. She waited until her relatives noticed her withdrawal, and by then they thought she was avoiding them. The absolute best time to orient family and friends to what awaits you for the next several years is when you first begin the dissertation. Without some advance notice, they will feel even more confused, bewildered, and angry. Like Ava's relatives, they'll start squeezing you.

Trying to compromise, Ava went on the week-long family reunion. She told me she took her chapter 2, hoping to do some work. That was, of course, wishful working. With all the activities, festivities, and late-night gab fests, she barely had time to change clothes. Ava came home more exasperated and more behind in her work than ever.

Like many or most of you, Ava was trying to juggle at least two lives. Graduate school is itself a "career" and often a second, simultaneous one. She had a husband and three kids, worked as an elementary school teacher, and crammed in dissertation time as she could. To give her credit, she did try to inform her relatives early. As she collected research, her printed articles overflowed her den and covered her dining room table in high-rise stacks. Using "one picture is worth" reasoning, she took photos of the two stuffed rooms and sent them to her relatives. She confessed to me, "The photos didn't penetrate. Everyone still kept calling."

STARTING OFF RIGHT

I've had clients, usually women, who went to one of two extremes: Laura took over the kitchen table and all the counters with her materials. She told her kids to make their own dinners around her while she worked. She was surprised when they hardly spoke to her. Taylor tried to do it all for her husband and children—shopping, cooking, serving, cleaning, listening to her husband's work woes every night, helping her children with homework every night, *and* simultaneously frantically trying to cram in her dissertation writing. She was surprised when she was exhausted all the time and hardly made a dent in her first chapter.

By the way, for the first time, women outpaced men in doctoral degrees as of 2009, with 60 percent earning doctorates. As of 2010–2011, the period of most recent data, women constituted 62 percent, with similar projections in the following years, and more women entering academia (Jaschik, 2010; Kena et al., 2014; National Center for Education Statistics, 2012).

A major part of your successful dissertation journey is to reach a balance that works for you between ignoring your family and trying to be *superspousepartnerparent*. See the following four enlightening books that deal with women doctorates who have chosen to remain in academe. The specifics may not apply to you, but the problems and experiences described and remedies may help you greatly.

The works are Connelly and Ghodsee's (2014) *Professor Mommy: Finding Work-Family Balance in Academia*; Evans and Grant's (2008) *Mama, PhD: Women Write About Motherhood and Academic Life*; Seto and Bruce's (2013) *Women's Retreat: Voices of Female Faculty in Higher Education*; and Ward and Wolf-Wendel's (2012) *Academic Motherhood: How Faculty Manage Work and Family*.

For your immediate situation and the sake of everyone, your family members should all be warned, and early. Whether you're the first to pursue an advanced degree or one of a long proud line of related PhDs doesn't seem to make much difference. Family members who haven't been through it have no idea at all; members who've earned the degree may have forgotten what it's really like and probably minimize their own struggles.

Ava confessed more. On top of the family reunion, she had succumbed to pleas for help. First it was a sister's impassioned request for babysitting her four-month-old twins while she went on job interviews. Then it was a cousin's entreaty for Ava's knowhow in completing her son's seventh-grade term project. In both cases, Ava's involvement lasted for months. "I couldn't say no," she said sheepishly. I advised her strongly to start practicing refusal or risk torpedoing her dissertation.

On the other hand, Randy, a single father with two children, enlisted his family near the beginning. He called his mother, aunt, and sister his "team." When we first started working together, he told me he sat them all down and explained what he would have to do in the next two years (at least). He asked for their support and advice, which they willingly gave. Randy knew that, directly and indirectly, they would help immeasurably on his journey. And they did, in practical and emotional ways, taking over many tasks and bolstering him at low points.

At one point, when Randy was dejected about his slow progress, his sister sent him a miraculously timely and reinvigorating email:

> Thinking of you, sweetie. I know we talk a lot, but I also know you're going through something that none of us has ever gone through—your doctoral program. You work at your job like crazy, you take care of your household and your two kidlets, and you constantly keep at your graduate work. With all of this, you stay positive. It's got to be difficult for you, yet you are ALWAYS here for us, your family.
> I include you in my prayers every night, and I think of you and love you every day! Please, don't EVER hesitate to call me when you need to release some mental stress or things just get too overwhelming. I've ALWAYS got your back!!!

I could have kissed that sister.

Selfish?

Unlike Randy's sister, who offered help whenever he needed it, sometimes relatives or friends will ask you for assistance, like Ava's. No one can argue with your concern for them, and it's wonderful and considerate to agree to help. But as I am preaching, there's a time and place for you to say yes or no. (For more discussion, see again my article in *Women in Higher Education,* Sterne, 2014.) A reminder from chapter 2: "It's Your Time": You've earned it and deserve it.

Saying No

When you agree to help a loved one, what may first seem like a harmless little pause in your doctoral program or dissertation or a short-term good deed can stretch into a permanent break that will never get you your degree. Ava started getting impassioned calls with more dire scenarios from her other sisters and cousins for similar "favors."

She didn't lose her compassion and genuinely felt for her relatives and their problems. I'm sure you do too. That's not the point. When you say no, you're preserving your own time and responding to the requesters, in Alcoholics Anonymous terms, with "tough love." They are forced to seek alternative solutions, and for all you know they may become more resourceful and stronger as they meet their problems themselves.

If an apparently critical situation entices you, think about your own goals and desires. Think about the life-altering, likely negative consequences to you of helping others at this crucial time. Need I remind you about Claudia in chapter 6?

Both you and the ones asking for help have other options. Talk with a neutral other person for possibilities and means you may not have thought of. Explore further resources, including other family members and agencies. Claudia might have been persuaded to help her friend without making such a radical move that brought her dissertation to a halt and bred more entangled problems than propagating octopuses.

Granted, saying "no" may be very hard, a "major challenge for most people," as emotional intelligence expert Travis Bradberry concluded (2014b, para. 11). Practice gently refusing, especially when you can offer alternatives. Then practice refusing more firmly. Bradberry (2014b) reminded us, "Saying no to a new commitment honors your existing commitments and gives you the opportunity to successfully fulfill them" (para. 11). So honor your desire to complete your dissertation and achieve your precious and hard-won doctorate.

Ava's experiences show that support, or lack of it, by those who are close can make the difference between a nightmarish dissertation experience and only an extremely uncomfortable one. The key to better situations is education and bribes.

SACRIFICES AND REWARDS: SHORT-TERM, MID-TERM, INTERMINABLE-TERM

Early intervention, as Randy proved, is a major strategy, and face-to-face is the absolute best (no emails or texts; Skype if you must). If you feel shaky about informing and inducing your relatives, remember your own sacrifices to get to the point of your doctoral pursuit—you've deprived yourself of vacations, time off, activities with your kids, sleep.

If you tolerate the intrusive words and actions of others, they won't go away. They'll stay at the same level or more likely escalate. By silence or apparent acceptance, you won't be fooling anyone either. Psychotherapist Greg Katz said, "Tolerations drain your energy and keep you unfocused and off balance" (personal communication, October 10, 2014). You get what you tolerate. Instead . . .

Educate Them

Don't flinch from telling those nearest and most hysterical that they're not the only ones who will be sacrificing visiting time, money, moments of satisfaction, and the luxury of trivial arguments. If your family members or friends have earned undergraduate or advanced degrees, rouse their memories of their own travails with term papers, master's theses, and capstone projects. They may nod in squirming or even empathic recollection. Then pounce: Tell them that the dissertation is at least five-times worse.

Sketch out, vividly, the kind of time and attention you need, especially with your many other duties. Refer them to a couple of the scenarios above. Ava's photograph didn't work, but when you're face-to-face, you can be dramatic in painting the word pictures and backing them up with evidence, like Edison.

Edison's mother and brother kept complaining about his absences from the traditional Sunday family dinners. He sat them both down and in a heart-to-heart detailed his monstrous dissertation schedule. He had one and a half hours a day to work on his dissertation, that is, if his boss didn't slap overtime on him. Weekends were out because his wife started to work as a nurse for the tuition he needed while he took care of the two kids, both under eight.

He told his family that with all the research necessary he could write about ten pages a week. That's 20 weeks, he continued, or five months to get 200 pages, the average length, and this time was just for the first draft. He then said that his chair always took more than the supposed requisite two weeks to return a draft and demanded all kinds of revisions.

After this summary, Edison pulled out the evidence: the chair's marked-up tracked-change draft, the university rubric, the printed chart in the university dissertation handbook of a typical timeline that spanned two years.

His mother and brother sat there, open-mouthed. Message delivered.

Bribe Them

After your ice-water shock to the relatives of the hard facts of your dissertation chase, and their recognition that they won't see you for at least eighteen months, it's time to bribe them. To prepare, refer to the list you made from chapter 1, "What Will the Degree Do for You?" Now convert these benefits to them.

Whatever version of "no pain, no gain" you choose, family members especially should know that *something good* awaits at the end of all the sacrifices and suffering. These can include your better job, promotions, prestige, more business, new business, time for a partner or child to resume a degree program, more time with the family, and, most importantly, mo' money. Remind them (and yourself) about all the payoffs.

The other type of bribe with both family and friends is to make promises for the future, AD (after degree). These can be special dates, an extended visit, a vacation together, offers of help with their special projects. To show your goodwill and seriousness, offer a bribe for a more immediate time. Geoff promised his wife that after he finished writing up his data collection methods, the very next weekend he'd take her out to their favorite restaurant on a mountaintop overlooking the majestic river. Madelyn told her ten-year-old daughter that the minute Mommy completed her proposal PowerPoint, they'd build the birdhouse together the girl was begging for.

If you ever want to finish, you must take the time to get family and friends to cooperate. They may never really understand, and they may cooperate grudgingly, but they'll finally leave you alone to do the work you need to do.

The suggestions in this chapter apply generally to both family and friends and many situations. In chapter 8, we'll get into more specifics of particular family storms that may threaten to drown everyone and sink your dissertation. I'll share ways to rescue yourself and keep your dissertation from going under.

EIGHT

Family

Choruses of Complaints, Songs of Support

Rick was beside himself. His wife had threatened to call a divorce lawyer. His teenage son wouldn't talk to him even more than usual. When the family sat down to watch television, his nine-year-old "princess" had stopped trying to squirm onto his lap.

Perplexed, Rick didn't know why his family had turned against him. So what if he went straight from work to the library, got home at 10 p.m., swigged half a beer, and flopped into bed? So what if he left early Saturday morning for his study group and forgot to call to say he wouldn't be home for lunch . . . or dinner? So what if, puzzling out his research findings, he nodded at the wrong places when his wife went on about their son's dubious friends or the leaking clothes washer?

Rick's experience is typical of family problems that can arise when one partner is writing a dissertation. In this chapter, despite my earlier counsel of sedative education and seductive bribes, I'll describe additional land mines you may be regrettably familiar with and give you some specific strategies for skirting them.

PARTNERS: "I DIDN'T BARGAIN FOR THIS" OR "I NEVER SEE YOU ANYMORE"

Have you heard either of these accusations? If your partner suddenly blurts one out, it's time to stop, look, and close your computer. Face it head on, or you'll be frantically pawing the pages to the "Troubled Waters" section of this chapter. Don't fall into the trap of "everything's fine."

When your partner nurses silent resentment and hurt, pretending everything is "fine," that's the opposite of fine for both of you.

Your initial educating moves should help, but if they don't, and it's understandable (they moan, "How much am I supposed to take?"), make time to sit down and let your partner talk and shout out the feelings, assumptions, misunderstandings, and accusations. You do the same. Allow each other the luxury of irrational feelings. You don't have to agree, but listen fully.

Then point out again the advantages of your degree. Agree to another session when either of you needs it to air any renewed or residual negative feelings that surface. If you have to go over the same ground, do so. When you don't bring up the negatives, they'll just go underground, pollute the family atmosphere, poison your relationships, and contaminate your efforts at the dissertation.

As in any good relationship, work out compromises. To assuage the "I didn't bargain for this" refrain, bargain. Offer to do three loads of dinner dishes (or make three dinners) for two hours of uninterrupted research time, an afternoon of yard work for a morning of library immersion, a trip to the mechanic to rotate the tires for a day at dissertation boot camp. To halt the "I never see you anymore" complaint, agree to, say, weekend dinners together, or evening cocktail half hours to reconnect. You'll feel better for the break, and then you can get back to work.

KIDS: "WE NEVER SEE YOU ANYMORE"

When your children voice the same complaint as your partner, the educate-and-bribe method can work well too. Sit the kids down—granted, you must make time for this, but it's worth it. Compliment their maturity, whatever their ages. Then explain that you've received a monstrous homework assignment from the Wicked Witch of the Desk. Older children can relate with their own special projects, essays, and term papers. If the kids have had or are having a hard time with their assignments, so much the better. If you've helped them with these projects, you can repaint in vivid colors the hard time you both had. They'll be able to empathize more.

Tell them too you'll be figuring out during your dissertation how to have special time with them to do things they like. Ask for their suggestions and tell them you'll think about how to plan the events. Ask too about special school events that are coming up and that they'd like you to attend. You can work these in as breaks around your dissertation time.

INVOLVE THEM: SHARE WHAT YOU'RE DOING

The temptation is strong to hole up and become a library troglodyte with clamped jaw or to pace at home in tortured silence wrestling the dissertation's murky hypotheses and intellectual quagmires. Both approaches foster distance, bitterness, and grouchiness with everyone in your family. Make time to talk to them about what you're doing. You can use the factual approach, with evidence, like Edison in chapter 7 ("Educate Them"), or a more conversational approach.

As you explain, and your partner and kids see your enthusiasm, they really will begin to get it, and even admire your dedication and the work. In bringing it to their level, explain your study in layman's terms. You'll not only see their eyes light up when they finally pierce through the mystery in answer to that perennial question, "What do you *really* do?" You too (miraculously) will begin to understand what you're doing.

Involving Partners

If your partner is in a profession or job related to your dissertation, you're ahead. Partners who work in healthcare and social services can relate to your study of the antecedents of domestic violence or correlations between cognitive therapy and positive outlooks. Partners in education can see why you are studying student achievement and principal leadership. If your partner is not in a related field, plunge in anyway. Any partner can appreciate your passion for studying what's obviously meaningful to you.

Ask for your partner's thoughts on your study. He or she will be flattered that you're asking. Share some research findings (you don't have to go into the convoluted statistics). Start a discussion. Your partner may contribute some real insights and questions you hadn't thought of.

If your partner offers help in finding articles, setting up interviews, or sending out surveys, *accept it.* Your partner wants to be involved. If you have to give explicit instructions, which I strongly suggest, do so beforehand. If you have to correct afterward, do so (tactfully). When you work together, your relationship will become stronger.

Involving Kids

Children want to be part of your life too. They may not comprehend everything about it, but they want to be included. Many new "doctors" thank their children in the acknowledgments, praising them for their understanding, patience, and support. I haven't found any children's books on Daddy's or Mommy's dissertation, but such books for kids of all ages would surely help parents explain and their children adjust to your long pursuit. (I may write one.)

Clients have told me how they involved their children. Rose enlisted her daughter, who was eleven, as a "special assistant." The girl delighted in alphabetizing note cards and making copies of Rose's propagating journal articles. Wade recruited his teenage son to do periodic Amazon searches for the latest books in the field and sign up for email alerts. Claude's college junior, the computer whiz, helped him mount his intricate PowerPoints.

A bonus: When you're a parent-doctoral student, you're a great role model to your kids. Your children realize that you've gone back to school voluntarily to better yourself and the family. They come to see more of the value of education, and they want to emulate you. I know one six-year-old who regularly works alongside her father at the dining room table on her own crayoned "dishtaysun."

SPECIAL DATES WITH PARTNERS AND KIDS

Much as you may feel you're tearing yourself away from more important matters, special dates are very important to maintain any sense of family. In the end, what's it all worth without their presence and love? Reassure them and make definite dates. Ask for their ideas too. The planned dates will motivate you to squeeze out another two pages beforehand, especially when you can't face another scholarly pontification or blank screen.

Dates With Partners

Here are some ideas my clients have used successfully with their partners.

- Plan evenings of romantic cocktails or special intimacy (difficult to make time for, Lord knows).
- Take a day of hiking and a picnic in the woods.
- Sit down together for an open-ended talk about mutual meaningful topics (future delicious vacation possibilities, revisits to happy memories, strategies for a needed renovation, even some erudite subjects you both like exploring—my husband and I are fascinated by early Christianity).
- Designate an afternoon together on a special project—cleaning out the attic, painting a spare room, visiting a new family down the block.
- Volunteer at a shelter to serve dinner.
- Get tickets for a concert or play (a musical, if you must).
- Go go-karting (good for venting advisor aggressions).

Spark any ideas? Go ahead. Make your own list, with both conservative and wild ideas. I bet your partner will love the wild ones.

Dates With Kids

Clients have also arranged these activities with their children.

- Take the family for a bash at Chuck E. Cheese or other neighborhood video arcade-crazy place.
- Schedule a special-interest outing with one or more of the children—a local humane society for your budding veterinarian, the planetarium for your mini-astronomer.
- Arrange a weekend dinner at home or a restaurant, at which everyone shares their week's accomplishments (including you on your dissertation).
- Cheer from the bleachers at your child's baseball or soccer game.
- Shoot hoops in your driveway.
- Host a party for your kid's special pals.
- Have a private and confidential heart-to-heart about your child's current anxieties.

Can you think of more? If you don't have kids, or they're grown and out, they may still like such ideas when they come back for a visit. These and other activities can also be used for your own brain-restoring breaks. See too the books I recommended earlier on academic women with families: Connelly and Ghodsee (2014), Evans and Grant (2008), Seto and Bruce (2013), and Ward and Wolf-Wendel (2012).

OTHER RELATIVES: "WE NEVER SEE YOU ANYMORE"

Like Ava and Edison in chapter 7, you may have heard this accusation more than once. First, put into action your version of the educate-and-bribe strategy. Of course, none of it will satisfy difficult Aunt Selma ("You don't even have time for your favorite old aunt who won't be around much longer?"). Train yourself to repel the guilt, and offer to buy Aunt Selma dinner in five years (I assure you, she *will* be around).

Educate and Bribe, Again

Nevertheless, work the educate-and-bribe tactic on your relatives. They may not understand at all, especially parents with very limited educations, and can hardly fathom the doctoral process. When you deliver your explanation with sincerity and passion, these feelings will be transmitted, and most relatives should be somewhat receptive.

On the bribe side, you can offer various incentives, similar to those with your nuclear family: making special dates for lunch, dinner, or museums; going to a few selected home-team sports events; scheduling heart-to-hearts; taking their kids to a local university campus (good role model value); and promising to appear for at least one of the coming holiday family get-togethers (see below). As with Aunt Selma, don't get roped in by guilt or apologies.

Sabotage, Unconscious or Not

Despite, or instead of, your best explanations and incentives, relatives can trip you up. On some level, they may not want to support you. Denise arranged to see me for a conference to discuss the crucial next steps in her dissertation. She lived about a half hour away and made the arrangements necessary: She informed her husband and mother, whom she lived with, that she would need a car. We prepared a detailed agenda.

The appointed time came and I waited. 5 minutes, 10 minutes, 15. The phone rang. Very agitated, Denise spilled it out. "I'm still waiting for my husband or mother to come back with a car. Dammit—they *knew* about our meeting! I called them, and they both said they didn't know when they'd be back. My mother said maybe an hour and a half."

That time wouldn't work because I had another meeting afterward. I told Denise to sit them both down as soon as she could and reiterate the importance of her dissertation work—to all of them. A happy ending: Denise's talk seemed to have worked. We rescheduled, and several days later she arrived on time. There were no more similar incidents.

Whatever may be your versions of relatives' sabotage, keep your eye out for it and zap it with courageous confrontation. Explain and set your limits. If you have to be firm and even harsh, so be it. It's your life and degree.

HOLIDAY STRATEGIES

This advice applies as well to holidays. With immediate family and other relatives, you can negotiate your holiday strategies. Their argument usually goes something like this: "It's only an afternoon (or day or weekend). Come on—you can take a break to see your family for *that* long." Maybe and maybe not. They may not understand your momentum or need for solitude or actual enthusiasm for your work, not to mention the pervasive holiday anxiety about seeing relatives.

You may recall last year's embarrassing holiday questions from the most intrusive relatives ("How come you're still single?") and realize they'll now have more ammunition knowing about your doctoral program (see below for hard questions and shut-'em-up answers). When we're with generations of relatives, most of us get thrown back into our earlier, family-defined roles and the rut of family dynamics (L. Esposito, 2014). If we've been sincerely working on growing emotionally, we can gain some distance and *not* react in our old ways, even though Great-Uncle Harley continues to try to suck us in. See below again.

For your holiday strategies, I recommend one of two basic positions:

1. Take the Scrooge position. Negotiate, bargain, promise, vow to do anything as long as everyone leaves you alone for most of the day. Remember Hugh in chapter 2 ("No Leisure"). He agreed to go to Christmas at a relative's and have dinner with everyone as long as he could retreat upstairs immediately afterwards to the spare room and work on his dissertation. Figure out your own variations appropriate to the holiday.
2. Take the Santa position. Get up early and put in two hours before you have to leave (your dissertation superego will be satisfied). Then hide your work under a red blanket with white trim and go stuff yourself. Listen raptly to your brother-in-law sounding off on the political commentator whom he love-hates. Cheer raucously with everyone at the basketball playoffs. Get into the backyard touch football game, with its own peculiar family rules.
3. Or praise (extravagantly and sincerely) the hostess's side dish recipes and ask for copies. Or let the kids climb all over you for the day. Watch cartoons and giggle with them (I love *Curious George*). The family will love you, and your brain will probably benefit from the respite.

Whatever position you take, decide on it beforehand and inform your most significant others. That way your spouse won't be shocked when you suddenly disappear after the hors d'oeuvres and before the traditional teary-eyed choruses around the piano. Or when you roll on the rug with kids pummeling your head.

TOXIC VOLLEYS AND TOUGH QUESTIONS

Like others, unfortunately family members can be "toxic people," those who barrage you with questions, belittle you no matter what you've accomplished, drain your energy, provoke great stress, and pull you down (Bradberry, 2014a). With some relatives, although you can avoid them the rest of the year, you can't at holiday gatherings. With others, they can assault you daily, especially if you have to live with them.

Your Neutralizing Responses

Your best defenses are understanding, maturity, and self-discipline. Understand that their constant putting down is a function of their own low self-esteem and maybe jealousy of what you've had the courage to embark on. Realizing these likely reasons, forgive them. Develop a sense of distance, even if they're close relatives. Have the largesse of heart to rise above their barbs and petty attacks; you are mature and secure enough to do so. Be kind if you can. ("Thank you for your concern, Esmée." Then turn to examine the vintage record collection nearby.)

Control your emotions and the urge to strike back with a particularly brilliant sarcastic retort about their waistline or dead-end job. By refusing to fight back or fall into the old family dynamic, you're refusing to engage in battle. You'll defuse the toxicity, and they'll go looking for someone else who's more fun to torture. See also Bernstein (2012), Bradberry (2014a), and Richardson (2009) for more support. See too the **AFFIRMATIONS** at the end of this chapter.

Hard Questions and Your Brilliant Answers

There's always at least one person in your family who asks those questions that make you squirm. Right up there with the in-your-face "Still single?" or "When are you going to have kids?" are questions about your dissertation. To help you field them, maintain your self-respect, and even jab a little in return, here are several of the most often-asked questions, with some variants, and suggested responses that have worked well with clients (definition of *worked well* = it shuts up the other guy). As always, tailor your responses as appropriate, although I suggest curbing your impulse to throw a punch.

- *How's it going? Aren't you done yet? You've been at it for so long. When will you finally finish?* Your answer: Thank you for asking. It's going very well. It's a long process, and you'll know when I've completed it when I do. And how is your miniature Arabian-horse-carving business?
- *What do you need a degree for? Why not get a job that's secure, like with the Post Office?* Your answer: I have a passion to make a difference in [your field/topic/inquiry]. Many employment opportunities are available, in teaching, research, and consulting. And how is your miniature Arabian-horse-carving business?

- *Aren't you a little old to be in school?* Your answer: I never want to stop learning. One of my professors is eighty-six and just got a fellowship to do research in Kuala Lumpur. And how is your miniature Arabian-horse-carving business?
- *Why don't you come to the family gatherings anymore?/Don't you care about us anymore?* Your answer: The dissertation takes a lot of time and concentrated effort. I love you. That will not change. And how is your miniature Arabian-horse-carving business?

See the pattern? A few sentences of reply, with no details. Delivered with certainty and confidence. Then turn the conversation back to them and their interests.

Alternatively, if your second cousin is a PhD and remembers her doctoral experience, she may be especially empathic and ask questions that aren't intrusive but savvy: "How responsive is your chair?" "Did you bring cupcakes yet to the research librarian?"

If this is the case, you are fortunate. Accept your blessing and invite your cousin to a private conversation in a corner of the sunroom. You can test the waters with slightly more detailed answers, and by the responses you may happily discover a willing listener, cheerleader, and academic friend. Just don't let the conversation bog down into recitals of committees' eternal nonresponses or horrific fellow students' failures.

TROUBLED WATERS: FIGHTS, SEPARATION, DIVORCE

Perhaps your most significant other has similar questions, voiced or held in. In either case, it's best to meet the objections and doubts head on. I am sad to say I have seen many clients through traumatic relationship breakups. Generally, the trouble started way before the dissertation and for different reasons, but graduate school and the dissertation undoubtedly exacerbate pressures and existing differences.

A sad saga I've heard variations of from more than one female client was Alina's experience. With a professional husband, Alina gratefully accepted her husband's financial and emotional support for her graduate program. He seemed excited and thrilled for her. As she earned top grades, garnered praise from her professors, and received her chair's blessing for her dissertation, Alina gained confidence in the program—and herself. Her husband began to alternate between cold silences and flaming rages; he actually accused her of feeling she was better than he. "I only have an MBA and you're getting a blasted doctorate."

Marilyn, the successful businesswoman I mentioned in chapter 1, said that when she decided to go for her degree, she had to move out of the house because her husband ridiculed her all the time (a version of "What do you need a degree for?"). They lived apart for a year while she did her work. She had hopes of reconciling, but he couldn't understand her passion for the challenges of college teaching after her success in business, having raised six successful children, and with eight grandchildren. The separation became longer and they eventually divorced. Marilyn now teaches college.

Hal told me his soon-to-be-ex-wife, a nursing home aide, said she felt he no longer had time for her. When they went to (requisite) academic cocktail parties, she never felt at ease with his intellectual friends. Hal had not informed her in advance what would be involved, and she hadn't admitted her feelings of inadequacy earlier. Hal said, his voice shaking, that they may have been initially attracted but not because of mutual values.

An unusual situation arose when Carson hired me as coach and editor. His wife, he told me, demanded to know why he couldn't finish his dissertation himself. She kept harping at him to "do it yourself" and referred to me in many less-than-complimentary terms. For every milestone he achieved, she rolled up a boulder of negativity. He—we—finally made it through, and six months later Carson moved out. They subsequently divorced.

These stories, and many similar ones, all have several things in common: The nondissertation half was not prepared for what was to come; the dissertation half did not prepare the other; the expectations by both were unrealistic that life together would not change; and, before or during, one or both did not face the issues that indicated their relationship was in real trouble. Friction "caused" by the dissertation is symptomatic of greater preexisting trouble in the marriage. The dissertation experience just intensifies it.

However, unlike collecting too many scholarly articles, family friction and divorce do not have to be an inevitable byproduct of graduate school and dissertation writing. With forethought, planning, compromise, and possibly uncharacteristic communication, as I recommended in chapter 7 ("Starting Off Right," "Educate Them," "Bribe Them"), you can do much to reduce the troubles, gain needed emotional and physical support from your primaries, and satisfy them that you haven't totally abandoned them.

You've got to have the courage to face up and 'fess up. If, for example, you entered the relationship without informing your Other that one of your life goals was to achieve the doctorate, and you never bothered to tuck that little fact into the conversation about which weekend movie to see, don't be surprised at the upheaval. If you just went ahead and enrolled and didn't talk about it beforehand, don't be shocked at the shocked face of the Other.

Some remedies: At the first sign of trouble, allocate a specific time for confronting the issues. Don't sweep them under the journals or hide behind your drafts. Encourage the expression of feelings and thoughts without interrupting. See how you can come to an understanding of the

Other's point of view, and voice it. This "mirroring" therapeutic technique can be very effective in showing your partner that you really do understand.

Then reach some agreements, like those I suggested earlier in this chapter ("Partners: 'I Didn't Bargain for This' or 'I Never See You Anymore'"), or others specific to your situation. Have as many of these meetings as necessary to keep clearing the air. Not only will you be saving your relationship, you'll also be able to work on your dissertation with a freer mind.

If you feel the issues are too deep and too much, seek professional help (one of my clients, a social worker specializing in conflicts with families, did so at a rocky point in her own marriage and dissertation). Perhaps the Other's expectations really were unrealistic, as were your own. Perhaps the Other couldn't take your self-development and growing self-assertion, as with Alina. Perhaps what drew you together was not really who you were or what you wanted from life, as with Hal.

It is true that sometimes relationships cannot be mended, as in my examples above. Both partners are better off without the encumbrance of the other. But many other primary relationships have survived the dissertation of one partner. Not only do they enjoy the rewards, but sometime the new doctor then supports the partner in the same quest, and both continue to grow (and brag at those academic cocktail parties).

SEE THEM WHOLE

Be cautioned. In this last section I give you two different spiritual techniques for smoothing the way when you must talk the hard talk with your family members.

Send Love Ahead

This first is a technique I learned in a spiritual study group. I've used it many times, to my still-surprised delight, and have written about it at some length (Sterne, 2013a). Here are the main steps:

- *Before* your big talk, sit quietly alone.
- Close your eyes and take some slow, deep breaths.
- If you've been resisting the situation or you're afraid ("I wish I didn't have to do this!"), admit it to yourself. Feel the dismay or fear.
- Do your homework—like Edison did in chapter 7 with his mathematical calculations, like Ava did with her photographs in the same chapter, or with your heartfelt explanation of the processes and your needs during this time. Write out what you want to say.

- Visualize the room or setting where you'll be talking. Choose a space you feel comfortable in.
- See the room shining in light.
- Picture yourself saying what you need to and every other person involved smiling. See them extending hands to you, nodding "Yes."
- Feel the light and peace envelop you and radiate out from you.
- Gently think about how you want to feel after it's over. What do you want to have accomplished or settled?
- Write down your answers: "I want to leave the talk feeling they understand me and what I need. I want to leave knowing they will support me. I want to leave feeling peaceful and grateful for their understanding and their knowledge that I will make it up to them."
- See everyone leaving feeling satisfied, fulfilled, happy with the outcome, and ready to take the next constructive action.
- Say to yourself, "I surrender all to God. I feel only love here." Repeat these statements every time you feel anxious about the situation or tempted to visualize anything less than perfect.
- Practice these steps twice a day.

See Them Supportive

Like aspects of sending love ahead, to see your significant others as loving and supportive isn't always easy. Do it anyway. See them as innocent, as babies or flowers, without malice or accusations, rages, or tears. See them accepting, understanding, encouraging you, telling you what you most want to hear about supporting you, offering to help, cheering you on. See them surrounded by light.

Practice holding to this highest picture of them. Even if they disagree, even if arguments escalate, even if frigid silences take over for a while, persist in seeing them whole.

These affirmations should help:

AFFIRMATIONS

You cooperate willingly as I continue and complete this dissertation.
I see you perfect and cooperative.
I see you loving, supportive, losing nothing from my dissertation.
I see you embraced with love, security, confidence.

Hokey as it may sound, visualizing and expecting others to act a certain way become a self-fulfilling prophecy, as shown early in Rosenthal and Jacobson's (2003) classic and chilling article on elementary schoolteachers' expectations and their students' corresponding performances and development. Quantum physics corroborates these observations: "Reality" changes with the observer. Hawkins (2012) wrote in *Power vs. Force,*

"The subjective and objective are, in fact, one and the same" (p. 44). Dyer (2004) instructed, "Change the way you look at things, and the things you look at change" (p. 173).

These assertions are the bases for the exercises here. They are very important to learn and practice and apply not only to your relatives but to yourself and everyone you meet. They apply to all the people (cohort members, chairs, committees, librarians, statisticians) and events (defenses conferences, presentations) in your dissertation journey. Mastering the techniques has more positive fallout: As you see others in the highest and most productive and cooperative lights, so you will see yourself.

With your family demonstrating right attitudes and support, friends' reactions may present other hurdles. As we'll talk about in chapter 9, friends' reactions may be disappointingly unfriendly.

NINE

Friends

Are They For You or Against You?

The piercing voice of Kathryn's best friend on the other end of the phone threatened to pierce her eardrum. "You're never around anymore! Why is this damn dissertation so important to you anyway? You think you're too good for me!"

Kathryn mumbled an excuse about the doorbell ringing, hung up, and started to sob. For twenty-two years, Penny had been her best friend, confidante, and supporter. Penny saw Kathryn through her mother's death, two pregnancies, a lawsuit with an impossible neighbor, and her daughter's first date, not to mention countless bad hair days and other infinite petty crises of daily life. Kathryn puzzled, Why was Penny reacting like this?

Penny's explosion is typical of friends who, like family members, simply don't understand what is demanded of you as an adult graduate student. As with your family, you can do much to resweeten curdled friendships. The remedies are similar, although customized for friends, and your responses demand dispassion, firmness, gentleness, explanations, promises, and frequent reassurance.

Again as with family, your best strategy is early heading-off-at-the-pass. Your friends may already know that you're neck-deep in a doctoral program. If they don't, it's way past time not only to inform them but also to draw a graphic picture (see chapter 7, "Educate Them"). In the process, be open to their (a) questions, (b) not-so-fond similar reminiscences if they've had graduate school experiences, and (c) indignation that they're different from everyone else and deserve your time and attention. If they throw tantrums, have your second strategy ready—bribes for later. Again see chapter 7 ("Bribe Them").

"COME ON—IT'S ONLY A QUICK LUNCH": JUST SAY "NOT NOW"

Friends will attempt to persuade you with invitations and especially with regular dates that, BD (before dissertation), you've made habits. These include weekly or monthly night or days out, habitual calls, and "quick" lunches. But we all know that quick lunches never are, especially in malls.

You may find it particularly hard to break the habit of a regular get-together. Explain to your friend in greater depth, using terms like *immersion* and *momentum* and *monstrous chair*. If you can relate your need for seclusion and concentration to similar needs in your friend's life, like studying for a real estate license or training for a triathlon, do so.

Remember too that quote in chapter 3 ("Rethink Your Priorities") from Charles Dickens (Godwin, 2008), in which he told why he refused invitations. When you decline, you can put the onus on yourself by adapting Dickens' words: "This is the penalty for writing a dissertation."

After your heartfelt explanation, how to respond to their invitation? Firmly: "Thank you, but no." Rehearse in the mirror if you have to. Offer a bribe: "How about meeting for our lunch on . . .?" With the incentive to yourself of finishing that section or chapter, you might even look forward to the "quick lunch" as a reward. Or suggest coffee or drinks at the end of the day, after you've satisfied the dissertation devil on your shoulder with a decent chunk of writing.

For other regular and sacrosanct connections with friends, the strategies are similar. Maybe you've had an hour-long phone call every Friday with your best friend for years that no event or act of God has ever interfered with. Now, the acts of chair have changed all that. Tell your friend how you love the calls, and now offer to talk every other week, and for twenty minutes. Or you've had an inviolable night out for pizza and drinks once a month with the still-loyal high school group. Decline and tell them how much you look forward to it, and you'll make it if you can.

COMMUNITY INVOLVEMENT AND VOLUNTEER ACTIVITIES: JUST SAY "LATER"

Giving your time to worthy endeavors is admirable. If you have been very active, your organizations and (other) officers may have become used to relying on you for help. You're called upon for everything, and you know better than I that, rabbit-like, one committee breeds the next. Or you've got a case of excessive involvement, like Trevor.

He was extremely active in his community. After work on Mondays, he volunteered for the neighborhood watch, on Tuesdays coached Little League, on Wednesdays ushered at his midweek church service and had two committee meetings afterward, on Thursdays met with the town voter registration officials, on Fridays tutored at-risk kids at the Y, and on Saturdays served dinner at the local shelter.

Trevor complained to me he wasn't making any progress on his doctoral work. He had declined to do the exercise I recommended in chapter 3 ("Find the Holes in Your Schedule"). Now I knew why. He had no holes.

I counseled Trevor to choose two—only two—of his weekly activities and promise himself he could resume the rest after his degree was awarded. He was appropriately contrite, and we generated specific scripts so he could withdraw gracefully from the other activities for the foreseeable future. Here are some scripts for you:

- I really love doing this [volunteering, coaching, dishing out stew], but I've got to concentrate now on my dissertation.
- I'm so sorry, but I can't do this [volunteering, etc.] until I wrestle my dissertation to the ground.
- Maybe you remember how it was with a big long, monstrous project. That's my doctoral dissertation. I've got to give it my all now, and I'll be in touch when it's under control.
- Regretfully, I must withdraw from this [volunteering, etc.] for the next eight months [or the time you feel you need, and add six months] because of my doctoral program. I look forward to helping coordinate the Christmas pageant [or another appropriate event in the future].
- As I resign for now, I know you'll find a qualified replacement. I'm glad to give him or her some pointers to ease the transition.
- Thank you for understanding. I look forward to resuming with you and the group.

See the pattern? Make your definitive statement, give your reason quickly without describing every wrenching detail, refer to a time frame that's comfortable, and make a promise for the future.

Another suggestion: I urge you to announce your withdrawal either in person or on the telephone, even though these methods take more courage than email or text. You may have to field a few questions or objections, but have confidence that you can (you've got practice with family members). To announce withdrawing from or curtailing volunteer activities, I believe emailing or texting are as rude as for breaking off a romantic relationship.

HANDLE JEALOUSIES AND PUTDOWNS

Friends, like family members, can be cruel in their disparagement, sarcasm, and sniping. Often their venom comes from grudging admiration and hidden jealousy that you're actually going for the degree. They may wish they'd had the courage and gumption to do it.

Your job is not to let anything they throw bother you. A tall order, granted. There's a trick, though, and it's one of perspective. Keep telling yourself this: *They needed to do that.*

I know—this statement may go against all your logic and the rage rising in your stomach. Realize, though, that your friends' stabs are very likely not aimed at you personally but stem from something completely unrelated and probably very deep. Not that I mean to psychoanalyze anyone, but the causes could be lack of childhood love and support, wrath at an absent parent, frustration at a stalled career, jealousy of everyone perceived as more accomplished, feelings of unworthiness and too-lateness.

In other words: *They needed to do that.*

I suggest too you repeat a concurrent perspective: *It was the best that they could do at that moment.*

When you realize that they needed to attack you for their own convoluted, unforgiving, transferential reasons, you can take in this principle easier. You're not condoning or excusing them. Rather, you realize that their level of maturity allowed them to act in the best way they knew how. In fact, given their current stage of development, they could have acted no differently and were doing the very best they could.

Not pretty for you, admittedly, but when you distance yourself with these two thoughts, you'll better maintain your equilibrium, deflect those poison arrows with a shrug, and just keep writing. For more discussion of these points, see my book *Trust Your Life* (Sterne, 2011, especially pp. 130–31).

You can respond to their barbs in one or more of several ways.

1. Answer with grace and consideration. "Marsha, you've accomplished a lot too—look at your influential contributions to the town council." "Doug, I'll be the same person with those letters after my name. We can still watch the hockey playoffs together."
2. Reply with boundary-setting. "Tim, I don't appreciate those deprecating remarks. If you can't give me support, let's not talk until my degree is awarded."
3. Respond with silent affirmations.

AFFIRMATIONS

I see you now, Bernard, in perfect happiness and satisfaction with your life.

I affirm for you, Lois, all good you wish for yourself.

LET GO OF THE CRAZYMAKERS

Sometimes, though, the putdowns get to be too much and, regretfully, you may have to let friends go. They are just too destructive. You spend too much time and energy intoning "They needed to do that" and fighting your urge to strangle them. Face the fact that they are toxic people and usually crazymakers.

Toxic people "push others' buttons, stymie projects, and inject pessimism into every situation" (Stillman, 2014, para. 1). Much has been written about crazymakers in the psychological literature, such as their narcissism and their easy escalation to physically abusive behavior. If you have any doubts or distrust your gut, these traits identified by master writing teacher Julia Cameron (1992) will help you identify—and chuck—the crazymakers in your life.

"Crazymakers are those personalities that create storm centers. . . . charismatic but out of control, long on problems and short on solutions" (Cameron, 1992, p. 44). They break and destroy schedules (yours), put their own schedule above everyone else's, expect special treatment, discount your reality (including your dissertation goals and deadlines), spend your time and money, set others you know against you and each other, are expert blamers, create unfounded dramas, hate order, and finally, deny they are crazymakers and turn the blame onto you (see Cameron's pp. 46–49). Any of this sound familiar?

A dissertation writer's mother chose the night before his final defense to demand that he put up her storm windows ("Winter will be here in only four months."). As another finally settled into his third chapter, his buddy appeared unannounced and pulled him away to celebrate the championship game of their grade school soccer team ("Hey, don't you want to support the guys?").

A candidate's friend broke her promise to watch her kids while the student had a hard-wrestled appointment, finally, with her chair ("I had to get my hair done, and they didn't have anything open for two days."). Another friend called the work- and writing-weary student at 1:00 a.m. to complain, yet again, about his wife and kept the candidate on the phone for an hour.

If you've got to deal with such crazies, either friend or family member, here are some ways to curb them (with thanks to Bradberry, 2014a, and Stillman, 2014).

- Say no. The high school soccer buddy should have been told, firmly, "Thanks, but no." The middle-of-the-night caller should have been told the same.

- Set your limits. Tell your storm-window mother you'll do it in a month. Give the dead-of-night caller a day and time that work for you.
- Choose your fights. Confront the crazymaker only when you feel you have time to get involved. Remember, though, that it's unlikely you'll "win"—they always have another rationale and seemingly endless energy to keep the battle going. It's what feeds them.
- Become aware of and control your emotions. Hard, for sure, and it's too easy to get sucked into the emotional drama, especially because they know exactly how to get you where it "guilts." The more aware you are of their tactics and your reactions, though, the more you can control them and tell yourself, "This is a crazymaker. I will not bite."
- Don't let their negativity, judgments, or condemnations pull you down. You are responsible for your own frame of mind. Their mindsets are toxic and do not serve you. Reject those mindsets and replace them with your own optimism, enthusiasm, and forward-thinking.
- Arm yourself with a few affirmations. Self-affirmations help set new habitual responses, and your brain actually changes when you repeat and believe them (Miller, 2014).

AFFIRMATIONS

I am unaffected by their mindset.
I don't have to win or reform them.
I deserve joy in everything I do.
I deserve friends who truly support me.

THOSE QUESTIONS AGAIN: "AREN'T YOU DONE YET?"

When you're neck-deep in the dissertation, friends can and do ask the same uncomfortable questions as family. We addressed these in chapter 8 ("Toxic Volleys and Tough Questions," and especially "Hard Questions and Your Brilliant Answers"). The responses suggested there apply here too, with adaptations for friends. Good friends will support you in your efforts; less good friends, or those secretly jealous of your drive and envious in advance of your getting the degree, will persist in not understanding, diminish your efforts, and denigrate your goals.

Don't let them. Their questions and replies to your answers are variations of toxicity. You don't need any of it. When the questions start, put a stop to them by saying something like this: "Thanks for asking but I appreciate your not asking again. I'll let you know about my milestones."

If they voice hurt feelings and point out that they're the exception to all your other friends, be warned. You're heading into a crazymaker's cyclone. Real friends will respond with understanding and can take your forthrightness. You'll know by the responses whether they're friend or foe.

ASSURE THEM YOU STILL LOVE THEM

For the real friends, a major and considerate strategy is to reassure them that your temporary sequestering has nothing to do with them but wholly with accomplishing your goal. Your plea for solitariness and refusal of invitations doesn't mean rejection, and you can repeat this thought as often as needed. Reassure them they're still loved, despite your unreturned phone calls and texts, ignored emails, solitary late nights, and what seem like gruff silences.

Explain again if you feel it will help why your uninterrupted concentration is critical and that the dissertation will be with you for at least another year (as the gods and your chair smile on you). You can also tell them you'll be in touch: You may need their encouragement, their ears and mind as a sounding board, or their dragging you out to the café when your brain is completely citation-clogged. When you ask if they welcome these requests, they'll likely nod vigorously, and they'll be very glad to hear your subliminal other message: You're not cutting them out of your life.

Reiterate your promises about resuming regular contact, and make a date for a week or several in the future. As you do so, your friends will see the force behind your words and accept them. They'll recognize that their best action at this point is to stay away. Both of you will then look forward to your next contact.

KNOW AND BELIEVE THEY ARE FOR AND WITH YOU

You can contribute further to your friends' understanding, support, and goodwill. In a spinoff of the quantum principle that change is in the mind of the observer (chapter 8, "See Them Supportive"), fashion your own self-fulfilling prophecies—positive ones. See your friends rooting for you.

I was warmed by an email my client Trudy showed me. Dejected at her slow progress, Trudy confided her feelings to a friend with whom she started the doctoral program. Her friend, now on the last two chapters of her own dissertation, wrote this to Trudy:

> Hey, Dear,
> Trust me, we've all been there. Press forward and continue on. I felt the same as you, and now I'm on the last part. Do not let it defeat you. It is our destiny to succeed!
> And keep me in touch.

That's a friend.

If your friends aren't quite as supportive as Trudy's, send them love, as you did with family members. As I described in chapter 8 ("Send Love Ahead"), send them love before talking with them about your present needs. You can also use the technique any time you think of your friends. I'm sure Trudy's friend needed a lot of love and support in her own dissertation trek, as she was giving to Trudy.

A few brush-up affirmations, revised for your friends:

AFFIRMATIONS

You support me willingly as I continue and complete this dissertation.
I see you perfectly cooperative in helping me to complete.
I see you understanding my needs now.
I look forward to getting together as I can.
I send you only love.

With your own right attitudes and expectations, your friends can be true blessings and blessedly for you. Later you can rejoice with them (and get drunk) when you're awarded your degree.

At work, you may encounter similar resistances as with friends. The same principles for combating them apply as to family and friends, but in a clean shirt and with less eye-rolling. In chapter 10, we'll talk about how you can keep working well on your dissertation and keep your job.

TEN

Make Peace and Time With Your Employer and Work Colleagues

It's not easy working full-time and writing a dissertation. Whether you're an employee or a self-employee with your own business, and especially if you have a family and kids, you've got many challenges. As we've talked about, progress on your dissertation requires planning, self-discipline, time, and saying no to many things.

A few doctoral students can quit work and devote themselves full-time to the dissertation. One student gave her reason for taking a leave from her job in favor of her dissertation: "I watched my coworker struggle through about three years of trying to write her dissertation and be professional full time" (McCoy & Gardner, 2011, p. 97). But many students cannot quit work. I assume you are among them. Nevertheless, you have options.

When you feel you cannot make any headway on your dissertation after a full work week (wholly understandable), this is the time to meet with your employer or supervisor. At the risk of sounding redundant, I remind you that the very same principles in chapters 7, 8, and 9 for good relationships with family and friends—orientation, education, bribery—apply also to your employer and coworkers during your dissertation duress.

Of course, you need to maintain more composure than with family or friends when you talk with your boss about your dissertation needs. And you need to appear reasonable. The more mature you feel, the better you will present yourself and the smoother your interaction to get what you need.

EXPRESS YOUR GRATITUDE AND EXPLAIN, EXPLAIN

Employers often encourage higher degrees, and some pay for them in whole or part. Your boss may be very supportive of your academic pursuit and willing to give you released time and preferential schedules to meet the demands of graduate work. To gain what you need, make a specific appointment for *that* talk.

Before you sit down together, confirm that you will be talking to the right person who can grant what you're asking. If you work on a team, the team leader may not have the authority to give you released time. Find out who has the final word.

Preferably with the boss's door closed, first express your gratitude as sincerely as you can and without fawning. After all, you're asking for a special dispensation, and you really are grateful for the hearing and (expected) accommodation.

Then explain why you are asking. Use a version of your explanations to family and friends from chapter 7 ("Educate Them") and chapter 8 ("Educate and Bribe, Again"). Go into as much detail as will make your case but without the theatrics that may be needed for family members. Here are some suggestions for scripts.

If your boss knows about your doctoral program: "Thank you for this meeting and for listening. I have reached the point in my doctoral program where the dissertation has to be written. (Wait for congratulations.) This 'book' requires blocks of concentrated time. I want to keep fulfilling my job duties completely while I write. I would be very grateful if you could arrange my schedule so I could double up on some days and have others off for the dissertation. I'm glad to answer any questions you may have."

A variation if your boss doesn't know about your program: "Thank you for this meeting and for listening. I may not have told you that I am in a doctoral program to get the [name of your degree]. I have been taking the courses online and doing the work nights. Now, I've reached the point of writing my dissertation. (Wait for congratulations.) This 'book' requires blocks of concentrated time. I want to keep fulfilling my job duties completely and would be very grateful if you could arrange my schedule so I could double up on some days and have others off. I'm glad to answer any questions you may have."

If your employer shows interest in your degree program and/or dissertation topic and asks for more information, by all means give it. The boss's genuine interest and intelligent questions, and your equally intelligent responses, will only help your case. By the way, not many articles seem to have been written on the difficulties of dissertation writing while working. I found only a few heartfelt blog posts. (Want to try it?)

In either scenario above, and you can adopt this formula to your own situation, you are doing the following: (a) expressing gratitude, (b) sharing your progress, (c) explaining what you need, (d) assuring your boss you will not neglect your job, (e) asking for what you want, and (f) leaving the final decision to the boss to agree to what you want and need.

Then, in a variation of your family strategy, offer job-related bribes . . .

POINT OUT HOW YOUR DEGREE BENEFITS THE COMPANY

Your employer may be supportive, cooperative, and generous, but to give you what you need may still need reminders of the benefits of your degree to the company. After your explanation, assure your boss that one of the reasons you are getting the degree is to help the company, and especially the boss's division (both true, right?). You will be putting to rest any suspicions that you're pursuing the degree to change jobs or careers (even though these may be part of your long-term plan).

Do *not* talk about the benefits to you personally, such as higher pay, bigger and better title, other and better opportunities, or the degree as an exit strategy.

Rather, volunteer the benefits of your degree to the company. Keep in mind, without voicing it, that all of the benefits you list will reflect well on the boss. If your degree is directly related to you job, great; if not, you can still point out many pluses. For example:

- This degree will increase my knowledge, skills, and abilities in doing my job.
- With the information I am collecting and absorbing, I will gain more expertise that can be applied to my work here.
- I will gain practice and application in contributing more innovative solutions for problems in my unit/section/department/division/the company.
- I will be able to train others more effectively.
- My leadership skills will be developed, and I will use them as appropriate.
- With the greater knowledge from the degree, my duties and responsibilities can expand as you need.
- With the degree, I will have more confidence in representing the company.
- With the degree, I will be more valuable to the company.

Then stop speaking. If you haven't already suggested what you want, let the boss ask or make suggestions for your revised schedule. And thank, thank, thank.

Your turn. To prepare for your presentation, start your own list of how your degree will benefit the company and, if you wish, to your boss in particular. Jump off from the suggestions above and create your list over several days—more will come to you at odd moments.

To make your presentation more immediate and meaningful, under each point give a specific example that applies. For example, "With the degree, I will have more confidence in representing the company. I will be able to meet with prospective buyers and show them what our product(s) can do to enlarge their markets."

The more you've thought in advance and let your creativity and applications to your work spring up, the more confident you will be in your representation of yourself to the boss.

NEGOTIATE WHAT WORKS FOR BOTH OF YOU

First, remember that your employer needs you and wants to keep you. You've been doing a great job (if you haven't, that's another book or at least an article). This reminder should strengthen your confidence to ask for certain things without jeopardizing your responsibilities or their impact on others. As a conscientious employee, your task is to negotiate your schedules and workloads that honor your job and allow for steady progress on your dissertation as well.

To reiterate, after your explanation of the writing pressures and necessities, wait for your boss to suggest a revised schedule. If this is not forthcoming, suggest your own. Think about it in advance; have your best plan in mind for time off and ways you can compensate. These can include taking work home, coming in on weekends, staying later some nights, and any other possibilities that could work.

Be prepared to negotiate as part of your first meeting with the boss, although a second may be necessary. Rehearse in advance and decide clearly what you will give up if necessary—instead of three afternoons off you'll settle for two. What time period do you want the arrangement to continue for? You may feel six months is adequate; the boss may suggest three. Compromise at four and a half.

Your boss may not be able to give you answers right away and may have to confer with others to arrive at a workable schedule and workload for you. You understand. Be gracious about the time and leeway needed. Don't show panic or urgency about your revised schedule. That only indicates weakness on your part and in your negotiation position.

Also promise to inform the boss of any changes in your situation. I know it's highly unlikely, but you may actually complete your draft earlier than anticipated. In that case, you may be able to handle a full week of work once again.

When you have the new arrangement worked out, get it in writing. It doesn't have to be formal (depending on the type of company and human resources department). A written agreement is very important. If you need it for any reason (although we don't want to entertain why you would), refer to the agreement and point to the date and boss's signature.

In the meetings, your conduct, your preparation, your thoughtful suggestions, and your poise show your employer that you care about your job and the company. All these, and your sense of responsibility, will demonstrate you are worthy of the special and temporary considerations you are asking for.

SUPERIOR JEALOUSIES

Many supervisors are enormously supportive of their subordinates' doctoral studies. Others are not, and generally for several reasons. They may envy your accomplishments and pending degree. They may feel that once you get the degree you will supplant them, and they'll be out of a job. Or that you'll get promoted over them (the humiliation!). Some may feel bitter and resentful that they never took the leap to do what you're doing, especially with a full-time job.

Carlton told me that his immediate supervisor in his social work agency "purposely" loaded him with the most difficult cases. The supervisor knew he was pursuing the doctorate, and she had a master's. A colleague had told Carlton he heard the supervisor complaining to a friend that Carlton "thinks he's better than us with mere master's." I pointed out to Carlton that his supervisor was likely afraid for her position and her best defense was to disparage him.

Recognize Toxicity

Carlton's supervisor, with her overload assignments and gossip about him, may well have been a toxic individual. In fact, Bradberry's (2014a) article I referred to above was intended for the work environment. His later article specifically on toxic bosses (Bradberry, 2015) pinpointed seven types and how to handle them. As damaging as family or friends, toxic superiors can undermine your morale, your work accomplishments, and your spirit.

They emphasize the problems and minimize solutions (not so great for supervisors) and can spread ill will about you to others. Dealing with them constructively so you keep your sanity is touchy, and you certainly don't need the stress on top of your dissertation.

Don't avoid the situation, pretend it doesn't exist, or ignore the cutting remarks and putdowns by silence. The toxicity will catch up with you, so meet the situations head on. Bradberry (2015) identified the buddy (inappropriate overfriendliness), the micromanager (attention to too many details—yours), the tyrant (dictating everything), the incompetent (not knowledgeable or effective), the robot (sees you as a statistic), the visionary (grand visions, no practical follow-through), and the seagull (swoops in and takes over).

If your boss fits any of these categories, look at Bradberry's (2015) remedies and how to apply them to your situation. For example, if your boss is a tyrant, when you're asking for released time for your dissertation point out how your topic was inspired by his latest talk to the employees. Give him credit (much as it may pain you). If your boss is a robot, speak her language in citing statistics of ABDs and doctoral dropouts. Tell her with passion you don't want to be one of them, and to establish human contact, share a couple of personal reasons why.

Also, refer back to chapter 9 and the discussion of toxic people ("Handle Jealousy and Putdowns" and "Let Go of the Crazymakers"). Review the suggestions; many will apply now because you have gained a relentlessly positive perspective and attitude.

Toxicity Antidotes

In addition to the suggestions I made earlier, you can do other things more specific to your work environment:

- Become more aware of the types and frequencies of interactions with the supervisor. Notice the patterns. As Bradberry (2014a) observed, you will start seeing what sets them off and that their behavior is predictable. When you recognize the patterns, you'll be able to decide when to confront, when to respond, when to swallow and nod, and when to minimize your contacts. You may not need to have frequent face-to-face interactions. Possibly most communication can take place in memos or emails.
- Schedule a meeting with the threatened individuals. Assure them you are not after their jobs or to show them up. Like them, you want to do your best in the job. Say you respect them and the responsibilities they have, and you want to support them.
- Examine your duties: They are certainly different from your superior's; otherwise you would be the supervisor. Ask for clarification of your duties, and as the supervisor explains, the differences will be underscored.
- If the supervisor is the big boss, the above suggestions can work. If the supervisor is below the big boss, talk to the boss. As graciously, tactfully, and kindly as you can, outline the situation. Don't couch your report in blame or accusations of the supervisor. Rather, voice your thoughts in the context of your being prevented from doing your best work for the company, and ask the boss for help and

support. The boss likely knows about the supervisor's attitude already, and you're just helping the arsenal that could lead to that individual's firing.

- If you must, seek other employment. I don't recommend this, though, while you're working on your dissertation. You have enough to handle without applying for, interviewing, and adjusting to a new job.

WORK COLLEAGUES' ENVY

Work colleagues' disparagements can be more difficult to take than supervisors'. After all, colleagues are supposed to be your friends, or at least equals on the job. How many times have you gone out for beers after work, commiserated about the boss, and shored up each other when one of you got caught mining Facebook? When you become a doctoral student, all that camaraderie can vanish.

My client Rudy, an older doctoral candidate who loved learning and truly desired to keep current in his field, told me he was "profoundly disappointed" in his work colleagues. They gave him no encouragement or support for his academic pursuits. "They believe the only reason to continue education is to get more pay, a better job, or prestige. They can't understand why a person my age loves to learn and is doing this."

Rudy had weathered the uncomfortable feelings of older graduate students in classes replete with those who could be their children (Kalambakal, 2014; McCoy & Gardner, 2011). He now felt the effects of his colleagues' stereotypical thinking in both values and assumptions about age.

What Rudy's colleagues didn't know is that the demographics of people pursuing advanced degrees have changed dramatically in the last decades. Fewer students are going directly from undergraduate to graduate programs (McCoy & Gardner, 2011). Especially with the proliferation of online degrees that allow flexibility in schedules, more people are enrolling in higher degree programs later (Larson, 2008), and the median ages are in the thirties (National Center for Education Statistics, 2013).

Some graduate students have had or continue to have full careers and yet still want to expand. For example, a fifty-one-year-old physician enrolled in a graduate degree program in liberal arts, with a concentration on writing. She didn't intend to give up her practice and hoped to combine the two fields (Larson, 2008). My experience with many clients corroborates this example. As I said in the introduction, most of my doctoral clients are professionals in their forties and fifties, and some are decades older. They are lifelong learners, passionate about adding to their knowledge and expertise, and restlessly creative.

If you get responses like Rudy did, gather your courage. You're not alone; many older doctoral students feel similarly (Gruber, 2012). Cite a few of the enrollment facts above. If coworkers persist in belittling remarks, ask them politely, neutrally, and firmly, to desist. A few possibilities:

- Thank you for supportive comments. Please do not share your negative remarks with me.
- With my graduate program, I am doing what I love to do. I wish the same for you.
- I never want to stop learning.

Depending on your relationships with colleagues, you can choose to share few or no details of your work. If some whom you've been close to accuse you of avoiding them or being "too good" for them, know that they are misjudging your refusal of invitations to the bar or yoga studio after work. Like others at work, they may really envy you because you're going for that degree—whatever or despite your age—and they're not. They may also fear the degree will get you promoted before them.

Use some of the same strategies you would with friends and toxic supervisors. You can adapt suggestions from chapter 9 ("Handle Jealousy and Putdowns," "Those Questions Again: 'Aren't You Done Yet?'" "Assure Them You Still Love Them"). If your colleagues are receptive, educate them about the constraints on your time. If they're doing something that also requires concentrated time, like taking additional training or studying for a professional exam, they'll understand. Then bribe them, promising a yoga weekend retreat together or drinks on you—later.

AFFIRM, VISUALIZE, AND PROJECT EMPLOYMENT PEACE

Peace in your workplace *is* possible. Whether you're an employee or an entrepreneur, if you think meeting rooms and meditation mats don't go together, look at David Howitt, CEO of the Meriweather Group. In an article titled "We Need More Entrepreneurs Who Are Healers" (Howitt, 2014), he declared: "I am living proof that we can be empathetic *and* own successful businesses, have a consistent meditation and spiritual practice *and* kill it in the boardroom, be loving and attentive parents *and* make a ton of dough. I am an executive, a CEO and a storyteller and healer. You too can be both" (para. 12).

Following Howitt (2014), apply a little spirituality. Expect your employer's and colleagues' cooperation and see them whole. If you expect and project dissonance, lack of cooperation, and pettinesses, you'll get what you expect. What we give out we get back.

So (watch it: **AFFIRMATIONS** ahead), affirm what you want for yourself and those you work with:

AFFIRMATIONS

I wish everyone I work with happiness and success.
I am grateful for my job and considerate and encouraging of others.
I recognize the company founder's vision and let it support and sustain me as I do my best to honor it.
On my way to work, and whenever I think of work, I send love ahead (see chapter 8, "See Them Whole" and "Send Love Ahead").

And visualize workplace harmony and peace:

AFFIRMATIONS

I feel and see only love here.
My boss, supervisor, and colleagues work in harmony with each other and me.
Here there is no competition, no backbiting, no fear.
We all cooperate on assignments and tasks for the company good and our own.

Use these affirmations and visualizations. They should help you in your job in both the immediate and long-range situations.

We've lingered at the workplace long enough. It's time to get back to that other work, your dissertation. In part IV, we'll tackle your relationships with others in your school environment. They may be puppies or piranhas, and sometimes both. First, in chapter 11, your committee.

IV

Good University Cops and Bad

ELEVEN

Your Dissertation Committee

The Best/Worst Friends You'll Ever Have

Chairs and committee members seem to hold dissertation writers' entire futures in their briefcases and inboxes. To grad students, these faculty are more powerful than Zeus in a thunderous rage or a spouse delivering the silent treatment. And with good reason; the committee and especially the chair (also referred to as advisor, primary advisor, research supervisor, or mentor), can help speed your dissertation through (if that's not an oxymoron) or delay you for years.

One client summed up her nightmare with precise, if horrific, detail: "Frustration is too tame a word for me in my PhD program. I have a long history of attempting to get through the program, and I am currently in my eighth year. I am on my second study—too long a story—and and my third complete committee overhaul. They never seem to be satisfied. Please, help!"

ARE PROFESSORS REALLY HUMAN?

Of course professors are really human. They have families, buy groceries, get the car serviced, even once in a while watch TV. Most of the time, though, whatever their rank, they are overworked, overcommitted, and wish they had more time with their families (Jacobs & Winslow, 2004; Peligri, 2014). Many hold positions at three or four or more universities, with several part-time course loads and full-time student loads, including dissertation candidates.

Often professors have 15 to 25 dissertation candidates when they should have 5, and they must give equal attention to their teaching loads, incessant committee meetings, requisite departmental cocktail parties, and the dean's expectations that they publish. Many faculty are burned out, see all students in a blur of sameness, and differentiate women from men only by their slightly tighter jeans. The professors are disillusioned with academe, have lost interest in their specialty, are nursing the hurt of their latest article rejection, embroiled in a divorce, just heard their closest colleague got the award for best scholarly book of the year, and wish they could disappear to a cabin by the lake and write their novel.

More kindly, they're trying to survive in a world they entered because they thought they loved the life of the mind. They've all come through the *rite de passage* you're struggling with. One professor told me he had "mercifully forgotten all the details" of his entire experience with the dissertation.

If the professors remember, they may still look back and feel mangled by their own experience of absent or grudging chairs and committees. It's possible, I'm sorry to say, that your committee members are now secretly and gleefully taking it out on their current students, including you.

I apologize if this characterization is unfair. But it's not fiction. Clients have told me that their chairs and committee members have been downright rude, sarcastic, and arrogant, not only slashing and burning their documents but also mock-whispering that the students shouldn't have entered the doctoral program in the first place.

It doesn't seem to matter either whether you have racial, ethnic, cultural, religious, or favorite baseball team commonalities with your chair. If you have differences, though, the lack of contact and communication can be disastrous:

> Students from different cultural backgrounds and learning styles can also be swept away by a professor's teaching style, lack of availability, or refusal to answer questions—a common practice in many graduate programs. Many students find themselves spending as much time trying to decode their professors as they do trying to absorb what he or she is teaching them. (Stokes, 2005, para. 7)

In a study at a Northeastern university of over 2,000 doctoral candidates (about 39 percent non-Caucasian), Barnes, Williams, and Archer (2010) asked for their students' positive and negative attributes of advisors. Students singled out as the most negative factors faculty's inaccessibility, unhelpfulness, and lack of interest in the students' work.

In a study of factors contributing to students' persistence despite barriers, the major barriers they discussed were a lack of collegial community, lack of meaningful relationships with advisors and chairs, and a loss of momentum toward completion (Fletcher, Gies, & Hodge, 2011). Education students in another study cited barriers of obligations outside the program, deficiencies in knowledge, and advisor struggles (King & Williams, 2014).

With a similar theme of deficient advisors, one student exclaimed in another study, "THANK GOD [caps in original] I am self-motivated because I would have been so delayed if I needed more guidance from my advisor" (West, Gokalp, Pena, Fischer, & Gupton, 2011, p. 318). Is it any wonder so many doctoral candidates have so many problems, take so long, complain to everyone in their path, re-re-renew their extensions, and instead of writing, numbly watch every season's reruns of *Breaking Bad*.

EXCRUCIATING OR EXCEPTIONAL?

As I've more than intimated, committees and chairs usually get a bad rap. Students frequently describe their committees as just wanting to push those dissertations through, get their pittance, devote their time to revising and publishing their own (hard-won) dissertation, and jockeying for tenure.

There's truth to this description. I have known and know of unpardonably neglecting chairs and committee members, with scholarly back-up (Barnes et al., 2010; Fletcher et al., 2011; West et al., 2011). Clients have wailed how they are ignored by the chairs, except for requisite quarterly form emails asking for updates. As one said, hers was "too quiet."

Another had the perfect nightmare of a chair: He didn't respond to voice messages or emails, didn't show up for appointments, kept changing and cancelling new ones, didn't read but only scanned the draft, as a result came to wrong conclusions about the material, and did not keep his promises about delivering the drafts to the other committee members. My client understandably questioned her own sanity and finally, after we talked at length, went to a higher authority (see chapter 12).

Students keep paying, semester after semester, revising their proposals until their fingers and mice have carpel tunnel, with little or no mentoring help in return. Despite my profession, which in a way depends on faculty's inability to deliver and students' desperation, I get very angry—the students are paying a great deal to the university and getting no or little attention or guidance.

Graduate students make the frequent mistake of thinking that their committees are reasonable, logical, well organized, prompt about returning phone calls and manuscripts, and with a balanced life and happy in their work. I recall one client who, before we started working together, sent yet another draft to the chair. He received an email from his chair informing him, with no encouragement or warmth, that the chair would let him know when he could send the next draft. Maybe the chair was attempting to manage his schedule, but this response certainly didn't hearten the student or help his momentum.

There is also untruth to these unflattering descriptions. I have known and know of chairs and committee members who are extremely conscientious, caring, and careful with their mentees' manuscripts. They respond quickly to emails, even phone the students, critique their manuscripts thoughtfully (generally in the fearsome tracked-change mode), and send reminders about deadlines and statutes of limitation. Sometimes, paradoxically, it is these very committee members who refer students to me for editorial help because the professors want the best possible products for their charges.

The professors on your dissertation committee can be your rosiest fantasies or worst nightmares, and even both. If you don't believe me, see the refreshingly honest, enlightening, and entertaining article by Gearity and Mertz (2012), "From 'Bitch' to 'Mentor': A Doctoral Student's Story of Self-Change and Mentoring." The range of horrid-to-fabulous chair/committee roles was captured perfectly by Grant and Tomal (2013): dictator, procrastinator, abdicator, aggressor, avoider, narcissist, utopian, comforter . . . versus collaborator and facilitator (pp. 35–36). You may be able to add a few more.

Nevertheless, you *can* choose a chair and committee who support you, for real, throughout the dissertation.

WHO CAN YOU WORK WITH AND HOW DO YOU KNOW?

Do not minimize this choice. A study of doctoral candidates and their chairs opened with this unequivocal student observation: "It is impossible to overestimate the significance of the student–advisor relationship. One cannot be too careful about choosing an advisor. This is both a personal and professional relationship that rivals marriage and parenthood in its complexity, variety and ramifications for the rest of one's life" (Zhao, Golde, & McCormick, 2007, p. 263).

As this student recognized, and many others have corroborated, your relationship with your chair is absolutely the most important in your entire doctoral haul. The relationship is fraught with hazards and yet can prove immensely satisfying and yield rewards much beyond your doctoral years and into your professional life (Cassuto, 2013b, 2014a; Grant & Tomal, 2013; Spaulding & Rockinson-Szapkiw, 2012; Walker, Golde, Jones, Bueschel, & Hutchinson, 2008; West et al., 2011).

If only there were a ChairMatch.com!

Until a completely exasperated doctoral candidate, hopefully not ABD, comes up with such a site or app, you have other options. A few universities assign chairs and committees, usually dependent on their (supposedly) light roster of doctoral students. In this case, you can only pray (see the end of this chapter).

More commonly, and more progressively, universities have provisions for you to choose at least your chair. This is a solemn undertaking, and I caution you—no, plead with you—not to rush into your choice but to do your homework and avoid "psychological land mines," as Grant and Tomal (2013, p. xxv) aptly put it. If you can possibly help it, you want to avoid musical chairs—going from one to another in the hope of a better experience (read: faster approvals).

Sometimes your choices are limited because the research interests and specialties of only a few senior faculty match yours. Nevertheless, with diligence and ingenuity, you can clarify what kind of chair you would work best with. One doctoral student took the search so seriously that she applied qualitative methods to the inquiry—and published her experience in a respected journal (Hernandez, 1996)!

So, take the preliminary steps (see also Sterne, 2015a).

Gather Plenty of Information

The first step is to gather as much information as you can from as many sources as you can find.

1. Use liberally the grapevines of your classmates, other peers, and recent doctors. Their insights and observations about reliability and consistency, especially in hindsight, can be invaluable.

   One of my clients, Sonia, said she wished she had paid more attention to her colleagues when she mentioned a certain professor's name. They raised their eyebrows and looked away. One finally called him erratic. Sure enough, midway through her proposal, she could no longer reach her chair. When she phoned him, she got disconnection messages, and her emails kept bouncing back. The story that circulated (I swear) was that one day he locked his office, left his wife, took his iPad and hiking boots, and disappeared into the mountains of Appalachia.
2. Talk to peers who are currently working with chairs you are considering. Are the students comfortable talking with the chair? How promptly do the students get responses? Does the chair remind them about university deadlines? Are the chair's critiques more substantial than correcting of typos? Do the students feel the chair prompts them to think in greater depth about the topic? Does the chair address the students at least civilly? How satisfied are the students with the experience?

   Fernando almost sobbed telling me of his chair's so-called critiques. They consisted of "correcting" every single instance in his

132-page draft of what the chair thought was misuse of numbers and condemning him for not knowing the "right conventions." As it happened, Fernando was using the latest required edition of APA (2010), which has its own rather eccentric rules about numbers. The chair obviously was not up on them. (I counseled him to refer the chair—politely—to the pages and paragraphs in APA that specify the number policies.)

3. Dig out faculty bios. Access the university/division/school/department website for faculty profiles. These should yield much: the primary research interests, courses taught, publications, presentations, awards, grants, universities from which the degrees were granted, journal affiliations, and whether the professor acts as a dissertation chair. Photographs are often included, and you can see if the professor has kind eyes (not infallible, but it helps). Make sure too the professor isn't on fourteen university committees.

   Dora chose the perfect chair, she thought. The only trouble was that he held onto her drafts for months because of his work on the accreditation committee, the tenure committee, the university governance committee, the ethics committee, the admissions oversight committee, the committee to establish a new master's program, the committee to found a scholarly journal, and the committee to choose pizza toppings for the faculty dining room orders.
4. Search out enemy literature.

   Professor Bruce Shore (2014), a longtime and award-winning professor and advisor to doctoral students, wrote a fine book ostensibly for chairs and advisors, *The Graduate Advisor Handbook*. In a colloquial, engaging style, he shares advice and cautions. They are tremendously humane and candid, peppered with personal anecdotes and practices. You can learn a lot about what to ask for, expect, and stay away from with your chair and committee. His perspective, revealed in the subtitle, should cheer you on: *A Student-Centered Approach.*

Next, ask questions.

Ask Questions About the Chair

What do you really want to know about a chair? What's really important to you? Based on the bio you accessed and other doctoral candidates' experiences, here are some suggestions (see also Calabrese, 2012; Grant & Tomal, 2013; Hernandez, 1996; Storms, Prada, & Donahue, 2011).

- Does the professor have the time for you?
- Are your research interests similar?
- Are you devotees of the same methodologies? If at a dinner party together, and you differ, avoid religion, politics, and research methodologies.
- Will the chair be—or get—knowledgeable about the research in your field?
- Will the chair be responsive to your emails and calls, not that you're going to be a pest?
- Will the chair critique your drafts in a reasonable time? Some universities specify professorial two-week turnarounds. Unfortunately, this "rule" guarantees nothing.
- Will the chair keep track of your drafts? Don't laugh; a client's chair kept losing her current drafts, confusing unedited with later edited versions, and repeatedly emailing her for the latest versions.
- Will the chair be available for meetings and generous with time within reason? You don't need to recount your life story leading up to the dissertation.
- Will the chair be encouraging and supportive in critiques and communication?
- Will the chair be reasonably "hard" in critiques? A chair who is too "easy" is doing you no favors. Don't be lulled. Later critiques by committee members and university reviewers can shock you, require revisions, and delay graduation. More important, "easy" chair critiques don't elicit your best work.
- Will the chair be clear in instructions?
- Will the chair be professional and friendly in your dealings?
- Will the chair work well with other committee members and "fight" for you with them if necessary?
- Will the chair be reasonably stable at the university? At a crucial time in a client's dissertation, his chair left the university abruptly under hushed circumstances. The client had to scrounge for another chair.
- Will the chair you are considering be open to a preliminary meeting or "interview"? Cassuto (2014b) suggested this strongly and noted that only one student asked to interview him of over two dozen students he eventually advised.
- Will the chair help you later in your career?

In that large study of doctoral candidates I referred to earlier (Barnes et al., 2010), students cited as the most positive traits of chairs those who were accessible, helpful, socializing, and caring. Your personal list may differ (I'm not sure too much socializing will serve you, as we'll see in the next chapter).

One university has an actual checklist and form for students to help them choose their chairs and committees, a laudable practice. The student completes initial questions on the topic, research design, methodology, and preferred faculty member area of expertise and names, if known. Three more sections follow, each with many key words to prompt the student: research design; faculty area of expertise; and central, faculty personal characteristics.

Some of the characteristics are opposites: supportive or hands-off, highly goal directive or minimally goal directive, soft critiques or sharp. Other characteristics would seem to constitute the perfect members: gives strong feedback, has a sense of humor, patient, collegial, calming to the candidate, committed to success, nurtures candidate's self-sufficiency, inspires intellectual growth, enthusiastic, and understands the dissertation and IRB processes, and more.

One more characteristic that I believe encompasses all others was singled out by Grant and Tomal (2013). The committee and especially the chair should "provide healthy development of the candidate's ego identity as a doctoral scholar" (p. 222). Obviously, when a chair is sarcastic and cutting, the candidate's understandable response is ego deflation. The "healthy development," though, presumes guidance about excellent writing, prompting of quality thinking, and continuous support of your budding scholarly mindset.

I am glad to say that because of good chairs (and my help, admittedly) I've seen many students learn, grow, and blossom intellectually, emotionally, and spiritually. After Melissa's proposal defense, she said she could feel herself "no longer afraid but taking hold." When Patrick published his dissertation findings, he told me that from his chair and our work together he had learned a great deal about scholarly expression. He continues to publish.

LISTEN INSIDE: GUT AND GUIDANCE

As I've hawked throughout, you really do know best. Your intuition or Inner Mentor (remember the IM?) is always available. If you need a brush-up, see chapter 3 ("Your Inner Mentor: Listening for Answers") and Brisk (2012).

Ask Questions of Yourself

Start asking questions of yourself as you did of prospective chairs. What do you want and need in a chair? Hernandez (1996), whom I admire for her scholarly, businesslike, and clever approach, and whose topic and approach are evergreen, asked herself, "What sorts of things do I need in a relationship?" (para. 37). Her responses were these:

- Space?
- Support?
- Guidance?
- Freedom?
- Security? (para. 37)

Hernandez (1996) also asked herself about her best timeline for completing the dissertation and what she wanted to do afterwards (for her, teaching and scholarship, private practice as a family therapist, or a combination). In this question was the implied one of whether the chair could help her attain her goals. Ask yourself the same in relation to your own career goals.

How Do You Feel?

After you do all your homework and due diligence, ask yourself the biggest question:

How do I *feel* about this faculty member?

Listen. Your IM will tell you. It tickles us in many ways (sinking feeling, nausea, black mood, headache; elation, excitement, joy) and is never wrong. Abraham (Hicks & Hicks, 2004) calls it our Emotional Guidance System (p. 57 and throughout), and it is among the greatest gifts we've been given. As you learn to heed it, without judging but simply feeling and inquiring, you'll have the answers you need.

You've already used your IM. When you meet someone new, you can tell immediately whether you like the person or not, right? If you had to figure out why, you might list a combination of physical traits and mannerisms. Yet you can probably think of other people you do like who have those same traits and mannerisms.

For your chair, if you think you should be reasonable and try to apply logic ("He's a well-known tenured professor!"), and your IM is telling you otherwise, it won't work. If you stack up all kinds of rational arguments to convince yourself of what *should* be the best choice ("She's got stellar publications and connections!"), it won't work. Your Emotional Guidance System will. That's why you really gravitate to the new associate professor who misplaces his glasses and stumbles over his words.

I implore you: Suspend your intellect (the only time I'll advise this). Listen to your IM and your emotions. They will guide you to your best chair and committee members.

DESIGN AND SEE YOUR PERFECT COMMITTEE

Paying attention to your feelings doesn't mean you can't help things along. Knowing how important your chair and committee are to your doctoral success and beyond, you're entitled to customize and visualize. Cassuto (2014a) advised his students, "You are the CEO of your own graduate education" (para. 7). You are the one who manages and is responsible for your dissertation and everything around it. He directed, "Know what you want, and expect what you're entitled to" (para. 12).

You can also do what Hernandez (1996) did. She wrote an innovative (and not really tongue-in-cheek) want ad, which I quote in its entirety because it embodies many of the suggestions above and may act as a guide for your own "want ad":

> Wanted: Dissertation Committee
> Doctorate in Family Therapy or related field required. This is approximately a two-year commitment, although positions can range from one to five years. Previous experience helpful, but not required. Expertise in systemic thinking, qualitative research, and academic writing absolutely necessary. Interest in student's content area (general now but to be refined later) extremely helpful.
> Sense of humor, creativity, and ability to generate visionary ideas necessary for this position. Members must be authoritative yet collaborative, patient yet assertive, and inspirational yet practical. Must be accessible in case of emergency (such as writer's block, flight of ideas, or delusions of grandeur), yet able to "back off" and provide "space" when necessary. Benefits are not guaranteed; however, benefit potential (in admiration, gratitude, and productivity) is great. (para. 47)

Now, can you write your own want ad or make a list of the ideal chair-committee characteristics? You may have noticed from my suggestions and exercises in chapters 1, 3, and 5 that I love lists. They are ways of clarifying your thoughts and act too as written affirmations for what you want to attract. The more you concentrate on them, the stronger your emotions and sense of deservingness become about what they declare.

In a variation of the exercises in chapter 8, you can also "send love ahead." You've made a list of your ideal committee traits. Now picture the as-yet-unknown committee with love, cooperation, harmony, collaboration, collegiality, and caring. Practice daily picturing the committee and ways in which they respond—a cheery cheering-on email, cogent questions on your draft, an invitation to visit the office to discuss a problem that has surfaced. The best chair and committee will appear.

True, I've outlined the ideal. Nevertheless, one of the reasons for this book is that chairs and committees don't always meet the ideal. An essential part of your higher education is to learn (a) how the committee members can fall short of the ideal, and (b) how best to deal with them so you don't wander in the ABD desert for forty years before reaching the Postgrad Promised Land. That's the oasis of chapter 12.

TWELVE

Dancing With the Committee

Your dance should be as pleasurable as possible, or, given the possibly Janus-like nature of your chair and committee, at least bearable. As you get to know their quirks and habits, in this chapter I'll help you meet them with equanimity and keep your committee on your side.

You may have already had frustrating, humiliating, and time-wasting experiences with your committee. Here, we'll talk again about principles that work to help you develop and maintain good or at least satisfactory interactions and avoid additional suffering and tuition chain-payments. The principles apply to both chair and members, one or more of whom may be more vocal (or, charitably, difficult) than the others.

WHOSE TOPIC?

First, I want to caution you about a phenomenon you may encounter early in the dance. This is the chair's "suggestion" that your topic be one of his or her choosing. Your chair may gently suggest you replicate the study he just had rejected, the study she's got in early stages, his secondary research interest, or her department head's major obsession.

In our second week together, my client Ryan called one morning at 8:13 a.m. "He wants me to take the topic he's been working on for six years! I have no interest in the snacking preferences of Millennials at the movies. What do I do?"

I knew how Ryan felt from personal experience. In my own doctoral seminar, one gray winter late Thursday afternoon, the chair cheerily passed around a sheet with five neatly typed topics. As I scanned the list, I recognized they were all *his* major research interests. The other students nodded and smiled and signed up. I'd given a topic some thought, as I mentioned in the introduction, and had just about decided what I wanted to do (an analysis of the minor poems of a major eighteenth-century author, Jonathan Swift). How I escaped signing on the list, I don't know, but I was the only one who did.

Generous soul that he was, my chair didn't hold it against me. In fact, he supported me throughout my dissertation and, as I also told you, helped me publish that (very) small article in a scholarly journal before my degree was awarded.

The phenomenon is more widespread than you might think. Cassuto (2014a), who chairs many dissertations, didn't hesitate to nail it. "If you think you're being collected like a bauble in someone else's collection, then steer clear. Or if you suspect that you're being recruited to run on someone else's hamster wheel, then run the other way" (para. 17).

Maybe chairs who suggest topics to their students are trying to help narrow the possibilities and make the choices easier. Maybe the chairs want to condense topic-fishing time. Maybe some students are grateful for the suggestions. Maybe these possibilities are too kind.

Whenever I hear stories like Ryan's or read (very scarce) admonitions like Cassuto's (2014a), I get angry (again). Chairs are supposed to be *for* their students, their students' interests and careers. Students are not slave labor. The collaboration is to help you produce the best dissertation you can; that's why you have the chair. As Cassuto (2014a) wisely observed, "collaboration has only one appropriate goal: It needs to be about you, and furthering your work and career" (para. 17).

Students think they must succumb to the chair's supposed suggestion. They fear that if they don't bow to the directed topic, they'll be punished throughout their dissertation experience (the chair's stalling with drafts, too few responses, too many critiques). Not true.

If your chair tries to bully you into a topic you can't stomach, gather your strength. Do a little script of the reasons for your choice: "I have always been interested in [your topic]." "My master's thesis was on [your topic] and I want to study this in more depth." "I will learn a great deal from [your topic] and it will help me in my career." Review chapter 5 ("Listen for the Topic That's Right for You") to reinforce your choice.

You can feel strong in your own interests and convictions. Your best will come through as you honor yourself. You cannot be hurt.

BUDDYING UP OR KEEPING TOO DISTANT

If your chair and committee are friendly, forthcoming, and responsive, you may be tempted to make moves toward becoming friends. If they are too formal and standoffish, you may be tempted to ignore them entirely (or as much as the required paperwork allows). Either extreme is a mistake, and you'll likely regret it later.

Chums

When professors are open and sociable, you may find it very easy to be the same. Your family, friends, and work colleagues don't really understand your dissertation-centered existence and all the slings and arrows you suffer. Your professors do.

Especially if you're in a campus situation, when you sit in the professor's office for your appointment, the chair may start complaining about the spouse, kids, teaching load, and all the other backbiting faculty (professors can live a lonely life too). Or your prof may invite you out for a beer (online it's a little harder to have a beer together).

You're understandably flattered, and after a few short ones assume that your new buddy-professor will quickly approve every first draft. When the manuscript is returned full up with critiques and hard questions, you're crushed. You wail, "But we're *friends*!" And you go into a funk that seriously puts you behind in your chapters.

The relationship with your chair especially is (or should be) close by nature, both professionally and personally. Yet boundaries should exist. Among other pitfalls, Grant and Tomal (2013) cited "relational conflict, and exploitations" (p. 32). Cassuto (2013b) chided chairs: Don't make your students your personal assistant (he cited one who had the student pick up his dry cleaning); don't employ them for research on a current project, even though they may need the funds.

If a professor asks or offers you opportunities for personal employment, you may feel special, singled out, and blessed. Watch out. Like the beer invitation, you may assume that if you assent, you'll be in the prof's good graces forever. Not so, never so. You *can* refuse politely, even though, as Cassuto (2013b) pointed out, students may feel they do so at their risk. As in your choice of topic, you can refuse here too graciously. "I am so sorry. I just don't have time, with my job, kids, parents, church work, and completing the IRB in time for its review. Thank you so much."

If a professor gets overly confidential or friendly, watch out again. Cassuto (2013b) admonished them not to brag or complain to their students about their job, not to compliment students on clothes or personal tastes, and definitely not to "friend" them on Facebook. You may be sorely tempted to reciprocate, but much as the professor may be willing to listen and empathize, the same advice goes for you.

In an attempt to stride the personal and professional tides, Cassuto (2014b) also discussed an aspect of the doctorate and life that mainly affects women. The title tells all: "When Your Graduate Students Have Babies: Should Advisers Keep Silent or Raise the Family Issue Early On?" He recognized the sensitive personal nature of the issue and that it was essentially none of his business. But knowing the extreme difficulties of balancing graduate study and a family, he felt it his responsibility to broach the matter. He assured the candidate that, whatever her decision, he would support her.

To my mind, Cassuto (2014b) did not overstep. "I chose to speak up because, like it or not, I play a role in my graduate students' whole lives, not just the dissertation part" (para. 8). This broader and admirable perspective reflects the nature of the lifelong, complex, mutually respectful personal-professional relationship of chair and candidate (Zhao et al., 2007).

The temptation for too much chumminess may loom more powerfully if the professor invites or insists on a mutual first-name basis, assuming professional collegiality. Please don't be lulled by this request. Call the chair by first name, as uncomfortable as you may feel, but remember that this is not a friend (for a related and interesting reprimand, see J. Esposito, 2014).

Georgina told me that her chair offered the key to his office and invited her to use his computer when he wasn't there. Recognizing possible unfortunate (read: accusatory) possibilities that could result, Georgina sensibly and gratefully declined. I applauded her.

Nor are your chair and committee members your father, mother, older sibling, or favorite aunt. You may certainly feel like a little lost child in the cavernous halls of academe, but go to others instead for your emotional supports: friends, family, even a therapist. Cassuto (2013b) pointed out the almost inevitable element of Freudian transference in the chair-dissertation student relationship. This is the projection of thoughts and feelings about an important past figure onto the present important figure, and this projection colors all present interactions.

The transferential relationship—both ways—cannot be denied. Your best defense is to acknowledge such thoughts and feelings: "He is like my never-pleased father." "She reminds me of my demanding, picky mother with her insistence on details." "He even looks like my older brother, whom I still idolize." "She's like the mother I never had—caring, nurturing, helping me in all ways." When you find yourself reacting, stop and ask yourself who you are really reacting to. Remind yourself that the chair is not your mother, father, and so forth.

A longtime dissertation advisor and distinguished sociologist, Michael Burawoy (2005), wrote an uncommonly frank essay that I think should be required reading for every dissertation writer. Comparing his own dictatorial style of advising to a woman colleague's, he noted that they were both "taken aback" by the other's approach: "She saw herself *in loco parentis*, caring for her students' many needs, knowing details about their lives and they about hers. I, on the other hand, care only about the dissertation and the rest will have to take care of itself, unless, of course, it interferes with academic progress" (p. 50).

Burawoy (2005) acknowledged too that the chair's chosen roles can be gender-related: Female chairs are usually more understanding and nurturing than male chairs. On the other hand, I've known of a few women chairs who match any despotic male. For an interesting and entertaining account, read Gearity and Mertz (2012), who documented both student's (Gearity) and chair's (Mertz) transformations in "From 'Bitch' to 'Mentor.'"

Remind yourself that your relationship with your chair is a professional one, as outrageous or enjoyable as it may be, and just get on with it.

Strangers

As you may know and we touched on briefly in chapter 11 ("Excruciating or Exceptional?"), some chairs and committee members keep too much distance for as long as they can. Their official policy is "hands-off" (Grant & Tomal, 2013, p. 49). Burawoy (2005) commented, "faculty are often only too happy to oblige with such a *laissez faire* model. It's neither intellectually taxing nor time consuming" (p. 51).

At the early chair-chasing stage, you may have rejoiced when your new chair consented to the honor, but then you never heard another word, voicemail, or text. You wondered but, a little apprehensive, kept pushing on.

Roberta came to me frantic because she hadn't heard from her chair in over a year. She had submitted her prospectus (proposal minus one) and waited patiently to hear from the woman. Roberta was too patient. I advised her to first call the department secretary and verify the chair's email and phone number (secretaries can be among your best friends, as we'll talk about in chapter 13). Then I told Roberta to email the chair, wait a few days, then phone, wait a few days, then text, and wait a few days. If she still got no response, I advised going to the department head and relate her efforts and the lack of response.

Finally, I'm glad to report, Roberta's chair responded, probably after pressure from the department head, and Roberta then received the guidance she had paid for.

In a reverse situation, if your chair demonstrates responsiveness but *you* feel you can push on without your chair's input, you're making an enormous mistake. When you maintain too much distance, your chair and committee may assume you are arrogant and overconfident about your topic and dissertation writing. They will likely feel ego-attacked; once they get their actual or virtual hands on your draft, they may attack it in return. Your entire proposal that took hard-labor months without committee input can be torpedoed in the blink of an email.

One of my charges, despite my entreaties to at least send his chair a greeting on every holiday, including National Ignore Your Chair Day, refused any contact. Finally, when the student emailed his proposal draft, the chair icily acknowledged receiving it. The student didn't hear from him again for six months. Although the chair may have been somewhat immaturely retaliating in kind, I couldn't entirely blame him. This student acted egotistically (see next section) and, I'm sorry to say, when he received the extensive critiques, he dropped out of the doctoral program and withdrew from my consulting.

The Ideal Balance

What's the best kind of relationship? On both sides, one that is friendly and professional, in which each of you is open yet discriminating of what not to share, both primarily interested in your topic, and focused on making it the best it can be. Be as considerate to your chair and committee as you wish them to be to you (the golden rule of committee gamesmanship). Admittedly, given all the psychodynamic implications of the relationships, especially with your chair, the balance is very fragile and can be tipped disastrously by one discourteous email. The following discussion should help you to determine your own ideal balance.

PLAYING HUMBLE STUDENT AND KEEPING YOUR SELF-RESPECT

One way to establish and maintain that ideal balance is a combination of humility and justified dignity. Humility before the perceived power of the chair is required, whatever your accomplishments. Not that you must kowtow to the committee—they'll know you're toadying. I've advised clients who have stellar long-term experience, titles, and positions, and likely make more annually than their chairs, not to mention owning lavish summer homes, to practice humility with the committee. In your dissertation experience, the chair is the authority.

Swallow Your Pride

William had sixteen years on his job, supervised forty-two employees, both division heads and their subordinates, and was getting the doctorate because it was his lifelong dream and would add substantially to his credibility in later consulting. His dissertation was based on several problems, which he knew intimately, in his human resources department. When his chair made several suggestions, William had difficulty in taking them—he called them "orders." He exclaimed to me, "I know more about this than she does!"

William made the mistake of having to be right. He felt superior to the chair, maybe somewhat justified because of his years of professional experience, and could not accept the criticism offered. I replied to him as softly as I could, "I'm sure you do know more about the topic, William.

She knows more about what's acceptable for dissertations." He finally got the point, grumbled only slightly, and made the corrections.

Raise Your Head

At the same time, you *can* maintain some self-respect and dignity without completely distorting your personality. As Grant and Tomal (2013) pointed out, overcompliance will not serve you or your dissertation. You don't have to take everything the chair or committee say or advise as gospel. They are not infallible. Nor will following their advice guarantee you approvals from the IRB or defense committee or minimal revisions by higher-up, very rigorous university research reviewers.

In a study of British and Swedish doctoral candidates, Gunnarsson, Jonasson, and Billhult (2013) found that disagreements between students and chairs had five major aspects: (a) important decisions involving the dissertation, (b) chair lacking current information, (c) chair giving questionable advice, (d) chair interceding with other members, and (e) interpersonal relationships. The disagreements also changed over time. Early conflicts generally indicated students' immaturity and later conflicts their maturing in knowledge and attitudes. Take heart: As this study shows, dissertation writers all over have similar experiences.

Wherever you are in the process and whether your conflicts are similar to those found by Gunnarsson et al. (2013), you can disagree. Just do so respectfully.

Have your arguments and scholarly support or precedence lined up. To plead your case, I recommend an in-person visit with your chair. Emails and texts can be misinterpreted as brusque and inhibit spontaneous exchange. At your appointment (men: no outerwear t-shirts; women: no stilettos), have two hard copies of your work ready, and give one to the chair. Present your reasons relative to the critiques in a neutral tone without griping. Let your passion for your subject, knowledge, and tight critical thinking shine through.

The chair may still object. If so, ask for suggestions. You can probably come to a compromise. Offer to revise the passage(s) and submit again. As you leave, shake hands and thank the chair. On your way out, you should feel clean and strong. Congratulations.

In the long run, the chair and committee will respect you for standing up for your convictions. After all, part of their job is to help you develop and hone your own academic perspectives as a growing scholar.

WHEN YOU'RE OLDER THAN YOUR PROFESSORS

I answered the phone and recognized Marlene's voice. One of the brightest and most conscientious students I have ever served, she didn't greet me but fumed for ten minutes. On her essay for the current course, her professor had track-changed almost every page and added a four-paragraph single-spaced letter stuffed with questions. Marlene shouted over the phone, "I'm calling the dissertation police!"

I understood why Marlene was so upset. At forty-eight, she had (bravely) just entered graduate school, and I was helping her with course papers. The professor for this course was much younger. Maybe she had to prove herself, but she challenged Marlene at every turn.

Marlene's situation is not unusual. More graduate students are entering advanced degree programs at older ages than ever before (National Center for Education Statistics, 2013). It can be hard, as in Marlene's case, to swallow the critiques of professors who, in some cases, could be your children or even grandchildren.

As I mentioned earlier, my clients range from their mid-twenties to their eighties; one woman entered a doctoral program at eighty-seven and sought my help (I aided her through the proposal, after which, unfortunately, she dropped out). Most doctoral candidates who come to me, and complete their degrees, are in their forties and fifties, with a surprising number in their early to mid-sixties. (They often blurt out their ages apologetically, and I immediately congratulate them for their guts, spirit, and drive.)

Of course, it's hard to accept critiques from younger committee members, but as much as you may choke, it's necessary. Online relationships can be a blessing—if you're an older student you don't have to stare into the fresh face of that superior (unless the professor insists on Skype conferences). Forget age and age comparisons ("He's half my age and already tenured/published/awarded twenty-three grants!") and remember why you're a graduate student and what your degree will do for *you*.

Maybe you'll be buoyed by knowing that older students are more persistent in reaching academic goals, more self-reliant, and more purposeful in mastering the required skills than younger ones (Kasworm, 2010; Offerman, 2011; Spaulding & Rockinson-Szapkiw, 2012).

Offerman (2011) observed encouragingly, "The contemporary doctoral student is older, more mature, and brings into the learning situation a wealth of real-world, career experience. The effective faculty member understands this and expects to learn as well as to teach, to act more as a colleague at times than a supervisor" (p. 27).

Whether or not your chair and committee have such an ideal perspective, the same rules apply for you to navigate successfully through your doctoral experience, whatever your age or status. Balance the professional and personal, treat your professors with respect, treat yourself with self-respect, do the work diligently, and do it well.

THE INFINITE LOOP OF REVISIONS

I hope you haven't experienced this infinite loop, but if you have, my condolences. The committee cry for obsessive revisions can stem from one of two main motivations. Some chairs and committee members can be perfectionist, vindictive, and petty, and their insistent revisions reflect less-than-healthy motivations (see chapter 11, "Are Professors Really Human?"). Other members push you for revisions because they want a quality work, for you and for them (by reflection). Their comments are not personal, and they're not out to get you. In fact, they likely see a publishable spinoff in your postdoc future. Keep these thoughts in mind.

At the same time, committee members vary greatly in the *type* of revisions they harp on. Students have shown me the most general comments, repeated and repeated, from their committees. The faculty members know that something doesn't feel or read right, but their comments don't really guide with specifics. With admirable candor, Grant and Tomal (2013) explained the possible reason: "faculty may have difficulty explaining all the nuances required to successfully complete and defend the dissertation" (p. 118).

In contrast, some committee members spray the student's work with the fussiest comments, line by line, comma by comma. When you make the corrections and hand in the document, they come back with more, sometimes contradicting their earlier comments. No wonder you get depressed. Spaulding and Rockinson-Szapkiw (2012) in their study of doctoral candidates' persistence in completing reported on one participant's frustration at a late stage: "I almost quit again right before the defense. . . . [I]t had to do with lack of direction and uniformity from the professors or their changing their mind when you think you are finished" (p. 208).

Of special interest here is Burawoy's (2005) confession to his advisees as a dissertation chair:

> I used to make detailed comments that would go on for pages and totally overwhelm and even paralyze you. Sometimes you would never come back. It was rather disingenuous of me to complain about your retreat since I suspect that my barraged aimed to establish my authority, my credibility as a young sociologist—with little thought as to what might be helpful to you. (p. 47)

If you are the recipient of a similar sheaf of critiques, whatever you do, don't act like an irate graduate student I heard of once. Without an appointment, he stomped into the chair's office, threw down his marked-up manuscript, which had his own brigade of sticky-note soldiers ready for battle, and argued with every point the chair had made. Needless to say, the candidate only reaped more endless-revision reprisals.

Instead, arrange to sit down with the chair or member, admit your doctoral frailties, and ask for clarification. As Cassuto (2013b) said, good advisors and chairs collaborate with their students. When you ask for a meeting, generally the professor will oblige, and respect for you and your maturity will go up a notch.

If you get caught in the infinite revision loop, assess your work honestly. Are there elements you don't understand? Can you ask a peer or recent "doctor" for help? After several volleys back and forth with his chair, Darryl came to me. He couldn't understand why he wasn't satisfying the chair's scribbles. When I looked at them and Darryl's rewrites, I saw that he had missed several crucial points. We talked, I coached him with several Socratic-like questions, he holed up to rewrite, and he finally produced an acceptable draft.

In another variation, Elena seemed trapped in an infinite revision loop with political overtones. Her chair and methodologist member had met with her and agreed that Elena should revise chapters 1 and 2. Subsequently the methodologist told Elena to revise chapter 3. But the chair had told Elena to work on revising chapters 1 and 2, which she (we) did. Then the chair refused to read chapters 1 and 2, saying Elena was to have worked on 3. By this time, Elena was completely confused and in tears to me on the phone.

This turn of events was an example not only of crazymaking (see chapter 9, "Let Go of the Crazymakers") and a dose of interprofessor politics but also of labyrinthine infinite revisions. Elena said she felt like a tennis ball. She momentarily thought of changing both chair and committee but we realized that at her relatively late stage, it wouldn't be smart to dump these people.

Instead, in a move that would elevate Elena's self-respect, I counseled her to refer her chair back to the original meeting (with email documentation), to summarize what the two members had decided and told her, and to hold the chair to her word. Finally, the chair agreed to read the first chapters and grudgingly acknowledged they were sufficient. Elena then worked on chapter 3 with the methodologist.

Incidentally, I cautioned Elena too not to complain to the methodologist about the chair. The politics were too precarious, and Elena could little afford at that point to alienate either of them. Eventually, with her patience, professionalism, and willingness to swallow her pride and to dismiss her rage, we got through it all and she graduated.

For Elena, it would have been extremely self-defeating to start hunting for another chair and/or committee. She also had no guarantee that she wouldn't be assigned other crazymakers. However, if you have discovered early that you just can't work with a professor, consider changing. Think carefully, though; your decision should be based on one or more considerations.

APPEALING TO HIGHER AUTHORITIES

Most universities have mechanisms for changes of chairs or members. Once in a while, professors themselves will suggest it. In Gearity and Mertz (2012), Professor Mertz came out swinging; in the first meeting to review Gearity's prospectus, which she had marked up liberally, she noticed his consternation and anger. She suggested—not once but three times—that he could change chairs.

Without specifying, Gearity told us readers he had no other options, possibly because of the topic or timeline. If you do have options, recognize that requests for changes take additional time, research, and application procedures. They can produce even greater stress than you may feel with your present chair and dilute your dissertation focus.

On the Ground

Before paying such prices and playing musical chairs, ask yourself a few questions:

- What are my university mechanisms for changing?
- Will my record have a "black mark" for changing? (Not usually.)
- How much time will it take me?
- Can I really afford the time?
- Have other students had similar hair-tearing experiences?
- Is the professor willing to sit down and discuss the conflicts with me?

In Your Head

A few more:

- Do the critiques arise from our underlying differences of approach or values?
- Are my complaints are justified?
- Is it really that I don't understand concepts, comments, or handwriting?
- Am I just pissed because I wanted to get done sooner?
- Are the changes requested reasonable?
- Will they make for a stronger work?

- Is it better to hang onto the plague I know than to contract a new one?
- What can I do to fix the situation without changing professors?

When you answer these questions for yourself truthfully, you'll gain a better understanding of the entire situation and the dynamics you're facing. To help you further, read on.

YOUR HIGHER SELF AND THEIRS

A more efficient way that won't take time away from your writing and will avoid another passel of paperwork is to see your chair and committee in the highest light. Alert: about half of this section consists of **AFFIRMATIONS**.

Psychologically Speaking

If the critiques and personalities seem particularly stinging, refer back to the principle in chapter 9 ("Handle Jealousies and Putdowns"): *They needed to do that*. My client Ted, an experienced and well-respected administrator of a community education program, was crushed at the many critiques by his chair. Despite his experience and knowledge, Ted knew his expertise did not extend to dissertation writing and structure. I could see he wasn't reacting out of a distorted sense of ego.

Ted was nevertheless disconcerted and a little humiliated. I suggested that he view the chair's comments not as a personal attack but as a step in the collegial give-and-take (talk about a mature viewpoint on disagreement!). His chair, I told Ted, was aiming for the best possible quality in the dissertation. To his credit, Ted took in this advice and perspective, and we dutifully mowed down all the critiques.

Because of pelting critiques like Ted received or other issues, you may strongly dislike the chair or a committee member. The traditional advice for anyone you absolutely have to work with is to make the best of it. If you can't grin and bear it but are grimacing and hardly bearing it, you can do other things. These require humility and honesty.

Bregman (2012) gave great advice, first pointing out that if you don't like someone, they likely know it. Their sensing your dislike may result in their not liking you, and this feeling makes working together all the harder. Second, Bregman recommended listing all the reasons you don't like this individual.

Once you do, then comes the squirming part. If, in a pertinent example, you dislike the chair because he must always be right, speaks in monosyllables, and keeps demanding more, look at yourself squarely. "Think about whether, in the dark shadowy parts of your psyche, you can detect shards of that disagreeable trait in yourself" (Bregman, 2012, para. 16). Uh, oh. Bregman had no mercy: " In other words, chances are, the reason you can't stand that person in the first place, is that they remind you of what you can't stand about yourself" (para. 18).

The payoff of this kind of introspection and forthright admission is that you gain compassion for your own nasty traits and, hopefully, a little more compassion for the person who grates on you so much. You might even find yourself, as Bregman (2012) did with his example, coming to like the person—in our case, that impossible chair.

Spiritually Speaking

Look into yourself more. Trust your Inner Mentor to guide you to the right questions and answers. Are you expecting a "bad experience"? Are you anticipating "trouble" because your peers have had upsetting experiences? Are you staying too aloof from your chair? Are you resenting every critique? You may be getting all of the same back.

We create our experiences (Dyer, 2004; Hay, 1987; Hay & Schulz, 2014; Hicks & Hicks, 2009). As we perceive, so we receive. You can change your perceptions of your chair and committee. Chopra (1994) must have had doctoral committees in mind when he wrote, "Whenever confronted by a tyrant, tormentor, teacher, friend, or foe (they all mean the same thing), remind yourself, 'This moment is as it should be'" (p. 59).

That is, you have attracted these disturbing relationships because you need them and need to overcome the issues raised. Dyer (2001a) reminded us, "If your relationship is lousy, it's because you think of it that way. . . . The only way you can experience another person is in your thoughts" (p. 89).

The conclusion? *Change your thoughts.*

How? Repeat and practice powerful affirmations:

AFFIRMATIONS

I am a great doctoral student to work with.
I deserve an excellent, responsive committee.
The chair is for me.
All members are for me.
The committee and I work together in perfect harmony.
I see all members in light.

Keep repeating one or more of these affirmations every time your teeth clench thinking of your committee. Repeat the affirmations until you believe them. You should feel more magnanimous, willing to confront differences, discerning the steps to do so successfully, and hopeful about the entire process. Your professorial relationships should (miraculously) improve.

Now that you've come to dance gracefully and graciously with your chair and committee, as you continue to write you don't have to bother them with the rash of questions and issues that inevitably arise throughout your dissertation. Other university resources await, as we'll see in chapter 13.

THIRTEEN

University Support

You've Got More Friends Than You Think

Graduate students on the road to doctoral Oz generally feel more isolated than a vegetarian at a barbecue. Especially if you have a laissez faire chair and committee, you may believe you're abandoned and unloved. You're not. Many other people in the university community can comfort and care for you.

FELLOW STUDENTS AS MENTORS

As you may know, fellow students and recently finished doctors can be great supporters and sources of hope ("If *he* got through, I sure as hell can."). Cohorts are among the only other long-sufferers who know what you're going through. They can relate and commiserate, usually with their own horror stories. They can urge you not to give up and assure you it will get better (as one cynic remarked, *after* you graduate). They can be very generous too with time and support.

Nan was flailing in the quicksand of her proposal's second chapter, the literature review. She sought help from a classmate who was nearing final defense. Over several nights, Nan's colleague sat down with her and tutored her through a full section of her review, even exacting rough drafts. From this immersion, Nan got the hang of it and eventually completed her chapter. When she sent it to me for editing, it was surprisingly competent.

Fellow students, though, as well-meaning as they may be, can also give you misguided advice. Remember, cohorts or new doctors are *not* your current committee. Your peers likely have or had a different set of professors; even if some of the requirements were the same, these and eccentricities may well change over time. Professors may respond differently to different candidates (meaning you).

Edmund gratefully accepted help from a recent graduate who had completed his dissertation with the same chair. Over my protests and admonition to check with his chair, Edmund proceeded to copy his friend's description of data collection procedures and sent it to his chair. Edmund was shocked, but I wasn't surprised, when the chair slashed almost the entire section.

Lesson: Gratefully accept support from your peers but be cautious about following their well-intentioned advice. Your chair, committee, and the current university dissertation manual call the shots.

What about peer dissertation support groups? Many dissertation guides advocate them for "solace, support and motivation" (Axelrod & Windell, 2012, p. 101) and sharing of information and writing techniques/hints (Bolker, 1998; Grant & Tomal, 2013; Joyner et al., 2012; Peters, 1997; Roberts, 2010; Rockinson-Szapkiw & Spaulding, 2014). Groups can be a great source of consolation, camaraderie, and empathetic grousing. By sharing your work, you hone what you're writing about, learn from others, exchange much information about work habits and university procedures, and gain a cheering section.

Watch out for problems, though. Bolker's (1998) discussion of the setup, pros, and cons of groups is excellent (pp. 104–15). Be alert to emerging problems, particularly because this is a leaderless group. Members may show off with constant oneupmanship, routinely tear down everyone else's work, burst into tears when their own work is critiqued, monopolize the sessions, pirate others' ideas, complain incessantly, relate disastrous chair stories, or flirt inappropriately. The group may deteriorate into a gossip fest, a social event, or a passionate comparison of Netflix discoveries. These activities may be pleasant but they are not why you should attend.

My own dissertation support group functioned primarily as a "gripe group." We all let off steam about the system and our nemesis chairs. For knotty problems with the dissertation, though, I did better alone holed up in the library (I've always been a loner).

Eventually you may feel you've gained what you need from your group in support, direction, and confirmation, and you realize you can now work better on your own. If you come to this realization, or you're in a group with negative issues, feel free to leave, thank everyone, and save the twenty-five-minute commute.

WHAT CAN YOU LEARN FROM LEARNING CENTERS?

Learning centers, or writing centers, as they may be called, constitute one of those university auxiliary supports that sound good and espouse noble goals. Regrettably, though, as students have told me, the centers are generally inadequate. One staff member, usually a graduate student, is assigned to every 627 students writing their dissertations. Appointments must generally be made four weeks in advance, and then the "editing" covers only the first few pages, with polite and encouraging notes to continue on your own.

From the work clients have shared with me, I see that the editing mainly pinpoints formats and grammar. An occasional writing center employee comments on clarity and logic of thinking, but such observations are rare.

If you're a very fast learner and want to or already have mastered the esoteric mysteries of APA, you know a good high school English teacher, or you want to invest in *English Grammar for Dummies* (Woods, 2010), the few writing center edited pages may help you complete the formats and grammar on your own. But don't expect your professors to correct such issues. Some will, but they are (and should be, in my opinion) rightfully concerned with your content and thinking. If they notice errors, they'll typically tell you to get an editor.

I admire the universities for the learning centers, but almost by nature they cannot adequately serve the many students who need help. I advise you to steer clear of the learning centers. Too many students have told me that they cause frustrations in wait time and inadequate or superficial commentaries.

YOU *CAN* SPEAK TO THE GEEKS IN THE COMPUTER LAB

Many universities have computer laboratories or technical support divisions to which students have access as part of their tuition. The labs are open long hours, and you can use the hardware and get help for those inexplicable electronic crises from the techies who live there. Online programs may have extended phone help as well.

Some universities also supply software to students for both quantitative and qualitative computer analyses. When you have access to such software but not the foggiest what to do with it, lab technicians can be of great help. Clients who have thrown themselves on the techs' mercy describe them as patient and clear, if somewhat monosyllabic. The geeks, as you may know, love to dazzle the rest of us with their knowledge.

They're kindly too. Once I went with a client to her university computer lab so we could revise together and she could print out the course paper that was due too soon. We staked out a computer about 9:00 p.m., and at the time neither of us was overly proficient in desktops outside our home bases. I politely asked the tech on duty for aid, and Bart came to our station, stood over us, and good-naturedly instructed us in inputting the changes needed. When we were ready with the document, he went into the print room and shepherded the birth. I'll always remember Bart with gratitude.

Some computer lab technicians work privately as well, and for reasonable sums. If they don't perform data analysis, they may recommend friends. In any case, make sure to specify that you need the results explained in *English.* Ask for their schedules too so you can confer face-to-face on printout as needed.

ADD TO YOUR TEAM: STATISTICIANS AND RESEARCHERS

If you don't locate a computer lab data analyst, private statisticians and researchers are worth considering for getting closer to your goal. Think of them like car mechanics: You wouldn't go to vocational school to learn how to fix your car (unless you're a Barrett-Jackson buff). You'd hire an expert.

Statisticians

Your university department may allow statisticians as technical associates for your data analysis. If, like me, you've never mastered the inscrutabilities and suffer from "statistics anxiety" (Lesser, 2014, p. 67), statisticians for your data analysis can save you time, aggravation, and that horrible feeling that you don't know what you're doing.

Some of my clients actually understand the concepts (I envy them) and look forward to doing the statistics themselves. For others like me, I counsel them to hire statisticians, if they can afford it. Ask in your department. Your university may employ staff statisticians expressly for students at no or nominal charge as part of your program.

Universities may also have lists of recommended professionals. Many specialize in student work and adjust their fees accordingly. Use your grapevine. Personal recommendations from professors or peers should better ensure your satisfaction with a statistician.

I've located and keep in touch with two or three statisticians to recommend to students. My favorite earned her doctorate and was a cohort of a former client. I contact her to verify clients' procedures and assumptions and learn a little more myself. She has infinite patience with my kindergarten questions and explains in a dialect I can grasp.

I'm always on the lookout for good statisticians. My client Jules reported that the statistician he found not only analyzed his data in record time but also supplied a typed and comprehensible explanation of each hypothesis. The stat also offered to consult by phone for anything Jules didn't understand. No wonder he praised the man to the Cloud, er, sky.

Researchers

Some universities have policies that frown on any researcher but the doctoral student. Depending on your time and the complexity of your topic, you may need or want to hire one. Granted, one of the goals of the doctoral program and dissertation is for candidates to "develop confidence and skills needed to become successful researchers" (Lesser, 2014, p. 68). Even if you hire a professional researcher to spill out a sheaf of articles, you must still scan them, determine if they're appropriate for your topic, make the decisions to keep or chuck them, and decide what aspects to incorporate into your dissertation.

Also, professional researchers may be librarians or have doctorates themselves. Both backgrounds are to your advantage; these researchers are familiar with and have access to many databases, both broad-spectrum and more specific to your field and topic. As you become acquainted and describe and explain your project (a good exercise for you), the researcher may suggest keywords, avenues of related or tangential research to pursue, and possibilities you can investigate.

My client Mario hired a researcher who had retired as a librarian from a nearby university. Mario had a full-time job, his wife worked, they shared the care of their three small children, and he needed to make substantial progress on his dissertation. Especially to write his literature review, he simply did not have the time for extensive research. His researcher was enthusiastic and ingenious in accessing materials, supplied the articles grouped by his subheads, and suggested how he might follow up more specifically on various topics. She told him she really enjoyed "the detective work." He thanked her profusely in his acknowledgments.

Both statisticians and researchers can become great supporters. They not only help you with the actual work but, understanding what you are going through, can act as welcome sounding boards for your dissertation miseries. If you plan to conduct additional research from your dissertation and publish, statisticians and researchers can also become part of your network of professional friends.

LIBRARIANS LOVE YOU, SECRETARIES STAND BY YOU

Like statisticians and researchers, librarians and secretaries can help you enormously in many ways as you plow through the dissertation (Bolker, 1998; Grant & Tomal, 2013; Joyner et al., 2012). Once you recognize the resources they have access to, you can enlist their aid to save time, effort, and runarounds.

Librarians

University library resources have bricks-and-books libraries and virtual libraries. One university spares students from having to buy those terribly expensive research books by making available electronic texts, a great service.

You can connect with the university librarians not only in person but also by email or phone. Today the librarians easily skate among and within the vast virtual databases, their own holdings, and, if needed, other libraries' through interlibrary loans.

Mario's experience with the retired librarian demonstrated her love of learning. She was not unusual. Librarians still love real books, journals, and people who wander in (I once came across an article called "Who Loves You Like the Library?"). Clients have told me librarians enjoy helping students. When I called one librarian to verify a reference, she confessed, "I love seeing that amazed and relieved look on the students' faces when I locate what they need or refer them to a trove of research on their topic."

A head librarian at a local university I knew felt so much empathy for the doctoral candidates that she held monthly seminars exclusively for them. When one or another would appear at the main desk looking lost, desperate, and frustrated, she would personally take them aside and instruct them in using the electronic resources and how to narrow down the references to their topic. (She also recommended my services to particularly needy students, but never mind that.)

Like this librarian, others can be not only kindhearted but also wonderfully cooperative and extremely knowledgeable about various dissertation-related matters. When you're stuck or research-weary, peck out an email or pick up the phone and pour out your dire needs to a university librarian.

Secretaries

Secretaries too can be great aids. Whatever big university honcho they're assisting, many are secretly on the students' side. Secretaries have superpowers: With one withering look, they can remind the chair that a doctoral student has been sitting in the waiting area for two days without food or drink, clutching the sweaty proposal draft. With apparent precognition, they can magically lift your manuscript to the top of the pile. With the speed of an e-text, they can transmit to a student the incredulous news of an approval.

My client Paula, who was on her last extension (see chapter 6, "Death by Rationale" and "Resisting the Extension Siren") and fighting a tight deadline, needed all the cooperation she could get from the departmental office. The chair's secretary had been pleasant but distant. Paula noticed a muffin wrapper in the woman's wastebasket. The next time she visited, she brought a batch of her homemade blueberry muffins (baking assuaged her dissertation anxieties). Delighted, the secretary thanked her, and they discovered a mutual love of old-fashioned bakeries and cookbooks. With the secretary's invaluable help, Paula walked at graduation.

As Paula did, notice secretaries' office accessories and engage them in conversation. Maybe you see their prized World Series baseball cap displayed on a file cabinet, a bobble-head of an action hero, or a photo on their desk of three kids at a lake. Ask about their families and show interest in their work and leisure activities.

With both librarians and secretaries, invest in the time to "warm them up." The principle behind this advice is well-known by business consultants. They counsel salespeople how to get through the buying executive's door by reminding them that there are no "little people." Those with the least impressive titles may be the ones who can do the most for you. Your efforts aren't hypocritical; look at them as reciprocal. Clients have told me that once they got to know secretaries, they've formed some very pleasant and even lasting friendships.

CONSIDER COACHES AND EDITORS

You must know by now I am prejudiced in favor of coaches and editors. Helping doctoral candidates in all aspects of their dissertations has been my joyful livelihood for three decades.

Some universities positively ban dissertation coaches and editors, some graze the subject with tacit acceptance, some sanction certain types of editing and not others (see below), and others almost require them. Depending on students' academic skills and confidence, they adhere to or ignore such strictures. The coach or editor shouldn't be expected to write the little beauty but to guide students in organizing their thoughts and managing their lives so they can write. And be their cheerleader and ally.

As Ingrid put it, "I need a friend and more. I need someone who can keep me motivated, yet who understands, someone who can listen and advise me without preaching. I need a weekly assignment, and to be held accountable. I need help managing my time and my life." I was glad to assist her.

Coaches

A dissertation coach is very different from your university chair or advisor. Chairs are paid by the university to execute many duties and functions—teaching, publishing, committee memberships, enthusiastic-seeming appearances at the dean's parties. It's unlikely that your chair has much time for you. He or she is grossly overburdened with students (see chapter 11, "Are Professors Really Human?") and can barely give you minimum attention.

Your coach, when you agree to work together, is paid by you and is (or should be) committed to give you the time and attention you need. Think of your coach as your academic personal trainer (with thanks to dissertation coach Rachna Jain; see Jain, 2011).

The experienced dissertation coach and founder of the University of Maryland's Dissertation House, Dr. Wendy Carter-Veale (2012), explained well a coach's functions:

> A thesis/dissertation coach . . . is paid to focus on you and help you finish your degree by listening to all of your concerns . . . academic or otherwise. In person or on the phone, they can discuss your project on an individual basis in absolute confidence, and also serve as a sounding board for stress relief. They can offer both emotional and academic support to help you complete important tasks, as well as provide the tools you need to achieve your goals, which enable you to accomplish more with less effort. . . . Their goal is to work in every possible way to help you write your dissertation, finish it, and get it published. (p. 38)

Your coach helps you choose an enticing topic, coaxes out your ideas, and prompts you to clarify them. Your coach asks you pointed questions ("Why do you want to do this study?" "What will it show/prove?" "How will it add to understanding of your topic?" "How excited are you about the topic?" "How will you collect your data?" "How feasible and efficient are your methods?"). Your coach listens empathically to your screaming about your writing blocks and offers techniques to help (see chapter 5, "Tricks to Tease and Ease Yourself Into It").

One client wrote me about a graphically metaphoric dream: "I saw something tightening around me head and hands." I replied that her dream was wonderful: It held the remedy to her writing block. I said, "If you can visualize that tightening, you can visualize a loosening of the grip around your head and hands." She acted on my advice and within a few days was writing again.

Your coach should continue to question you on all important aspects of the dissertation, assist you in planning your procedures, and consistently praise you for small and large triumphs (getting the library hours straight, receiving a letter of permission from your research site, obtaining IRB approval). Your coach should encourage you forward, see you through to the final draft, shore you up for the defense, applaud your final deposit, and even, at your invitation, sit in those uncomfortable seats watching you graduate.

Your coach can also help you with officially nondissertation matters, such as problems with family and friends (like Andrew's wife in chapter 8, "Troubled Waters: Fights, Separation, Divorce"). Everything in your life *does* have to do with your dissertation progress, and I have often counseled clients with the advice I give you in chapters 7, 8, and 9, as well as prayerful guidance.

Editors

Coaches may or may not include editing in their services. I include it because I see how many dissertation writers need it. I include editing too because, as many have told me, they learn from studying my editorial changes and questions. Among faculty, it is a given, unfortunately, that few graduate students are prepared for scholarly writing. Van Aswegen (2007), a faculty member and editor at a technology university, published a horrendous list of student inadequacies. They apply to many other-than-technology students.

Van Aswegen (2007) also pointed out that "an unwritten assumption" among many chairs seems to be "that no aspects of writing and/or bibliographic citation fall within their bailiwick" (p. 1148). I have had clients with chairs on all points of the continuum: from extensive tracked-change revisions on the document to a few comma insertions and the admonition to follow APA, with or without an editor.

To locate an editor, inquire of your departmental secretary; the department may keep a prepared list of recommended editors. Look on university bulletin boards for flyers, click on websites provided, explore graduate student organizations' directories (such as the Association for Support of Graduate Students), or search the Internet for "dissertation editors." As with other specialists such as statisticians and researchers, the best way may be to get recommendations from colleagues.

Editorial businesses vary greatly. Editors may be employees of large companies that promise instant turnaround, have 1,000 eagle eyes on call in all parts of the world, and get your hard-squeezed manuscript dumped in their inbox at random. These organizations generally do not offer personal contact with the editor. You fill out the contact form, send in your work, and light a candle to St. Jerome, patron saint of librarians, scholars, students, and abandoned children (and dissertation writers).

Editors may be part of a consortium or small organization in which personal contact and service are emphasized. Editors may also be part of a smaller organization—one individual, like me and several colleagues—who prefer to render highly individual services and take on only a few clients at a time so we can render the most in-depth help. I have little experience with the "factory"-type of editorial services, although the website testimonials glow. When because of overloads or conflicting schedules I refer doctoral students to other editors, I make sure to get acquainted, get testimonies, and get feedback.

Dissertation editors may also specialize in one or more levels of editing. A study was actually conducted on thesis and dissertation editors' perceptions and practices with types of editing (Kruger & Bevan-Dye, 2010). Here are the generally accepted levels:

- Copyediting or light editing, often called "mechanics." The editor corrects spelling, grammar, punctuation, capitalization, and similar issues.
- Medium editing, also called standard or basic editing. This level includes all of the above as well as consistency of formatting and usage in accordance with your university handbook and chosen style manual—APA, Chicago, MLA. Consistency applies to chapter headings, spacing, acronyms, rules about numbers, all other style rules, agreement of table of contents with text headings, lists of tables and figures with their text titles, and correction of citations in the text and references, in accordance, again, with your style manual.
- Substantive editing, sometimes called or including developmental editing. This type of editing requires the editor's thoughts about and engagement with your subject. Actual revisions, repositioning, and suggestions to improve the work are made in chapters, subheads, paragraphs, and sentences. The editing decreases redundancy, confused points, and inappropriate tone and word use (in scholarly writing, for example, colloquialisms and popular jargon); and increases organization, clarity, focus, flow, and grace of expression.

All three levels include proofreading, in which the editor corrects typos and other small editorial errors. Note: Proofreading is *not* editing. If you ask for proofreading (generally lower fees), you will get only minor corrections. Fees increase with the level of editing agreed on.

Be sure to clarify what type of editing the individual does and what type(s) you need. Some do one thing, some do more. Two of the editors I recommend with confidence do only light to medium editing, and I alert candidates to their chosen ranges of services. I do it all and in fact enjoy jumping into the manuscript and immersing, all to the glory of a better and more understandable and cohesive dissertation.

I am sorry to say that some editors do not carry out what they promise or advertise. A student wrote me, after having paid an editor on her university's list, urgently pleading me to edit her manuscript. She had submitted the "edited" work to her chair and received this missive: "Whoever you sent it to previously did not read it. There are so many, too many, writing errors. Please—have a professional go through this document."

Also, some editors, like the one above, do only "one-shot" editing: a single pass over the manuscript for the agreed-on fee. This means that if your chair doesn't see/like/approve, when you go back to the editor you incur another fee. I work differently. My fees include *all* editing to address committee complaints and suggested amendments until appears the magic word "Approved!" As I tell clients, I stick with them until they make that historic walk in their cap and gown (Hallelujah!).

Remember that engaging an editor of any type doesn't at all guarantee that miracle of instant blessing by the chair and committee. As we know, they may still find plenty to comment on. As a substantive editor, I assure clients that I have two goals: to please them and to please their committees (or maybe that order should be reversed). I also assure candidates of confidentiality unless they tell me otherwise.

Once, though, I had a rather unusual experience. After James kept submitting unsatisfactory revisions of his proposal to his chair (see chapter 12, "The Infinite Loop of Revisions"), the chair finally recommended hiring an editor and asked to be informed. James and I agreed to work together, and as requested he told the chair he had an editor. James included my assurance that with my help the proposal would be satisfactory. (As I said earlier, I continue with candidates until all approvals are gained.)

The chair wrote back to James, wanting to know my name, and referred to my promise. She pointed out, reasonably, that my standards of acceptability might not be hers. I reiterated my dual purpose to James: to please him and meet the committee's standards. I was and am willing to cooperate to oblige them within academic integrity.

Occasionally, however, chairs and committee members object to word or symbol usage because they're not up on the latest, greatest APA edition. As I mentioned earlier with Fernando (chapter 11, "Gather Plenty of Information"), when a client tells me of such objections, I unearth the page and paragraph citations and ask the student to humbly inform the committee members of these. For other matters, such as the committees' virulent preference for either "the researcher" or "I" in your text, make certain your coach or editor is willing to compromise if necessary and defer (within reason) to the chair's and committee's predilections.

OLD COURSE PROFESSORS DON'T HAVE TO FADE AWAY

A great resource for dissertation troubles is former professors whom you've particularly liked, who've liked you, given you A's, or you've even shared a few beers with. These professors generally welcome contact from former students (I know I have warm spots for previous clients who get in touch). These professors don't have your present committee's vested (ego) interests. From your past professors' combat experience in the academic trenches, they can offer you sane perspectives, suggest research materials and sources, and provide salving moral support.

Cassuto (2014a) commented on the rewards of maintaining contact with your chair (the exceptional kind, as in chapter 11, "Excruciating or Exceptional?"), and the benefits apply also to previous professors. This relationship, when it's begun and sustained rightly, as Cassuto (2014a) observed, "turns into a lifelong, productive, ever-evolving relationship of mutually rewarding collegiality. It often levels off into a friendship between peers" (para. 4).

My client Reynold had such an experience. When he emailed a favorite former professor and told him about his dissertation and difficulties finding prior research, the prof answered immediately, congratulating Reynold for reaching the dissertation stage. The professor included too a citation of an important recent study close to Reynold's that no one else had turned up.

Generally, previous professors will be happy to hear about your ambition and progress in pursuing the doctorate and may even have earlier encouraged you to do so. A caution here, though, and it will apply later in chapter 15 ("Plan Your Payoffs"). The professor may exclaim, "Your dissertation is *so* important! Have you thought about publishing it?"

Meaningful pause. . . . Then the kicker: "How about coauthoring it?"

At first you may be understandably flattered, but think a little more. It's your dissertation; you did all the work. Not that I mean to malign a well-intentioned professor, but the deal is usually that in exchange for the professor's name and (assumedly) prestigious affiliation, or personal acquaintance with the chosen journal's editor, you will still do all the work. You'll be the one to condense those sweat-ringed 200 pages to 25 or 30 for the journal.

The professor may generously offer to review your article and comment. If the article comes back with the journal's peer reviewer critiques—and these can be worse than any maleficent chair's—the professor will cheer you from afar and ask you to send a copy once you've made all the revisions.

Of course, not all former professors are opportunistic. Consider contacting one or more. They can mightily support you, prod you on, and become friends during your entire dissertation journey.

PICTURE THE PERFECT UNIVERSITY FRIENDS YOU NEED

For perfect previous professors and all others we have discussed in this chapter, figure out who you will really need, and when.

Make a simple list of all the university friends you can think of. Next to each, add when to contact them: Now, Later, Never, and with dates if you can.

As you know by now, I'm a big list maker—not only for groceries and computer supplies but for visualizing perfect anyones. A list of your perfect helpers and their ideal characteristics will help you focus your thoughts and draw to you the individuals you need in the wider university community. Here are some affirmations to use or adapt.

AFFIRMATIONS

Fellow students: I now attract the most helpful, generous, savvy, cheering-me-on fellow students. As they help me now, I will help them later.

Computer tech: The most confident, communicative, clear, knowledgeable tech appears now, ready and willing to instruct me patiently in all technical matters.

Statistician: I now see before me the perfect statistician—highly proficient, used to working with doctoral candidates, understanding, able to translate the findings into English for me.

Researcher: The most creative, innovative researcher is now here, familiar with all the databases, interested in my topic, cooperative, and eager to keep searching for buried scholarly treasure.

Librarian: I draw to me the best librarian in the university system, who loves helping students, has access to all university and outside resources, and shows me the mysteries of digital life beyond the card catalog.

Secretaries: All the secretaries and administrative assistants of my chair and committee members are poised to help me in whatever I ask. They are friendly and accommodating and keep me informed about the department's/school's/university's requirements and paperwork.

Coach: My perfect coach is here now—ready to immerse in my topic, advise me wisely, and reprimand me (gently) when needed, all with good will, humor, and love.

Editor: My perfect editor is here now—prompt, affordable, coherent, committed to my work, knowledgeable about my university, friendly, supportive, tactful, funny, brilliant, handsome, tall, dark-haired, ripped, charming . . . .

Former professors: They are delighted to hear from me, remember me, and are very happy to learn of my progress. They make great suggestions and are committed to my completing the dissertation and using it in my career.

Finally, two blanket affirmations for attracting your ideal university friends. The first is from Hay (1987):

AFFIRMATIONS

> I use my affirmative thinking to create exactly what I want. . . . I think differently. I speak differently. I act differently. Others treat me differently. (p. 90)

The second is adapted from Hicks and Hicks (2006, p. 11):

> I, [Your Name], see and draw to me, through divine love, those beings who can supply me with instruction and enlightenment. The sharing will elevate us both, now.

Keep your mind on the perfect university friends in all these areas. Listen to your Inner Mentor for guidance. You may find that sources, resources, and people spring up "magically." You'll stumble on a website with the information you've been searching for, you'll bump into a former professor at the gas station, a colleague will call and alert you to a particularly relevant article, your aunt's friend the PhD will offer special assistance, even your chair will respond more promptly. Keep visualizing and affirming, through the fogs and storms.

Recognize too that although you are asking for help from others, you are also giving them a great deal: business, attention, respect for their expertise, appreciation of their knowledge and ability to help, need for them and their accomplishments. They probably admire you as well for your persistence and seriousness, and they are likely very glad, and flattered, to help. The exchange at its best is one of mutual esteem and love.

As you work with everyone who can aid you in following all the necessary steps to produce your dissertation, incredulous as it may seem, you will inch closer and closer to completion. After all the rocks in the road, with something like elation, you'll glimpse the finish line. To make the sprint to your victory smoother, in part V, starting with chapter 14, I'll give you suggestions for finishing your dissertation so you leave the doctoral program with a sense of completion, completeness, closure, and grace.

V

Graduation: It's Only a Walk Away

FOURTEEN

Am I Really Almost Done?

Believe it! You really are almost done. A few crucial considerations remain, though, to make sure your long haul is entirely satisfying. Your dissertation experience will haunt you forever, so don't neglect any part. Here I'll guide you through the final phases so you avoid the depression of having reached this momentous goal and ease back into the (relatively) normal spheres of family and work.

REHEARSE YOUR PERFECT DEFENSE

Almost everyone who has a doctorate has a final defense story. A friend of mine was obviously pregnant at her defense. After she successfully passed, her chair told her that her entire graduate education was a "waste." Outrageous, I know. I'm very glad to say she proved the chair wrong. Later, with two kids, she became an award-winning professor at Brandeis.

Family, doctorate, and academic career can be and often have been accomplished. I admire any woman who combines them. Admittedly, the choices and priorities are hard, as several books I recommended earlier attest (Connelly & Ghodsee, 2014; Evans & Grant, 2008; Seto & Bruce, 2013; Ward & Wolf-Wendel, 2012).

Back to defense stories: At my defense, during the two hours, my foot had fallen asleep. As I rose for the verdict, I almost fell over the table into a committee member's lap. I still blush reliving it.

One of my doctoral cohorts, by far the most brilliant of us all, felt he did so poorly at his defense that he cancelled a long-planned prepaid vacation to Scandinavia with his fiancée. I never heard whether he went on the trip later or got married. This was mea culpa at its most severe.

The professor friend I quoted earlier must have had an equally traumatic time because he said he "mercifully forgot" it all.

Candidates are either petrified of the defense or try to underplay it. They imagine the committee asking impossible questions, like an explanation of how the multivariate analysis of variance was applied to their forty-two variables, or asking "fluff" questions, like their opinion of the university cafeteria food.

Many candidates either spend every possible moment cramming or avoid preparation entirely. Viola, a bright candidate I coached, told me that, despite my admonitions, she minimized her defense and barely squeaked by. She knew the material but her nervousness and lack of preparation got the best of her. She recently wrote me that she regrets to this day not following my advice.

Recognizing that both extremes are, well, extreme, for clients I developed a long list of suggestions for a good final defense. Here's a distillation.

- The defense is on *your dissertation*. Remind yourself that you are the expert.
- Read the university manual on defense protocols. It can actually be helpful and should tell you if a PowerPoint presentation on your dissertation is required, and if so the number of slides and time allotted for your portion.
- Ask your chair for advice. After all, the chair is supposed to be your collaborator and defense preparer. Schedule an in-person or phone conference and discuss the range of questions that could be asked by all committee members. With this conference, you'll be able to prepare answers and will feel on much more solid ground.
- Attend a few defenses before your own. You'll get the gist of the questions asked and the format for the whole thing. Observe how the candidates respond, and make notes on the positive behavior (poise and direct eye contact with the committee) and negative behavior (a lot of "uhs," "ahs," and slouching). Your attendance will go a long way to eradicating your fear of the unknown.
- Study other candidates' final PowerPoints, especially if they've had your chair.
- When you're ready for your own PowerPoint, use your proposal slides and other candidates' as templates. Creating the new slides will help you review and summarize everything.
- Think of the worst questions you don't want to be asked. Write them down.
- Once you have a bank of questions, type out your answers. You can refine them later. Make sure your dissertation backs up your answers (for example, correct number of participants, statistical results, themes revealed).

- Rehearse with a relative or friend (something you can involve them in, as I suggested in chapter 8, "Involve Them: Share What You're Doing").
- Know your material. Some candidates mark a hard copy of their dissertation at the pages reflecting anticipated questions. If you do, you can turn to the pages quickly.
- If you don't know an answer to a committee member's tough question, don't fudge. Instead say, "That's a really good question. I'll have to think more about it" or "I'll do more research on that." This advice, based on chapter 12, "Playing Humble Student," will increase the committee's admiration for you.
- After the defense, expect some revisions. Just because it's the "final" defense doesn't mean the committee can't change its collective mind and swoop down on niggling and not-so points (remember chapter 12, "The Infinite Loop of Revisions").
- The day before, decide what you'll wear (even if the defense is by teleconference). Choose clothes that look and feel professional. Don't forget the deodorant.
- The night before, go to the movies or do something physical. Get a good night's sleep.

AFFIRMATIONS

For at least a week beforehand, every time panic hits, practice a few defensive affirmations:

My defense goes perfectly.
The committee is for me.
I know everything I need to know, instantly.
I am divinely directed.

Visualize the movie of your perfect defense. See yourself poised and confident, talking easily about any aspect of the work, adlibbing from your PowerPoint, and graciously receiving the committee's congratulations and hearty handshakes at the end. You have become an academic colleague!

You'll thank yourself for all that overpreparation.

YET ANOTHER FACULTY REVIEW

Sorry to tell you, but after the final defense, in a growing number of universities your work must go through yet another round of reviews. These may be a final format review and/or content review, by beings variously named university research reviewer, procedural reviewer, final dissertation reviewer, quality reviewer, or some fancy permutation. Argh!

With no academic distractions such as plague your committee members, these individuals are charged solely with reviewing your dissertation for all kinds of errors and gaps. Of course, your committee is supposed to have helped you plug the leaks, but the final reviewer will find things no one else thought of, from the obvious to the esoteric (they stumped me on APA a few times).

If you university doesn't have such a person, consider yourself fortunate. On the other hand, whatever the reviewer finds, take it in good faith. At least someone is giving your work undivided attention. Whatever you correct, as agonizing as another delay may feel, your dissertation will be stronger for it. I wish you Godspeed and only typos.

MASTER THE RED TAPE

My advice: In a word, master it. Too many ADDs (almost done doctors) have faltered, slipped, and fallen off the cliff of current deadlines because of red-tape misinterpretations and misunderstandings. Some universities have an alphabet full of forms to file, others have one or two. Again, check your dissertation manual; the forms are often printed in the back. The paperwork can dribble on for months, so become familiar with all the successive deadlines and be sure to meet them.

One of my clients looked forward to graduation and the deserved celebration with his family. They were all flying in from 3,000 miles away, and he'd made hotel and restaurant reservations. The night before the big day, he found out that, because of a single form not filed, his graduation would take place six months later. I don't know who paid for the hotel and dinner arrangements.

To prevent such calamities, and if administrative work isn't your forte, reacquaint with one of those secretaries you've already warmed up. They will generally guide you patiently through all the requisite forms and committee members' signatures—and on time. Or your university may have an administrative office for just such matters. A member of this office may also be charged with reviewing every dissertation for adherence to format issues, such as correct margins, pagination placement, and other basic style matters. Be grateful for their recommendations.

HOW TO ENJOY YOUR OWN GRADUATION

The first rule is this: Make sure, with the help of a kind administrative assistant, that all that paperwork is filed in the right university offices and in the national dissertation database (required). Make sure all copies of the dissertation are submitted to the university library with the proper paper and binding specifications (also required). You can now rest in the knowledge that you've met all the requirements, and you won't be horribly surprised like my client with all the relatives.

The second rule is this: Decide to go to your graduation. So you may have missed your high school, college, and master's graduation ceremonies, pretending they didn't mean much to you, or you were reacting with youthful misguided counterculture rebellion. This degree is the culmination of your education, and you've suffered, worked, and sweated for it long and hard. Unless you plan to enroll in another program for another doctorate (ha!), *go, go, go*!

Some ADDs attend graduation with special dispensations from chairs or deans to have their final work straggle in later. Through such an exception, my client Matthew was allowed to "walk" in the May graduation ceremony and did not complete his work until the following October. He said, "My parents took pictures of me in the cap and gown. But I really didn't feel like it was real." Nevertheless, even delayed a few months, graduation *is* real.

The third rule is this: Prepare for interrogations by well-meaning family and friends. Remember *those* questions from family in chapter 8, "Hard Questions and Your Brilliant Answers," and from friends in chapter 9, "Those Questions Again: 'Aren't You Done Yet?'" Now the questions may escalate to the next level.

- "So what are your plans with your doctorate in animal art?"
- "I just read an article about the cutbacks in hiring doctorates throughout the country."
- "You know, you can always come to work for Uncle Clevis at the bakery. Just call."

Consider these questions your post-final defense, and be ready with snappy responses.

- For the doctorate in animal art: "The metropolitan zoo is considering a graphics wing, and I've applied for a consultancy."
- For the cutbacks: "I'm starting at community colleges and will work my way up. Two colleges are already interested."
- For the bakery: "Sure, with my doctorate in business, I can balance his books, do his ROI, and make comparative bar graph and pie chart projections on the profitability of a gourmet kale loaf bread line or ham and brie croissants."

Your turn. Like you imagined those shuddering questions for your defense, imagine a few your family and friends could zing you with.

Write out as many questions as you can think of. "Was it really worth all that money . . . and all those loans?" "What if you don't get a job right away?" "Will you move back in with your parents?" "Are you now finally going to get married (alternative: have a baby)?"

We all know the answers to such questions are none of anyone's business but your own, and their assumed dismal scenarios may never take place, especially with your positive and expectant attitudes. Nevertheless, you'll feel much more at ease, and even enjoy everyone, equipped with your response-ammunition.

Now that you're fully prepared, the fourth rule: Celebrate—you deserve the accolades! The girlfriend (later wife) of my client Wayne completely organized a party for him at a hotel ballroom(!) and sent out cute computer-generated invitations to everyone they both knew. For my client Elizabeth, her husband and daughter planned a lavish party for her at a well-known restaurant. She danced up a storm and had a beautiful album made of the many photos of the event. When I saw the photos, I admired how she enjoyed herself, drank it all in (and drank), and accepted the compliments and full credit for her achievement.

And then there's the morning after . . .

AVOID POST-PARTING DEPRESSION (PPD)

Janet should have felt great, but for the last month she couldn't understand her persistent feelings of discomfort. Her dissertation had been approved, she had one more stint of paperwork to file everything, she'd received the graduation packet, a new job offer was almost set, and her family had stopped nagging her about finishing. What was wrong?

As you contemplate LAD (life after dissertation), like Janet you may suddenly sense a great void, also known as post-dissertation depression (PDD) or post-parting depression (PPD). (I suffer from AA—acronym addiction.) That empty feeling in your stomach is not protein deprivation but sudden withdrawal of focus on a long-cherished objective. The goal you've yearned for and hated for so many years has finally been met. It may even feel like mourning.

Like Janet, you may also feel you really didn't do your best work on the dissertation. You ran out of time, steam, money. Even though the dissertation was approved, you know you're capable of much more. You may regret that you didn't spend even more time and attention on the dissertation.

If you feel this way, read doctoral coach Rachna Jain's (2005, no. 6) very wise words: "Realize the dissertation is not a test of your intelligence." She pointed out that completion reflects more your skills in organizing, researching, and writing on a specific topic rather than "defining your native intelligence." Remember too that your mastery of the skills has to do with learning the academic jargon and what's acceptable and reprehensible, and rather rigidly sticking within certain parameters.

I must disagree with Jain on one point, though. A certain kind of intelligence *is* required for the organizing, researching, and writing. In all these aspects, you must use critical judgment as it applies to your topic. You probably developed this faculty as you got more familiar with the subject, became immersed in others' scholarly productions, and let your subconscious do much of the leg-, er, mind work. Nevertheless, especially after all the ego bashing you've received at so many points along the way, Jain's (2005) is good advice to keep in mind.

With commendable perspective, a new doc told me, "I am not my mediocre dissertation. I am still a successful person." I thought his dissertation was better than mediocre and that he was being too hard on himself. I told him so, and reminded him that, if he desired, he'd have other chances for brilliant scholarship with presentations and articles based on his dissertation.

Achieving a doctorate is a lot like finally losing a hundred pounds or getting married. One expects that all problems will disappear and life will instantly become fabulous. In academic lingo, these expectations aren't operationally generalizable, internally consistent, or externally valid or reliable.

Despite a dramatic loss of pounds or gain of a partner, the hard truth is that only as one changes inside does life get better outside. In the same way, despite loss of the massive weight of the dissertation and endless furrowed brows, your life as a new academic doctor changes only with conscious attention.

Given the high attrition rates, scholars have found, in which may be a massive understatement, that "'deciding to do a Ph.D. [or other terminal degree] is a high-risk strategy'" (Brailsford, 2010, p. 15, as cited in Spaulding & Rockinson-Szapkiw, 2012, p. 200). You've overcome many momentous challenges. You've demonstrated high motivation, self-directedness, goal setting, capactiy to juggle all your responsibilities, flexibility between creativity and slavish rule-following. You've shown willingness to make all kinds of sacrifices, weather all kinds of unexpected events, plan successfully (most of the time) and cope with almost unremitting stress.

Congratulate yourself for persisting to the end! You now have the treasured doctorate and can look forward to the next phase of your life and career. In chapter 15, we'll look at how you can ease and please yourself into the many facets of LWOD: life without the dissertation.

FIFTEEN

Waking to Your Dream

After the graduation ceremony, parties, backslaps, congratulatory cards, telegrams, emails, texts, and your love affair with your new business cards trumpeting those prized letters after your name, you, the grad student, are student no more. Nervously, you may be wondering how to adjust to LWOD. How to scale back? How to accept that the deed is done? How to switch gears, preferably smoothly? In this chapter I offer some guidelines to assist you.

THE MOST DANGEROUS TIME . . .

It's a motivational truism that the most dangerous time is when you've reached a goal. This is the origin of what many candidates experience, the new dissertation-birthed depression. Consciously and unconsciously you've been pushing hard for so very long. Preoccupied with the intensity and innumerable details of the work itself, you may have lost sight of the larger purpose of the dissertation and degree. You do want to use it, right?

First, though, take in that you've actually done it. Bask. Take some deep breaths, literally and figuratively. Take a break—a weekend, one week, two. But watch out. It's not as if you're retiring (a lethal practice, it's now well known). Maybe you need to clean the house, the refrigerator, the car, your desk. Maybe you need to load up the car with cartons of toilet paper from the discount warehouse. Maybe you need to liberate the dining room table and surrounding floor from all the prisoner-books and articles. Fine. Take a few days.

Then decide on the day/date you'll resume. Don't take too long or you'll lose your momentum. The secret now is to remind yourself of your dream and *set new goals*.

Go back to chapter 1 and review why you embarked on the doctorate in the first place. What exciting dreams did you dream? Feel the excitement again. Dig out those exercises you did:

- How is the degree part of *your* life dream?
- What will the degree do for *you*?

Reviewing your paragraphs now, you may want to make some amendments. Philippe, whom I mentioned in chapter 1, pursued the doctorate to gain the credential for a position in his native ministry of education to help increase literacy. During his research, he investigated many successful microloan programs in developing countries. He realized that, although literacy was certainly crucial, he could make a greater impact founding and administering a microloan program for villagers to develop local skills and industries, learn entrepreneurship, and earn profits.

Philippe saw that such programs not only help alleviate the poverty and unemployment but also could, like many other microloan programs, later incorporate literacy courses. Philippe was so excited at this idea that three days after graduation he flew home and began conferring with government officials to get the program started.

ENVISION YOUR FUTURE, TAKE THE STEPS

Whether or not you've adjusted your dream, remember another suggestion from chapter 1: "Visualize Your Dream." Perfect position, perfect office, perfect clients, perfect colleagues, perfect compensation . . .

The stronger are your desires and motivation, the stronger will be your mental pictures. What you concentrate on grows. What you mentally picture you attract (Fox, 1992; Hicks & Hicks, 2004, 2008, 2009). Practice your pictures again, with the greatest details you can muster. Add some affirmations:

AFFIRMATIONS

My perfect position is here now.

The Universe sends the perfect clients to me now.

I listen for all the exact right ideas for using my degree in the most beneficial ways.

My perfect picture is actualized now.

Next, take the steps. Tackle your latest goal with techniques similar to those for the dissertation (it worked there, didn't it?). In chapter 3, "Find the Holes in Your Schedule," I recommended writing up a master list of all the steps you see are needed and allocating specific times for each.

Now, instead of searching databases, maybe you'll search office real estate listings. Or clear out your guest room for a home office. Spruce up your vita. To locate teaching jobs, for example, ask your chair and committee members (don't forget former professors) for leads. Ask them (nicely) for recommendation letters. Set up appointments and interviews. Talk to current faculty members or employees of your desired institution. Draft introductory letters to department chairs or administrators.

Make this master list as comprehensive as you can. The more you think about it, the more will come to you. Thoroughness is good. As with the dissertation (chapter 3 again, "Find the Holes in Your Schedule"), note down the activities in your main calendar book or equivalent. Space out your tasks over days and weeks. With a sane distribution of your daily and weekly goals, you won't feel overwhelmed. If you do, use again the Diaper Method (chapter 5, "Tricks to Tease and Ease Yourself Into It").

PEEK AT YOUR LONG-NEGLECTED LATER LIST

Another step in combating PPD and affirming your next goals is to review "Your Later List" from chapter 3. Depending on how concentrated your efforts in your career goals and how long your master list, choose a balance of targets and actions. For example, if one of your doctorate goals is promotion in your present company, you won't need much time for job-hunting or resume sprucing. If your postdoc goal is establishing an online business, you'll want to devote most of your time to the steps to get it off the virtual ground.

Now you have the relative "leisure" to pursue not only career-related goals but also the things nagging at you that you've postponed for too long. The Later List, like any other, is a convenient compendium for getting all those nags out of your head. (I have several Later Lists for all kinds of things—carton weeding, clothes shopping, furniture rearranging, bulk buying, novel resuming.) As you look at your Later List, see whether your priorities and desires have changed. Maybe you already gave away your old gym clothes or no longer feel the need to write your memoir. Maybe new priorities have surfaced.

When Lucas, a client who had just graduated, looked up from his desk, he realized his three kids were suddenly teenagers. At the top of his Later List, he wrote, "Now. Spend more time with them!" Other clients have resumed poetry writing, bookshelf building, volunteering, camping with the family, aesthetic welding.

Postdissertation too, guard against feeling you must mow down the whole Later List in a frenzy of activities. As you may already know, the sun always rises and to-do lists never end. We're also supposed to enjoy our activities (at least some of them). If you haven't already, add some pure fun things you've deprived yourself of for so long—arranging a long-postponed fancy lunch with a friend, poking around the new fake-quaint mall, going to drag races, seeing four first-run movies in succession and munching from one of those huge horrible popcorn buckets.

Use your new, revised Later List as another master list to spin off short-, mid-, and long-term goals (Allen, 2002). Your practice with the dissertation should hold you in good stead here, and remind yourself it all doesn't have to be done now.

If you get overwhelmed, recognize the symptoms—shortness of breath, churning in the stomach, inexplicable dread. Go somewhere quiet and sit quietly. Focus on your breathing. Ask yourself: "What would I really like to do . . . today, this weekend, next week?" Listen inside. As always, your Inner Mentor knows and will gladly give you answers. Relax.

REENTER YOUR FAMILY'S ATMOSPHERE

Undoubtedly, some of the items on your earlier Later List involved your family. It's time to reconnect and keep your promises. Look at the promises from chapters 7 ("Bribe Them") and 8 ("Special Dates With Partners and Kids"). It's now AD (after degree). Even though you may have (and should have) had a bunch of special dates during your dissertation dark ages, it's time for more rewards for all of you.

So gather the family, have a big meeting if that's your style, or just blurt out your thoughts while everyone is standing up grabbing dinner before dispersing. Tell them you want to make good on your promises, whether it's a family vacation, working on a project together, going to a special restaurant or show, wrestling on the living room floor, or any of the many other things on your bribe-and-promise list.

Alternatively, you could ask each family member separately what they'd like to do together. What favorite promise do they want you to keep to them? You'd be shocked how kids remember. Maybe it's making a LEGO village with your seven-year-old, a special bumper car date alone with your thirteen-year-old, or a resort weekend with your partner.

Your family may be skeptical ("Sure, Dad, keep promising."). Show them you're serious by asking for dates, times, places. Flash some green that you've set aside specially. Remember too that these promises aren't chores. They should be fun for you too.

Reentry may take you more adjustment from the mindset of the troglodyte scholar you've been than you realize, and the same goes for your family members. Like a soldier who returns from war after a long period (the simile is apt), you may find that family life without you has changed. In your long absence, part of your family's support may have included taking over a lot of the duties you had.

For example, your wife or partner may have gotten used to handling things you used to (sorry if I'm stereotyping)—car repairs, cable guy, noisy neighbors. Your husband or partner may have mastered the mysteries of the things you used to take care of—the dishwasher, casseroles, ferreting out the bargains from the grocery flyers. It's probable your partner not only got used to handling "your" things but got to like doing them and felt proud and independent. And even worked out some creative shortcuts.

Part of your smooth reentry may be recognizing such shifts, sitting down together, sharing feelings, and talking about a new or amended division of duties. After my client Ivan became Dr. Ivan, he couldn't understand his wife's distant responses. When he asked her what was wrong, she finally admitted that during his dissertation immersion, she felt like "the man of the house" and discovered many aptitudes she hadn't known she had—like wielding a mean screwdriver. Ivan was relieved to hear her thoughts, and they worked out some new household arrangements.

PLAN YOUR PAYOFFS

Reconnecting with you family is certainly a payoff. You've undoubtedly dreamed of professional payoffs too. If you're like most new doctors, you'll want to land a prestigious (or any) teaching or corporate position and produce scholarly articles, books, and conference presentations.

Positions

If your immediate aim is a teaching job, apply. Treat the process like a serious project (you've got experience now, yes?). As I suggested earlier, plan and take the steps. Revise your vita and review your interviewing skills. Get help if you need it. See a manual like Kelsky's (2015) *The Professor Is In: The Essential Guide to Turning Your Ph.D. Into a Job*. Make a list of universities you'll consider and find out what it takes to apply. Plan to attend several professional conferences—most have employment prospects sections. Mine the current scholarly journals and organization websites in your field. Subscribe to newsletters; many have regular job listings.

Request letters of recommendations from your chair, committee, and former favorite professors (and be sure and thank them). Notify everyone else you know and tell them you're interested. Talk to colleagues you know who are teaching. As a start, consider part-time campus or online adjuncting.

Yes, the academic job hunt can be demoralizing. Herrmann (2012) painted a particularly mordant picture: "'I Know I'm Unlovable': Desperation, Dislocation, Despair, and Discourse on the Academic Job Hunt." It doesn't have to be this way.

Use the power of your mind, your affirmations, and your visualizations. An adaptation of that Hicks and Hicks (2006, p. 11) declaration in chapter 13 ("Plan the Perfect University Friends You Need") can help assuage panic and set your expectations right:

AFFIRMATIONS

> I, [Your Name], see and draw to me, through divine love, those chairs and departments who need and appreciate my subject and teaching expertise.

A couple more:

> What I am seeking is seeking me.
>
> The perfect position is waiting for me now. I am ready. I accept it. I am grateful.

Publications

As a newly anointed scholar, you will naturally want to publish your work. Publication is still the road to academic advancement, and you deserve recognition as well as additional benefits from all you've invested. Your chair or a committee member may have already suggested publication. As you know from your professors and lit review, the dissertation can be revised for journal articles and presentations, entire books can be based on the dissertation, and new projects can be extensions of the dissertation (remember your "Recommendations for Further Research").

Creating a scholarly article is a daunting task. You already have all your material, and that's part of the problem. It's a challenge to condense your 200-odd pages into 25 or 30, the number required by most scholarly journals.

There's an art to converting your dissertation into an article, and you may want to devote time to research on the topic. The APA website has a section of tips for conversion, and you can find other articles on the Internet. Possibly the best "schooling" is to study articles in the journals you'd like to publish in. Notice the subheads, their length, the writing style. With articles, you don't have to keep "proving" your points, citing basic research books, quoting voluminously, or spilling out extensive literature reviews. Chop and summarize.

Once you submit your article to a peer-reviewed journal, be ready for revisions. Acceptance without revisions is almost unheard of. Peer reviewers' critiques, as I mentioned in chapter 13 ("Old Course Professors Don't Have to Fade Away"), can be more brutal than those of any chair or committee.

You can also ask colleagues and professors to critique your article draft. Watch out for professors, though. When professors get too "close," as Cassuto (2013b, 2014a) observed (see chapter 12, "*Whose* Topic?" and "Buddying Up or Keeping Too Distant"), you can get into trouble.

Recall too my caution in chapter 13 ("Old Professors Don't Have to Fade Away"): former professors may suggest "coauthoring," a code for you to do all the work of reducing your dissertation to a coherent article and then sending them the draft for "review." They get first mention and fully half the credit. If you decide to accept "coauthoring" for any of its perceived perks (greater possibility of acceptance, professor owing you one), go in with your eyes open.

Dissertation-to-book is another animal, and a trickier one. Your book audience is generally broader than a scholarly one, and so your diction and length must be adjusted accordingly. Even if an academic press is interested, your book must maintain reader interest and tell a "story."

You will likely have another whole year's project ahead of you. If you're serious, see the authors' guidelines of academic presses, the fine book on dissertation-to-book by Germano (2013), and Mulholland's (2011) candid and thoughtful experiences metamorphosing his dissertation into a book. (If you decide to turn your dissertation on abused women into a Lifetime movie, you won't need any academic guidelines.)

Several of my clients who have gone into academia have published successful articles (often with my editorial help). Madison had an article accepted about his work in progress during his proposal stage—extremely unusual. He's since published many articles from different perspectives of his dissertation. His research interests have also expanded, and he's delivered presentations (by invitation) at many national conferences. My client Celestine used two of the interviews from her dissertation to create a memoir of Haitian immigrants. It was recently published by a university press.

Admittedly, scholarly publication takes persistence, perseverance, and dedication. Even Madison was not immune. His first rejection from a peer-reviewed journal had several single-spaced pages of highly detailed critique. He commented to me, "Boy, you gotta have a thick skin!"

True, and you've got to want to do it and believe in your work. Use not only your intelligence and well-developed critical thinking skills but also your inner wisdom. Listen for the right guidance in process, time allocation, possible journals, and the daily drafts.

AFFIRMATIONS

My IM guides me throughout this process.
I relax, breathe, listen, and obey.
"I am Divinely led in all ways." (Murphy, 1982, p. 51)
I succeed *now*.

CELEBRATE YOUR PROFESSIONAL AND PERSONAL GROWTH WITH GRATITUDE

As the degree becomes a more natural part of your new identity, you will profit by taking some time to reflect on the entire experience.

I watched George walk off the stage in his doctoral gown, his gray hair peaking from his tasseled cap. As I stood nearby, he hugged his best friend, also in cap and gown. "Well, Jake," he said, "we did it—and we grew old in the process."

At the same graduation, in the parking lot, just before opening his car door, Richard, another new doctor, shook my hand warmly and said, "Thank you. I grew up in the process."

These two comments point up the difference between just getting the degree and getting everything possible from it. It should be evident by now that completing a doctoral program is much more than writing a complex book-length paper, challenging as that is. As you turn the very wide corner from a university-focused life to a career- and productivity-focused one, you can draw many lessons that will serve you well on your future path.

Here are some reflective questions and suggestions. Your reflections should show you how far you've come and how you've grown. You might even get a few articles out of the musings, or at least a letter to the editor.

1. What have you learned about the system?
   If you want to stay in it, as you did with the doctoral program, follow the rules. Some battles are worth fighting, others are not.
2. What have you learned about people?
   Your chair and committee can become lifelong professional colleagues and friends. They've encouraged your passion (Cotts, 2015). Cassuto said, "I have many former students who are

friends. . . . One of the best parts of the job is relationships, and it's artificial to cut them off at the end" (Cotts, 2015, para. 16). Your family and friends? You may be greatly moved to have discovered how much they have supported you. Count the ways.

3. And politics?

   Undeniably, they exist. You don't have to buy into the backbiting and competition that can spread like an epidemic throughout departments. Treat others as you would have them treat you. Be considerate, give credit, thank others for favors, do your best work, show up. Your graduate school experience has socialized you for the academic life in more ways than you may realize, although you'll still have plenty to learn (Austin, 2002).
4. How to allow for idiosyncrasies?
5. You've likely already discovered that professors have preferences and quirks. If you're going to continue to live with them, honor these—you might even make little "collegial profiles" to remind yourself that Professor A hates anyone barging into his office without knocking and Professor B prefers all communications by texts. Especially when you're asking for favors, keep the quirks in mind: If you ask a professor to review your article and she will only do so if mailed hard copy, groan and go to the Post Office.
6. What have you learned about your topic?

   Your findings may be corroborative or revolutionary. In either case, they are worth publishing. In your future dissertation research section, you've already written about how the topic can be expanded—different participants, locations, demographic characteristics, hypotheses. Give your scholarly creativity free reign, and keep reviewing that all-important command from Chapter 5, "Listen for the Topic That's Right for You." You're entitled to get passionate again about an extension of your topic.
7. What have you learned about yourself?

   When I attended Nalida's defense, I could see from her demeanor her almost literal growth in confidence, poise, knowledge, and speaking skills. Afterwards, she told me how much she felt it all, and she beamed with her new self-awareness.
8. What have you learned about your working habits? Perseverance? Persistence? Creativity? Intelligence? Scholarly confidence? Ability to say no? Sense of balance? Patience? Spiritual growth? Inner guidance? Give yourself credit.

With such self-assessments, you will recognize the true value of your doctoral experience, internalize its lessons, and gain new appreciation of yourself in many ways. Now you are ready to use the degree to shape your professional activities and fulfill long-cherished dreams in a productive and satisfying career. And spend some time with your family and dog. And be willing to share your experiences. When asked, now you can generously counsel, warn, prod, and support current struggling doctoral students. You will help them complete their dissertations with less torment and at least a little more enjoyment and, finally, become doctors.

Conclusion

Why I'm Still an Academic Nag

Why do I continue to be an academic nag? Perhaps the best answer came from a former client's remarks. After our work together and award of his degree, he progressed to an extraordinary academic career, with many accolades, promotions, publications, conference presentations, and continued invitations.

He wrote, "I realized the lifelong impact that you have on my work and life. It goes far beyond the actual writing of the dissertation. I am a better scholar, professor, and person. Thank you!"

Thinking about this wonderful comment, I realize that when I see candidates through to completion of the doctoral degree, the work together means much more. My guidance helps them grow in ways they may never have expected or intended, expand their life's work and its meanings, and recognize and embrace the opportunities that come for their self-fulfillment.

Another answer to my academic nagship is agreement with Burawoy's (2005) eloquent explanation of the chair's perspective of the student's dissertation journey:

> It is not just the intellectual excitement, but there's a passion . . . to seeing a dissertation through to its end, overcoming the most variegated obstacles. When students finish I have flash backs to the beginning of their careers—our first meetings, their first research, a startling paper, their early disappointments, crises of despair, disturbing confrontations, dead ends that are now forgotten—and then to the moment their dissertations suddenly, magically crystallize, and then surge forward. (p. 56)

I too have found this fruition exciting, stimulating, invigorating, and immensely satisfying as students have allowed me to be a part of their evolution. As I said earlier, my great joy is to help doctoral candidates create the very best dissertation possible. However much or little I have to nag, they take it in stride, and most are grateful. They understand, like I trust you do from the nagging imperatives and exercises in this book, that the prods are meant only to reach the goal.

As you continue in your dissertation writing, for wisdom, inspiration, and support at the right times and sequences, keep in mind these words from Hay (1987):

AFFIRMATIONS

I open myself to the wisdom within, knowing that there is only One Intelligence in this Universe.
Out of this One Intelligence comes all the answers, all the solutions, all the healings, all the new creations.
I trust this Power and Intelligence. (p. 15)

I see you working on your dissertation steadily, and I hear you saying this:

AFFIRMATION

My work on this dissertation goes easily, effortlessly, intelligently, speedily, joyfully, and lovingly to perfect completion.

Use these and other affirmations regularly, and you will meet all dissertation challenges and overcome all troubles.

As you continue in your career, academic or otherwise, remember the undergirding lessons of this book. You are the creator, director, and writer of your story. You can create it in ways that bring the greatest satisfactions to yourself and others (Unity, 2015a). And despite your new accomplishment, remember that you, like all of us, are still the student. You will continue on the path of success knowing that God is your Teacher (Unity, 2015b).

I hope that this book helps you create your very best dissertation experience, with recognition not only of the necessary content mastery but also of the many emotional, interpersonal, and spiritual issues that arise and must be dealt with for successful completion.

Finally, I see you having produced the perfect dissertation that serves you, your field, your family, your mission, and your passion. And going on gloriously from there.

References

Note. The first year in parentheses refers to the edition I used. For older works, (e.g., Butterworth), the year of original publication follows.

A Course in Miracles. (2007). *Combined volume* (3rd ed.). Mill Valley, CA: Foundation for Inner Peace.

Achor, S. (2012). Positive intelligence. *Harvard Business Review, 90* (1/2), 100–102. Retrieved from http://www.di.univr.it/documenti/OccorrenzaIns/matdid/matdid467193.pdf

Alidina, S. (2014). *Mindfulness for dummies* (2nd ed.). Hoboken, NJ: John Wiley.

Allen, D. (2002). *Getting things done: The art of stress-free productivity.* New York, NY: Penguin.

American Psychological Association. (APA). (2010). *Publication manual of the American Psychological Association* (6th ed.). Washington, DC: Author.

Ampaw, F. D., & Jaeger, A. J. (2012). Completing the three stages of doctoral education: An event history analysis. *Research in Higher Education, 53*(6), 640–60. Retrieved from http://perryjil.pairserver.com/files/Three_Stages_of_Doc_Ed.pdf

Army War College revokes Senator John Walsh's degree after plagiarism investigation. (2014, October 10). *Huffington Post Politics.* Retrieved from http://www.huffingtonpost.com/2014/10/10/john-walsh-degree-revoked_n_5966930.html

Austin, A. E. (2002). Preparing the next generation of faculty: Graduate school as socialization to the academic career. *Journal of Higher Education, 73*(1), 94–122.

Axelrod, B., & Windell, J. (2012). *Dissertation solutions: A concise guide to planning, implementing, and surviving the dissertation process.* Lanham, MD: Rowman & Littlefield Education.

Bailey, J. W. (2014, July 24). The Senator John Walsh plagiarism scandal. *Plagiarism today.* Retrieved from https://www.plagiarismtoday.com/2014/07/24/senator-john-walsh- plagiarism-scandal/

Barbor, C. (2001, May 1). The science of meditation. *Psychology Today.* Retrieved from http://www.psychologytoday.com/articles/200105/the-science-meditation

Barnes, B. J., Williams, E. A., & Archer, S. A. (2010). Characteristics that matter most: Doctoral students' perceptions of positive and negative advisor attributes. *NACADA Journal, 30*(1), 34–46.

Benson, H. (1975). *The relaxation response.* New York, NY: HarperCollins.

Benson, H. (1997). *Timeless healing: The power and biology of belief.* New York, NY: Simon & Schuster.

Bernstein, A. (2012). *Emotional vampires: Dealing with people who drain you dry* (2nd ed.). New York, NY: McGraw-Hill.

Blum, L. D. (2010). The "all-but-the-dissertation" student and the psychology of the doctoral dissertation. *Journal of College Student Psychotherapy, 24*(2), 74–85.

Bodian, S. (2012). *Meditation for dummies* (3rd ed.). Hoboken, NJ: John Wiley.

Bolker, J. (1998). *Writing your dissertation in fifteen minutes a day: A guide to starting, revising, and finishing your doctoral thesis.* New York, NY: Owl/Henry Holt.

Bradberry, T. (2014a, October 21). How successful people handle toxic people. *Forbes.* Retrieved from http://www.forbes.com/sites/travisbradberry/2014/10/21/how-successful-people-handle-toxic-people/

Bradberry, T. (2014b, December 9). How successful people squash stress. *Forbes.* Retrieved from http://www.forbes.com/sites/travisbradberry/2014/12/09/how-successful-people-handle-stress/

Bradberry, T. (2015, February 4). How successful people overcome toxic bosses. *Business Insider.* Retrieved from http://www.businessinsider.com/how-successful-people-overcome-toxic-bosses-2015-2

Brailsford, I. (2010). Motives and aspirations for doctoral study: Career, personal, and inter- personal factors in the decision to embark on a history Ph.D. *International Journal of Doctoral Studies, 5,* 15–27. Retrieved from http://ijds.org/Volume5/IJDSv5p015-027Brailsford283.pdf

Bregman, P. (2012, September 12). What to do when you have to work with someone you don't like. *Harvard Business Review Blog Network.* Retrieved from http://blogs.hbr.org/bregman/2012/09/what-to-do-when-you-have-to-work-with-someone.html

Brisk, S. (2012, November 26). How to develop your intuition. *Shine/GALTime.com.* Retrieved from http://shine.yahoo.com/healthy-living/develop-intuition-160900146.html

Burawoy, M. (2005). Combat in the dissertation zone. *American Sociologist, 36*(2), 43–56.

Butterworth, E. (1992). *Discover the power within you.* New York, NY: HarperCollins. Originally published 1968.

Calabrese, R. L. (2012). *Getting it right: The essential elements of a dissertation* (2nd ed.). Lanham, MD: Rowman & Littlefield Education.

Cameron, J. (1992). *The artist's way: A spiritual path to higher creativity.* New York, NY: Tarcher/Putnam.

Cantor, N., & Englot, P. (2013). Beyond the "ivory tower": Restoring the balance of private and public purposes of general education. *Journal of General Education, 62*(2/3), 120–28. Retrieved from http://www.newark.rutgers.edu/files/Beyond-Ivory-Tower-Cantor-Englot.pdf. doi: 10.1353/jge.2013.0019

Carter-Veale, W. Y. (2012). *PhD completion: If you can write a master's thesis you can write a dissertation: Helpful hints for success in your academic career* (Vol. 1). Phoenix, AZ: Dr. Carter's Educational Group.

Carter-Veale, W. Y. (2013). *PhD completion methods journal.* Phoenix, AZ: Dr. Carter's Educational Group.

Casanave, C. P. (2008). Learning participatory practices in graduate school: Some perspective-taking by a mainstream educator. In C. P. Casanave & X. Li (Eds.), *Learning the literacy practices of graduate school: Insiders' reflections on academic enculturation* (pp. 14– 31). Ann Arbor, MI: University of Michigan Press.

Casanave, C. P., & Li, X. (2008). Introduction. In C. P. Casanave & X. Li (Eds.), Learning the literacy practices of graduate school: Insiders' reflections on academic enculturation (pp. 1-11). Ann Arbor, MI: University of Michigan Press.

Cassuto, L. (2013a, July 1). Ph.D. attrition: How much is too much? *Chronicle of Higher Education.* Retrieved from http://chronicle.com/article/PhD-Attrition-How-Much-Is/140045/

Cassuto, L. (2013b, April 22). Remember, professor, not too close. *Chronicle of Higher Education.* Retrieved from http://chronicle.com/article/Not-Too-Close/138629/

Cassuto, L. (2014a, July 21). Spotting a bad adviser—And how to pick a good one. *Chronicle of Higher Education.* Retrieved from http://chronicle.com/article/Spotting-a-Bad-Adviser-and/147757/

Cassuto, L. (2014b, September 2). When your graduate students have babies: Should advisers keep silent or raise the family issue early on? *Chronicle of Higher Education.* Retrieved from http://chronicle.com/article/WhenYourGraduateStudents/148535/

Cerf, B. (1948). *Shake well before using: A new collection of impressions and anecdotes mostly humorous* (3rd ed.). New York, NY: Simon & Schuster.

Chopra, D. (1994). *The seven spiritual laws of success: A practical guide to the fulfillment of your dreams.* San Rafael, CA: Amber-Allen/New World Library.

Chopra, D. (2004). *The book of secrets: Unlocking the hidden dimensions of your life.* New York, NY: Harmony Books.

Chopra, D. (2011). *The seven spiritual laws of success: A practical guide to the fulfillment of your dreams* (rev. ed.). San Rafael, CA: Amber-Allen.

Connelly, R., & Ghodsee, K. (2014). *Professor mommy: Finding work-family balance in academia.* Lanham, MD: Rowman & Littlefield.

Côté, J., & Allahar, A. (2007). *Ivory tower blues.* Toronto, Canada: University of Toronto Press.

Cotts, C. (2015, January 21). Top of the class: Some of NYC's leading professors share their secrets. *New York Observer.* Retrieved from http://observer.com/2015/01/top-of-the-class-nycs-top-professors/

Covey, S. R. (2000). *Living the 7 habits: Stories of courage and inspiration.* New York, NY: Free Press.

Covey, S. R. (2013). *The seven habits of highly effective people.* 25th anniversary edition. New York, NY: Simon & Schuster. Originally published 1989.

Cozart, S. C. (2010). When the spirit shows up: An autoethnography of spiritual reconciliation with the academy. *Educational Studies, 46,* 250–69. doi:10.1080/00131941003614929

Crosby, W. (2012, December 5). Former doctoral student sues Duquesne. *Duquesne Duke.* Retrieved from http://www.theduquesneduke.com/former-doctoral-student-sues-duquesne-1.2965542?pagereq=1#.UXFqBLXCaSo

Dames, K. M. (2008). Turn you in: Scholarly ethics in a culture of suspicion. *Information Today, 25*(6), 23–25.

Dossey, L. (2006). *The extraordinary healing power of ordinary things: Fourteen natural steps to health and happiness.* New York, NY: Harmony Books.

Dossey, L. (2011). *Prayer is good medicine: How to reap the healing benefits of prayer.* New York, NY: HarperCollins.

Driscoll, E. (2013, January 28). Higher education trends to watch for in 2013. *Fox Business.* Retrieved from http://www.foxbusiness.com/personal-finance/2013/01/28/higher-education-trends-to-watch-for-in-2013

Duhigg, C. (2014). *The power of habit: Why we do what we do in life and business.* New York, NY: Random House.

Dyer, W. W. (2001a). *Dr. Wayne Dyer's 10 secrets for success and inner peace.* Carlsbad, CA: Hay House.

Dyer, W. W. (2001b). *You'll see it when you believe it: The way to your personal transformation.* New York, NY: Quill/HarperCollins.

Dyer, W. W. (2004). *The power of intention: Learning to co-create your world your way.* Carlsbad, CA: Hay House.

Emory, M. (2011, December 15). Dr. Herbert Benson on the mind/body connection. *Brain World.* Retrieved from http://brainworldmagazine.com/dr-herbert-benson-on-the-mindbody-connection/

Esposito, J. (2014). "Students should not be your friends": Testimonio by a Latina on mothering one's own, othermothering, and mentoring students in the academy. *Equity & Excellence in Education, 47*(3), 273–88.

Esposito, L. (2014, December 19). Holiday anxiety—The gift that keeps on giving. *U.S. News & World Report.* Retrieved from http://health.usnews.com/health-news/health-wellness/articles/2014/12/19/holiday-anxiety-the-gift-that-keeps-on-giving

Evans, E., & Grant, C. (Eds.). (2008). *Mama, PhD: Women write about motherhood and academic life* . New Brunswick, NJ: Rutgers University Press.

Exkorn, K. S. (2014, February 22). The top 5 excuses for not practicing mindfulness and how you can do it anyway. *Huffington Post.* Retrieved from http://www.huffingtonpost.com/karen-s-exkorn/mindfulness-practice_b_4763160.html

Fletcher, E. C., Gies, M., & Hodge, S. R. (2011). Exploring persistence, challenges, and barriers of doctoral students. *Multicultural Learning and Teaching (Online), 6*(1). doi:10.2202/21612412.1073

Fox, E. (1992). *Around the year with Emmet Fox: A book of daily readings* (2nd ed.). San Francisco, CA: HarperSanFrancisco. Originally published 1958.

Frank, J. (2014, October). In soundproofing we trust. *Author Magazine.* Retrieved from http://www.authormagazine.org/articles/2014_10_frank.html

Gearity, B. T., & Mertz, N. (2012). From "bitch" to "mentor": A doctoral student's story of self-change and mentoring. *Qualitative Report, 17*(Art. 59), 1–27. Retrieved from http://www.nova.edu/ssss/QR/QR17/gearity.pdf

Germano, W. (2013). *From dissertation to book* (2nd ed.). Chicago, IL: University of Chicago Press.

Gilbert, E. (2006). *Eat, pray, love: One woman's search for everything across Italy, India and Indonesia.* New York, NY: Penguin.

Godwin, G. (2008, January). Tips on getting unstuck. *The Writer, 121*(1), 34–37.

Goethe, J. W. (2000). *Faust: A tragedy.* New York, NY: Norton. Originally published early nineteenth century.

Goldberg, N. (2005). *Writing down the bones* (2nd ed.). Boston, MA: Shambhala.

Golde, C. M. (1998). Beginning graduate school: Explaining first-year doctoral attrition. *New Directions for Higher Education, 101*, 55–64.

Grant, C., & Tomal, D. R. (2013). *How to finish and defend your dissertation: Strategies to complete the professional practice doctorate.* Lanham, MD: Rowman & Littlefield Education.

Grasso, M., Barry, M., & Valentine, T. (2009). *A data-driven approach to improving doctoral completion.* Washington, DC: Council of Graduate Schools.

Greene, S., & Lidinsky, A. (2014). *From inquiry to academic writing: A text and reader* (3rd ed.). Boston, MA: Bedford/St. Martin's.

Gruber, C. W. (2012). Lifelong learning-doctoral studies in middle adulthood. *Procedia-Social and Behavioral Sciences, 46*, 216–21.

Guiley, R. E. (1998). *Prayer works: True stories of answered prayer.* Unity Village, MO: Unity Books.

Gunnarsson, R., Jonasson, G., & Billhult, A. (2013). The experience of disagreement between students and supervisors in PhD education: A qualitative study. *BMC Medical Education, 13*(1). Retrieved from http://www.biomedcentral.com/1472-6920/13/134

Harra, C. (2009). *The eleven eternal principles: Accessing the divine within.* Berkeley, CA: Crossing Press/Crown/Random House.

Hawkins, D. R. (2012). *Power vs. force: The hidden determinants of human behavior.* Carlsbad, CA: Hay House. Originally published 1995.

Hay, L. (1987). *You can heal your life.* Carson, CA: Hay House.

Hay, L. (1998). *Heal your body A–Z: The mental causes for physical illness and the way to overcome them.* Carlsbad, CA: Hay House.

Hay, L. (2011). *21 days to master affirmations.* Carlsbad, CA: Hay House.

Hay, L., & Schulz, M. L. (2014). *All is well: Heal your body with medicine, affirmations, and intuition* (4th ed.). Carlsbad, CA: Hay House.

Hernandez, L. L. (1996). In search of a dissertation committee: Using a qualitative research approach to study a lived experience. *Qualitative Report, 2*(4). Retrieved from http://www.nova.edu/ssss/QR/QR2-4/hernandez.html

Herrmann, A. F. (2012). "I know I'm unlovable": Desperation, dislocation, despair, and discourse on the academic job hunt. *Qualitative Inquiry, 18*(3), 247–55.

Hicks, E., & Hicks, J. (2000, July 18). *Abraham Workshop recording* [CD]. St. Louis, MO.

Hicks, E., & Hicks, J. (2004). *Ask and it is given: Learning to manifest your desires.* Carlsbad, CA: Hay House.

Hicks, E., & Hicks, J. (2006). *The law of attraction: The basics of the teachings of Abraham.* Carlsbad, CA: Hay House.

Hicks, E., & Hicks, J. (2008). *Money, and the law of attraction: Learning to attract wealth, health, and happiness.* Carlsbad, CA: Hay House.

Hicks, E., & Hicks, J. (2009). *The vortex: Where the law of attraction assembles all cooperative relationships.* Carlsbad, CA: Hay House.

Homer. (2006). *The Odyssey* (R. Fagles, Trans.). New York, NY: Penguin. Written c. 800 BCE.

Howitt, D. (2014, June 20). We need more entrepreneurs who are healers. *ATT Business Circle.* Retrieved from https://bizcircle.att.com/articles/need-entrepreneurs-healers/#fbid=amFqKQF3tgW

Jacobs, J. A., & Winslow, S. E. (2004). Overworked faculty: Job stresses and family demands. *Annals of the American Academy of Political and Social Science, 596*(1), 104–29.

Jain, R. (2005). *15 tips for Ph.D. completion.* Retrieved from www.CompleteYourDissertation.com

Jain, R. (2011). *Get it done: A coach's guide to dissertation success.* Gaithersburg, MD: Moonswept Press.

Jain, R. (2014a, October 19). The culture of suffering. *PhD365.* Retrieved from http://completeyourdissertation.com/blog/575/the-culture-of-suffering/

Jain, R. (2014b). *Feel better first.* Retrieved from http://completeyourdissertation.com/blog/54/feel-better-first/.

Jaschik, S. (2007, December 7). Hope on Ph.D. attrition rates—Except in humanities. *Inside Higher Ed.* Retrieved from https://www.insidehighered.com/news/2007/12/07/doctoral

Jaschik, S. (2008, September 9). Ph.D. completion gaps. *Inside Higher Ed.* Retrieved from http://www.insidehighered.com/news/2008/09/09/gaps

Jaschik, S. (2010, September 14). For first time, more women than men earn PhD. *USA Today.* Retrieved from http://usatoday30.usatoday.com/news/education/2010-09-15-womenphd14_st_N.htm

Josephson, M. (2012, March 29). "Those who mind don't matter and those who matter don't mind."—Bernard Baruch. *What Will Matter.* Retrieved from http://whatwillmatter.com/2012/03/quote-be-who-you-are-and-say-what-you-feel-because-those-who-mind-dont-matter-and-those-who-matter-dont-mind-dr-seuss/

Joyner, R. L., Rouse, W. A., & Glatthorn, A. A. (2012). *Writing the winning thesis or dissertation: A step-by-step guide* (3rd ed.). Thousand Oaks, CA: Corwin.

Kalambakal, V. (2014). The advantages of being an older student. *Back to College.* Retrieved from http://www.back2college.com/advantage.htm

Kasworm, C. E. (2010). Adult learners in a research university: Negotiating undergraduate student identity. *Adult Education Quarterly, 60*(2), 143–60.

Kearns, H., Gardiner, M., & Marshall, K. (2008). Innovation in PhD completion: The hardy shall succeed (and be happy!). *Higher Education Research and Development, 27*(1), 77–89. doi:10.1080/07294360701658781

Kelsky, K. (2015). *The professor is in: The essential guide to turning your Ph.D. into a job.* New York, NY: Crown/Three Rivers/Random House.

Kena, G., Aud, S., Johnson, F., Wang, X., Zhang, J., Rathbun, A., . . . Kristapovich, P. (2014). *The condition of education 2014* (NCES 2014-083). U.S. Department of Education, National Center for Education Statistics. Washington, DC. Retrieved from http://nces.ed.gov/pubs2014/2014083.pdf

King, S. B., & Williams, F. K. (2014). Barriers to completing the dissertation as perceived by education leadership doctoral students. *Community College Journal of Research and Practice, 38*(2/3), 275–79.

Kruger, H., & Bevan-Dye, A. (2010). Guidelines for the editing of dissertations and theses: A survey of editors' perceptions. *Southern African Linguistics and Applied Language Studies 28*(2), 153–69.

Lakein, A. (1989). *How to get control of your time and your life.* New York, NY: Signet/Penguin.

Larson, C. (2008, October 22). Older, and wiser, students. *New York Times.* Retrieved from http://www.nytimes.com/2008/10/23/business/retirement/23DEGREE.html?_r=0

L'Engle, M. (1971). *A circle of quiet.* New York, NY: HarperCollins.

Lesser, L. M. (2014). Overcoming statistics anxiety and being successful in data analysis. In J. A. Rockinson-Szapkiw, & L. S. Spaulding, (Eds.), *Navigating the doctoral journey: A handbook of strategies for success* (pp. 65–76). Lanham, MD: Rowman & Littlefield.

Marte, J. (2013, August 19). 10 things grad schools won't tell you. *MarketWatch*. Retrieved from http://www.marketwatch.com/story/10-things-grad-schools-wont-tell-you-2013-08-15

Martin, A. (2005). Plagiarism and collaboration: Suggestions for "Defining and Avoiding Plagiarism: The WPA Statement on Best Practices." *WPA: Writing Program Administration, 28*(3), 57–71. Retrieved from http://www.wpacouncil.org/archives/28n3/28n3martin.pdf

Mayo Clinic (2014, July 19). *Meditation: A simple, fast way to reduce stress*. Retrieved from http://www.mayoclinic.org/tests-procedures/meditation/in-depth/meditation/art-20045858?pg=1

McCoy, D. L., & Gardner, S. K. (2011). The transition from full-time employment to full-time graduate student: A qualitative exploration of master's and doctoral students' experiences in higher education programs. *Enrollment Management Journal, 5*(1), 84–109.

Melnick, M. (2013, April 30). Meditation health benefits: What the practice does to your body. *Huffington Post*. Retrieved from http://www.huffingtonpost.com/ 2013/04/30/ meditationhealth-benefits_n_3178731.html

Miller, C. A. (2014, December 16). The surprising science of self-affirmations. *Caroline Adams Miller MAPP*. Retrieved from http://www.carolinemiller.com/surprising-science-self- affirmations/

Mitchell, M. (2013, May 29). Dr. Herbert Benson's relaxation response. *Psychology Today*. Retrieved from http://www.psychologytoday.com/blog/heart-and-soul-healing/201303/dr-herbert-benson-s-relaxation-response

Mulholland, J. (2011). What I've learned about revising a dissertation. *Journal of Scholarly Publishing, 43*(1), 39–51.

Murphy, J. (1982). *Quiet moments with God*. Marina del Rey, CA: DeVorss. Originally published 1958.

Murphy, J. (1986). *Your infinite power to be rich*. Paramus, NJ: Prentice Hall.

Murphy, J. (1987). *Special meditations for health, wealth, love, and expression*. Marina del Rey, CA: DeVorss. Originally published 1952.

Murphy, J. (2001). *The amazing laws of cosmic mind power* (Rev. I. D. McMahan). Paramus, NJ: Prentice Hall.

National Center for Complementary and Alternative Medicine. (2013). *Relaxation techniques for health: An introduction*. Retrieved from http://nccam.nih.gov/health/stress/relaxation.htm

National Center for Education Statistics. (2012). *Digest of Education Statistics. Table 310.* Degrees conferred by degree-granting institutions, by level of degree and sex of student: Selected years, 1869-70 through 2012-22. Retrieved from http://nces.ed.gov/programs/digest/d12/tables/dt12_310.asp?referrer=report

National Center for Education Statistics. (2013). *Digest of education statistics. Table 324.80.* Statistical profile of persons receiving doctor's degrees, by field of study and selected characteristics: 2009–10 and 2010–11. Retrieved from http://nces.ed.gov/programs/digest/d13/tables/dt13_324.80.asp?current=yes

National Center for Education Statistics. (2014). *Digest of education statistics: 2012*. Retrieved from http://nces.ed.gov/programs/digest/d12/ch_3.asp

Offerman, M. (2011). Profile of the nontraditional doctoral degree student. *New Directions in Adult Continuing Education, 129*, 21–30.

Parry, M. (2010, January 26). Colleges see 17 percent increase in online enrollment. *Chronicle of Higher Education*. Retrieved from http://chronicle.com/blogs/wiredcampus/ colleges-see-17-percent-increase-in-online-enrollment/20820.

Peligri, J. (2014, July 27). Underpaid and overworked: Adjunct professors share their stories. *USA Today.* Retrieved from http://college.usatoday.com/2014/07/17/underpaid-and-overworked-adjunct-professors-share-their-stories/

Peters, R. L. (1997). *Getting what you came for: The smart student's guide to earning a Master's or Ph.D.* (rev. ed.). New York, NY: Farrar, Straus & Giroux.

Ph.D. Completion Project. (2014). *Project information: Overview.* Retrieved from http://phdcompletion.org/information/index.asp

Pinker, S. (2014, September 26). Why academics stink at writing. *Chronicle of Higher Education.* Retrieved from http://m.chronicle.com/article/Why-Academics-Writing-Stinks/148989/

Pinker, S., Munger, M. C., Sword, H., Toor, R., & MacPhail, T. (2014). *Why academic writing stinks and how to fix it.* New York, NY: Chronicle of Higher Education. Retrieved from http://chronicle.com/article/Why-Academics-Stink-at/149105?cid=inline-promo

Plimpton, G. (1986). E. L. Doctorow: The art of fiction no. 94. *Paris Review, 101.* Retrieved from http://www.theparisreview.org/interviews/2718/the-art-of-fiction-no-94-e-l-doctorow

Richardson, C. (2009). *Take time for your life.* New York, NY: Broadway Books/Random House. Originally published 1999.

Richmond, C. J. (2007). *A study of intake and assessment in solution-focused brief therapy* (Unpublished doctoral dissertation). Western Michigan University, Kalamazoo, MI. Retrieved from ProQuest Dissertations and Theses database (ProQuest document ID: 445049571).

Rico, G. (2000). *Writing the natural way.* New York, NY: Tarcher/Putnam.

Roberts, C. M. (2010). *The dissertation journey: A practical and comprehensive guide to planning, writing, and defending your dissertation* (2nd ed.). Thousand Oaks, CA: Corwin.

Rockinson-Szapkiw, A. J. (2011). Improving doctoral candidates' persistence in the online dissertation process. Faculty Publications and Presentations. Paper 184. Retrieved from http://digitalcommons.liberty.edu/educ_fac_pubs/184

Rockinson-Szapkiw, A. J., & Spaulding, L. S. (Eds.) (2014). *Navigating the doctoral journey: A handbook of strategies for success.* Lanham, MD: Rowman & Littlefield.

Rosenthal, R., & Jacobson, L. (2003). *Pygmalion in the classroom: Teacher expectation and pupils' intellectual development.* Norwalk, CT: Crown House Publishing. Originally published 1968.

Rothenberg, A. (1979). *The emerging goddess: The creative process in art, science, and other fields.* Chicago, IL: University of Chicago Press.

Rudestam, K. E., & Newton, R. R. (2014). *Surviving your dissertation: A comprehensive guide to content and process* (4th ed.). Thousand Oaks, CA: Sage.

Schaffenberg, I. (2014, November). Three ways to reignite our writing. *Author Magazine.* Retrieved from http://www.authormagazine.org/articles/2014_11_schaffenburg.html

Sclamberg, A. (2014, October 1). 4 things you need to know to get a life you love. *Huffington Post.* Retrieved from http://www.huffingtonpost.com/alexis-sclamberg/4-things-you-need-to-know_3_b_5898094.html?utm_hp_ref=meditation

Seppala, E. (2013, October 17). Benefits of meditation: 10 science-based reasons to start meditating today [Web log post]. *Emma Seppala, Ph.D.: The Science of Happiness, Health & Social Connection.* Retrieved from http://www.emmaseppala.com/10-science-based-reasons-start-meditating-today-infographic/#.VCNhbPk7tr8

Seto, A., & Bruce, M. A. (Eds.). (2013). *Women's retreat: Voices of female faculty in higher education.* Lanham, MD: University Press of America.

Shore, B. M. (2014). *The graduate advisor handbook: A student-centered approach.* Chicago, IL: University of Chicago Press.

Siegel, B. S. (1998). *Love, medicine and miracles: Lessons learned about self-healing from a surgeon's experience with exceptional patients.* New York, NY: HarperCollins.

Siegel, B. S. (2013). *The art of healing: Uncovering your inner wisdom and potential for self healing.* Novato, CA: New World Library.

Smallwood, S. (2004, January 16). Doctor dropout: High attribution from Ph.D. programs is sucking away time, talent, and money and breaking some hearts, too. *Chronicle of Higher Education, 50*(19), A10. Retrieved from http://chronicle.com/weekly/v50/i19/19a01001.htm

Sousa, D. A. (2011). *How the brain learns.* Thousand Oaks, CA: Corwin Press.

Sowell, R. T. (2010, November 9). *The CGS Ph.D. Completion Project: A study of doctoral completion at selected universities in the US and Canada.* Presentation at 2010 North Carolina State Graduate School Symposium, Raleigh, NC. Retrieved from http://www.ncsu.edu/grad/about-grad/docs/cgs-phd-completion-project.pdf

Spaulding, L. S., & Rockinson-Szapkiw, A. J. (2012). Hearing their voices: Factors doctoral candidates attribute to their persistence. *International Journal of Doctoral Studies, 7,* 199–219.

Stallone, M. N. (2004). Factors associated with student attrition and retention in an educational leadership doctoral program. *Journal of College Teaching and Learning, 1* (6), 17–24. Retrieved from http://www.cluteinstitute.com/ojs/index.php/TLC/article/view/1952/1931

Sterne, N. (1983). *Tyrannosaurus wrecks: A book of dinosaur riddles.* Harper Trophy edition. New York, NY: Thomas Y. Crowell/Harper & Row. Hardcover edition 1979.

Sterne, N. (2011). *Trust your life: Forgive yourself and go after your dreams.* Unity Village, MO: Unity Books.

Sterne, N. (2012, December 28). My life (not quite) in academia. *The Irascible Professor.* Retrieved from http://irascibleprofessor.com/comments-12-28-12.htm

Sterne, N. (2013a, August 26). Send love ahead. *Transformation Magazine.* Retrieved from http://www.etransformationguide.com/guide/article/send-love-ahead.html Also published in *Transform your life: Expert advice, practical tools and personal stories* (2014, pp. 159–61). Clearwater, FL: Transformation Services.

Sterne, N. (2013b, September 25). The diaper method. *Authors' Blog, Author Magazine.* Retrieved from http://authormagazineonline.wordpress.com/2013/09/25/the-diaper method/

Sterne, N. (2014, October). Dissertation interruptus: 7 cautionary tales. *Women in Higher Education, 23*(10), 16, 17, 19.

Sterne, N. (2015a, April 21). How to choose your chair. *GradShare.* Retrieved from http://www.proquest.com/blog/gradshare/2015/How-to-Choose-Your-Chair.html

Sterne, N. (2015b, Spring). How to choose your perfect dissertation topic. *Graduate Schools Magazine,* pp. 12, 13, 15.

Stillman, J. (2014, October 2). 7 techniques to handle toxic people. Inc.com. Retrieved from http://www.inc.com/jessica-stillman/7-techniques-to-handle-toxic-people.html.

Stokes, D. (2005). Graduate culture. *Diverse: Issues in Higher Education.* Retrieved from http://diverseeducation.com/article/4730/

Storms, B. A., Prada, M. J., & Donahue, E. N. (2011). Advising doctoral candidates to degree completion. *Educational Leadership and Administration: Teaching and Program Development, 23,* 85–92.

Sword, H. (2012, June 3). Inoculating against jargonitis. *Chronicle of Higher Education, 58*(38). Retrieved from http://chronicle.com/article/Inoculating-Against-Jargonitis/132039/

Teilhard de Chardin, P. (1961). *The phenomenon of man.* New York, NY: Harper Torchbooks. Originally published 1955.

Trafton, A. (2011, May 5). The benefits of meditation. *MIT News.* Retrieved from http://newsoffice.mit.edu/2011/meditation-0505

Unity. (2012, November 30). Clarity. *Daily Word, 150*(9), 41. Unity Village, MO: Author.

Unity. (2015a, January 4). Authenticity. *Daily Word, 153*(1), 17. Unity Village, MO: Author.

Unity. (2015b, February 9). Guidance. *Daily Word, 153*(1), 58. Unity Village, MO: Author.

Van Aswegen, E. S. (2007). Postgraduate supervision: The role of the (language) editor: Sed quis custodiet ipsos custodes? (Juvenal, Satire 6, 346–48) [Who will guard the guardians?]. *South African Journal of Higher Education: Postgraduate Supervision 2007: Special Edition, 8, 21,* 1142–54.

Walker, G., Golde, C., Jones, L., Bueschel, A., & Hutchinson, P. (2008). *The formation of scholars: Rethinking doctoral education for the twenty-first century*. Stanford, CA: Carnegie Foundation for the Advancement of Teaching.

Ward, K., & Wolf-Wendel, L. (2012). *Academic motherhood: How faculty manage work and family*. New Brunswick, NJ: Rutgers University Press.

Ward, P. R. (2012, November 12). Doctoral student sues Duquesne U. over unfinished dissertation. *Pittsburgh Post-Gazette.* Retrieved from http://www.post-gazette.com/stories/business/legal/doctoral-student-sues-duquesne-u-over-unfinished-dissertation-661665/

Warner, J. (2008). The conversation. In E. Evans & C. Grant (Eds), *Mama, PhD: Women write about motherhood and academic life* (pp. 3–10). New Brunswick, NJ: Rutgers University Press.

Weil, A. (2000). *Spontaneous healing: How to discover and embrace your body's natural ability to maintain and heal itself.* New York, NY: Ballantine Books.

Weil, A. (2007). *8 weeks to optimum health: A proven program for taking full advantage of your body's natural healing power*. New York, NY: Ballantine Books.

West, L. C. (2014). Communicating needs and nurturing familial relationships. In J. A. Rockinson-Szapkiw & L. S. Spaulding (Eds.), *Navigating the doctoral journey: A handbook of strategies for success* (pp. 19–30). Lanham, MD: Rowman & Littlefield.

West, I. J., Gokalp, G., Peña, E. V., Fischer, L., & Gupton, J. (2011). Exploring effective support practices for doctoral students' degree completion. *College Student Journal, 45*(2), 310– 23.

Wheatley, M. (2006). *Leadership and the new science: Discovering order in a chaotic world.* San Francisco, CA: Berrett-Koehler.

Wiener, J. (2012). *Historians in trouble: Plagiarism, fraud, and politics in the ivory tower.* New York, NY: New Press.

Wilbur, R. (1969). Walking to sleep. In *Walking to sleep: New poems and translations*. New York, NY: Harcourt Brace & Jovanovich World.

Williamson, M. (2000, October). Meditation. *O, The Oprah Magazine,* Retrieved from http://www.oprah.com/spirit/Marianne-Williamson-Trust-is-Shorthand-for-Going-With-the-Flow

Woods, G. (2010). *English grammar for dummies* (2nd ed.). Hoboken, NJ: Wiley.

Zhao, C. M., Golde, C. M., & McCormick, A. C. (2007). More than a signature: How advisor choice and advisor behaviour affect doctoral student satisfaction. *Journal of Further and Higher Education, 31*(3), 263–81.

Xia, J. (2013). *A mixed method study on students' experiences in the selection of a dissertation topic* (Unpublished doctoral dissertation). Arizona State University, Tempe, AZ. Retrieved from http://repository.asu.edu/attachments/114540/content/Xia_asu_0010E_13176.pdf

Selected Resources

Note: These are just a few resources that clients and I have found particularly helpful. Many more could be added, but you have enough to read.

Abraham-Hicks. The teachings of Abraham. http://www.abraham-hicks.com/lawofattractionsource/about_abraham.php

American Psychological Association of Graduate Students (APAGS). http://www.apa.org/apags/index.aspx Also their magazine: *gradPsych.* http://www.gradpsych-digital.org/gradpsych

Association for Support of Graduate Students. http://www.asgs.org

Chronicle of Higher Education. http://chronnicle.com

A Course in Miracles. http://acim.org/index.html

Deepak Chopra. http://www.chopra.com

Diverse: Issues in Higher Education. http://diverseeducation.com/

Huffington Post: College. http://www.huffingtonpost.com/college/

Grad Resources. http://www.gradresources.org/menus/about.shtml

Graduate Schools Magazine. www.gradschoolsmag.com

National Association of Graduate-Professional Students. http://nagps.org

Qualitative Report. http://www.nova.edu/ssss/QR/index.html

The Thesis Whisperer. http://thesiswhisperer.com

Unity. http://www.unity.org

A Short Glossary of Important Acronyms

ABD: All but dissertation [the traditional]
ABD: Ain't barely done
ABD: All but disgusted
AD: After dissertation
ADD: Almost-done doctors
ADHD: Almost-doctor hot dog
AYDY: Aren't you done *yet*?
BD: Before dissertation
DGI: Don't give up
DUH: How you feel reading your results
FFD: Finally freakin' done!
FFR: Final frustrating review
IRB: Irritating rattling brass
IRDI: I really did it!
LAD: Life after dissertation
LWOD: Life without the dissertation
PHM: Please hire me
PDD: Post-dissertation depression
PPD (alternate): Post-parting depression
TDAFM: Terminal degree that almost finished me
YAY: Yippee! OO-RAH!

Index

Note: Names appearing in text citations and the reference list are not indexed here.

ABD. *See* "all but dissertation" (ABD)
Abraham (spiritual guide), 30, 31, 37, 56, 119. *See also* Hicks, E.; Hicks, J.
academic language, 60. *See also* writing, academic
Academic Motherhood: How Faculty Manage Work and Family (Ward & Wolf-Wendel), 71, 81, 153
academic nag, xxii, xxiii, xxiv, xxix–xxx, 21, 171
academic writing. *See* writing
affirmations: for academic job hunts, 162, 166; courageous for plunging into proposal, 43; for your defense, 155; for discipline, 58; for dissertation challenges, 172; doctoral-related, 8–9; for employers and coworkers, 106–107; for family support, 88–89; for friends, 94–95, 98; for harmony with committee and chair, 135; on health, 57; higher self, 36; about the Inner Mentor, 21; for letting friends go, 96; for life after dissertation, 164; while meditating, 9; mentioned, xxviii, 24, 84, 120, 134; post-dissertation frenzy, 164; for publications, 168; on realizing your dream, 162; on resisting temptation to take a break, 58; on right position after degree, 166; for right time and timing, 27; self-programming, 16; self-talk as, 15; for settling in, 50; for sticking with it, 65; for strengthening your life dream, 8–9; time management, 26; on topic selection, 40; for university support sources, 149–150; for work and coworkers, 107; for workplace harmony, 107. *See also* spirituality
Alice in Wonderland, 43
Alidina, S., 10
"all but dissertation" (ABD), xv, xx, xxiii, 3, 13, 52, 104, 114, 121, 185
Allen, D., 41, 63
American Heritage Dictionary, 48
American Psychological Association (APA) Manual (2010), xxviii, 48; use of APA style, 115, 146, 147, 156, 166
anthropomorphisms, 48
APA. See *American Psychological Association (APA) Manual* (2010)
Archer, S.A., 112

Barnes, B.J., 112
Baruch, B., 15
Benson, H., 9, 56
Benson-Henry Institute for Mind Body Medicine, 9
Bernstein, A., 84
Billhult, A., 129
Bodian, S., 10, 20
Bolker, J., 138
Bradberry, T., 73, 84, 95, 103, 103–104, 104
brain, using both sides of, 61
breaks: balanced, 62, 63; with family, 64; scheduling, 65
Bregman, P., 134–135
Brisk, S., 118
Bruce, M.A., 71, 81
Burawoy, M., 126, 127, 131, 171
Butterworth, E., 29

Calabrese, R.L., 42

calendar scheduling, 23, 26. *See also* time management
Cameron, J., 95
candidates, xix; attrition rate of, xix–xx, 159; demographics of, xxvi–xxvii; increasing numbers of, xix; learning to say no, 71, 72–73; major barriers to success, 112–113; profiles of, 4–5; reasons for pursuing a PhD, 4–5. *See also* graduate students; lifestyle changes; personal growth
Carter-Veale, W., 41, 42, 144
Cassuto, L., 117, 120, 124, 125–126, 126, 131, 147–148, 167, 168
chair(s), xxiii; changing, 132, 132–134; conscientious, 114; continued professional relationship with, 168; demands for revisions from, 74, 117, 131–132, 145, 155; estranged relationship with, 127–128; friendly relationship with, 124–127; ideal relationship with, 128–129; lack of guidance from, xxiv–xxv, 113; letters of recommendation from, 166; thanking, 166; and topic selection, 123–124; working through differences with, 134–135. *See also* chair selection; professors
chair selection, 114–115; gathering information for, 115–116; gut reaction to, 119–120; positive traits of chair, 117–118; questions to ask about chair, 116–117; questions to ask yourself, 118–119. *See also* chair(s)
chaos theory, 60
children: complaints from, 78; dates with, 81; involving for support, 79, 79–80. *See also* family(ies)
Chopra, D., 20, 29, 32, 33, 34, 135
clarification, 131–132
coaches, 143–145, 149
coauthoring, 167
colleagues, envious, 105–106
college courses, 11
colloquialisms, 48
committee(s): changing, 132, 132–134; continued professional relationship with, xxiv, 168; demands for revisions from, 74, 117, 131–132, 145, 155; designing the perfect, 120–121; estranged relationship with, 127; letters of recommendation from, 166; negative characterization of, 113; thanking, 166; working through differences with, 134–135. *See also* professors
committee chair(s). *See* chair(s)
committee chair selection. *See* chair selection
computer lab technicians, xxiii, 139–140, 149
Connelly, R., 71, 81
contractions, 48
A Course in Miracles, 20, 30
Covey, S.R., 7
coworkers: dealing with, 99. *See also* workplace
Cozart, S.C., 35

Dearman, J., xx
defense, xxiii; experiences, 153–154; suggestions for, 154–155; visualization of, 155
degree (PhD): benefits to your company, 101; as major accomplishment, 159; others' reasons for pursuing, 4–5; practical application of, xxiv, 6; your reasons for pursuing, 5–6, 74, 162
Diaper Method, 46, 163
Dickens, C., 22–23, 92
discipline, 59
Disney, W., 8
dissertation(s): challenges involved in writing, xxi; components of, xxi–xxii; consistency of format and style, 146; converting to an article, 166–167; dedication and acknowledgements, xxix; fear of finishing, 57–58; making the proposal, 41–43; organizing in files, 43, 45; problem statement (PS)/ statement of the problem, 42; publication as book, 167; requesting an extension for, 53–54; revision demands, 131–132; right topic

considerations, 38–40; topic considerations, 38; topic selection, 41. *See also* defense; extensions; leave of absence; post-dissertation
dissertation committee. *See* committee
dissertation committee chair. *See* chair(s)
dissertation committee chair selection. *See* chair selection
"Dissertation Interruptus: 7 Cautionary Tales" (Sterne), xxviii
dissertation seminars, 12
doctoral candidates. *See* candidates
Doctorow, E.L., 47
Dossey, L., 56
dream(s): affirmations for strengthening, 8–9; degree as part of, xxii, xxiii, 4–6; visualizing, 7–8, 162
Dyer, W., 8, 34, 37, 89, 135

Eat, Pray, Love (Gilbert), 20
editing, levels of, 146
editors, 143, 145–147, 149
The Emerging Goddess (Rothenberg), 61
Emotional Guidance System, 119
emotional words, 48
employers: dealing with, 99; enlisting support from, 100–101; informing of advantages of your degree, 101; jealous, 103–104; negotiation with, 102–103; toxic attitude of, 103–105. *See also* workplace
English Grammar for Dummies (Woods), 139
Esposito, J., 126
euphemisms, 48
Evans, E., 71, 81
Exkorn, K.S., 10
exercise (physical), 63–64
exercises (mental): icon identifying, xxiv; list what your degree will do for you, 6; listening to your Inner Mentor, 21; meditation, 9–10; write out your dream and the place of the degree in it, 5–6
extensions: limits on, 54, 55; requesting, 53–54
faculty review, 155–156
family(ies), xxiii; attempts at sabotage by, xxiii, 82; bribing for support, 74–75, 80–81, 82; complaints from children, 78; complaints from partners, 77–78; educating, 73–74, 82; after graduation, 164–165; holiday strategies, 82–83; involving children for support, 79, 79–80; involving partners for support, 79; pressure from, 58, 70, 71, 81; questions from, 84–85, 157–158; support from, 71–72, 85; taking breaks with, 64; toxic influence of, 83–84. *See also* children; partners
Faust (Goethe), 33
fear of finishing, 57–58
Fox, E., 32
Frank, J., 30
friends, xxiii; assuring them of your love, 97; jealousies and putdowns from, 94; need to let go of, 95–96; opposition from, 91; pressure from, 52, 58, 70, 92; supportive, 97–98; taking breaks with, 64; tough questions from, 96
"From 'Bitch' to 'Mentor': A Doctoral Student's Story of Self-Change and Mentoring" (Gearity & Mertz), 114, 127, 133
From Inquiry to Academic Writing (Greene & Lidinsky), 49

Gardiner, M., 57
Gearity, B.T., 114, 127, 133
Germano, W., 167
Ghodsee, K., 71, 81
Gilbert, E., 20
Glatthorn, A.A., 42
goal setting: after graduation, xxiii, 161–162; "later list", 26–27, 163–164
God consciousness, 35. *See also* Inner Mentor (IM)
Goethe, J.W. von, 33
Golde, C.M., 69
Grad Resources, xxix
The Graduate Advisor Handbook (Shore), 116
graduate courses, xix, 11

graduate school culture, 69
graduate students: as mentors, 137–138, 149; older, 130. *See also* candidates
graduation, xxiii; enjoying, 156–157, 158; preparation for, 156; regaining momentum after, 161
Grant, C., 71, 81, 114, 115, 118, 125, 129, 131
gratitude, 168
Greene, S., 49
Gunnarsson, R., 129

Harra, C., 20, 29
Harvard Medical School, 9
Hawkins, D.R., 88
Hay, L., 8, 56, 149, 172
Hernandez, L.L., 118–119, 120
Herrmann, A.F., 166
Hicks, E., 30, 150, 166
Hicks, J., 30, 150, 166
holiday strategies, 82–83
Homer, 54
Howitt, D., 106
humility, 128
"'I Know I'm Unlovable': Desperation, Dislocation, Despair, and Discourse on the Academic Job Hunt" (Herrmann), 166

illness, 55, 55–56; connected to dissertation work, 56; mind-body connection of, 56
Inner Mentor (IM), 19–21; and the chair selection process, 118, 120; guidance from, 47, 135; involvement in the writing process, 47, 50; post-dissertation advice from, 164; as provider of answers, 20, 30–32; and university support, 150. *See also* God consciousness; spirituality
Inner Writing Judge, 46–47
intention, 33–34

Jacobson, L., 88
Jain, R., 45, 158–159
jargon, avoiding, 48, 49
Jonasson, G., 129
Joyner, R.L., 42, 48

Katz, G., 73
Kearns, H., 57
Kelsky, K., 165

Lakein, A., 26
"Later List", 26–27, 163–164
Law of Detachment, 34–35
Law of Intention and Desire, 33–34
Law of Least Effort (Law of Relaxation), 32–33
learning centers, 139, 149
leave of absence, 51, 53, 54
L'Engle, M., 49, 50
letters of recommendation, 166
librarians, xxiii, 141–142, 143, 149
Lidinsky, A., 49
lifestyle changes, xx, xxiii, 11–12; declaring readiness, 15–16; lack of leisure, 13–15; lack of structure, 12–13; making adjustments, 15
list keeping, 26–27

MacPhail, T., 49
Mama, PhD: Women Write About Motherhood and Academic Life (Evans & Grant), 71, 81, 153
Marshall, K., 57
Massachusetts General Hospital, 9
meditation, 9–10, 64
Meditation for Dummies (Bodian), 10
mentors, fellow students as, 137–138, 149
Mertz, N., 114, 127, 133
Mind/Body Medical Institute, 9
Mindfulness for Dummies (Alidina), 10
Mulholland, J., 167
Munger, M.C., 49
Murphy, J., 8
"My Life (Not Quite) in Academia" (Sterne), xxviii

New Thought teachings, 20
Newton, R.R., xxi, 42
New York City Academic Network, xxvii

Odysseus and the Sirens, 54
Odyssey (Homer), 54
Offerman, M., 130

partners: complaints from, 77–78; dates with, 80; friction with, 85–87; having "hard talk" with, 87–88; involving for support, 79. *See also* family(ies)
passive verbs, 48
peers: dissertation support groups, 138, 149; as mentors, 137–138, 149
personal growth: and gratitude, 168; questions for reflection, 168–169
PhD. *See* degree (PhD)
Ph.D. Completion Project, xix, xx
Pinker, S., 48, 49
plagiarism, 49
politics, xxiii, xxiv, 169
post-dissertation: advice from Inner Mentor, 164; affirmations, 168; applying for positions, xxiii, 165–166; dream visualization, 161; and the "later list", 163–164; planning your payoffs, 165–167; publication, 166–167; questions from family, 157–158; reconnecting with family, 164–165; regaining momentum, 161; schedule for career actualization, 163; setting goals, 161–162
post-dissertation depression (PDD), 158
The Power of Intention: Learning to Co-create Your World Your Way (Dyer), 34
Power vs. Force (Hawkins), 88
priorities, 21–23
problem statement (PS)/statement of the problem, 42
The Professor Is In: The Essential Guide to Turning Your PhD Into a Job (Kelsky), 165
Professor Mommy: Finding Work-Family Balance in Academia (Connelly & Ghodsee), 71, 81, 153
professors: commitments of, xix, 111–112; former, xxiii, 147–148, 149; former, letters of recommendation from, 166; former, thanking, 166; grudges and biases of, 112; lack of common background with, 112; negative attributes of, 112; relationships with, xxiv. *See also* chair(s); committee
publication: of articles, 166–167, 167; coauthoring, 167; of dissertation as book, 167

questions : from family members, 84–85, 157–158; from friends, 96; for reflection, 168–169

red tape, 156
redundancy, 48
The Relaxation Response (Benson), 9
researchers, 141, 149
revisions: committee and chair demands for, 74, 117, 131–132, 145, 155; made by editors, 146, 147; for peer review journals, 148, 167
rewards, 22, 46
Richardson, C., 84
Richmond, C.J., 19
Rico, G.L., 61
Rockinson-Szapkiw, A.J., 131
Rosenthal, R., 88
Rothenberg, A., 61
Rouse, W.A., 42
Rudestam, K.E., xxi, 42

Schaffenberg, I., 63
schedule, for career actualization, 163
scholarly writing style. *See* writing, academic
Schulz, M.L., 56
secretaries, 141, 142–143, 149
self-assessment, 168–169
self-discipline, 59–60
self-respect, 129, 130
self-sabotage, 57
Seto, A., 71, 81
Seven Spiritual Laws of Success (Chopra), 32
Shore, B.M., 116
Siegel, B.S., 56
Sisyphus metaphor, 42
sleep benefits, 64
Sowell, R.T., xix, xx
Spaulding, L.S., 131
spiritual laws: Law of Detachment, 34–35; Law of Intention and Desire, 33–34; Law of Least Effort (Law of

Relaxation), 32–33
spirituality, xxii, xxiv, 7–8, 19, 20; acknowledgement of, 35–36; defined, 35; spiritual nature of humans, 29–30. *See also* affirmations; Inner Mentor (IM)
statisticians, 140–141, 149
Sterne, N., xxv, xxviii, 23, 94, 147, 153
Stillman, J., 95
students. *See* candidates; graduate students
style, consistency in, 146
support: coaches, 143–145, 149; editors, 143, 145–147, 149; peer dissertation groups, 138, 149. *See also* family(ies); friends; university support
Swift, J., xxv, 124
Sword, H., 49

teaching jobs, applying for, 165, 166
tech support, xxiii, 139–140, 149
Teilhard de Chardin, P., 29
television watching, 64
"Three-Winged Bird" (Wheatley), 60
time management, 23–24, 58; calendar scheduling, 23, 26; keeping promises to self, 24–25; listing of tasks, 24; principle of doing something, 25
Tomal, D.R., 114, 115, 118, 125, 129, 131
Toor, R., 49
toxicity: in family relationships, 83–84; in work relationships, 103–105
Trust Your Life (Sterne), xxv, xxviii, 19, 94
Turnitin, 49
"two minute rule", 63
Tyrannosaurus Wrecks: A Book of Dinosaur Riddles (Sterne), xxviii

Unity Village, 20
university support, xxiii, 148–149, 150; computer lab technicians, 139–140, 149; fellow students as mentors, 137–138, 149; learning centers, 139, 149; librarians, 141–142, 149; peer dissertation support groups, 138, 149; previous professors, 147–148, 149; researchers, 141, 149; secretaries, 141, 142–143, 149; statisticians, 140–141, 149

Van Aswegen, E.S., 145
visualization, 7–8, 88, 155
volunteer activities, postponing, 92–93
"Walking to Sleep" (Wilbur), 31

Walsh, J., 49
Ward, K., 71, 81
Warner, J., 15
Weil, A., 56
"We Need More Entrepreneurs Who Are Healers" (Howitt), 106
Wheatley, M., 60
"When Your Graduate Students Have Babies: Should Advisers Keep Silent or Raise the Family Issue Early On?" (Cassuto), 125
Why Academic Writing Stinks and How to Fix It (Pinker, Munger, Sword, Toor, & MacPhail), 49
"Why Academics Stink at Writing" (Pinker), 48
Wilbur, R., 31
Williams, E.A., 112
Williamson, M., 20
Wolf-Wendel, L., 71, 81
women: in academe, 71; as committee chairs, 126; family pressures of, 70–71, 72; lifestyle adjustments of, 15; vulnerability to diversions, 52; and work-life balance, 153
Women's Retreat: Voices of Female Faculty in Higher Education (Seto & Bruce), 71, 81, 153
workplace: demands of, xxiii; fostering peace in, 106. *See also* coworkers; employers
writing: academic, 48–49; allowing time for, 50; backing up files, 47; continuing at a nonlinear point, 60–61; distractions from, 52; getting started, 44, 45; help from Inner Mentor, 47; and the issue of balance, 62; and loss of momentum, 51; optimal conditions for, 62–63; reasonable breaks from, 62, 63–54; starting with the obvious/easy, 45;

style of, 47–48; taking leave of absence from, 53, 54; timing yourself, 46
writing centers, 139, 149

You'll See It When You Believe It (Dyer), 7

About the Author

Dr. Noelle Sterne has served doctoral students of all ages, nationalities, and backgrounds for thirty years in her academic coaching and editing practice. Having earned the PhD in English and comparative literature from Columbia University, she taught college composition and literature for several years. She was cofounder of the New York City Academic Network, a service organization of editorial professionals. She also coedited the dissertation style manual of the Office of Doctoral Studies, Teachers College, Columbia University, and a handbook answering doctoral students' most frequently asked questions.

Several articles have appeared based on *Challenges in Writing Your Dissertation*. These are in *The Irascible Professor, Women in Higher Education, Graduate Schools Magazine,* and *GradShare*. Additional articles are forthcoming.

A lifelong writer (mostly nonacademic), Dr. Sterne has published over 300 articles, essays, guest blogs, and columns in print and online venues, including *Author Magazine, Chicken Soup for the Soul, Children's Book Insider, Funds for Writers, Inspire Me Today, Pen & Prosper, Transformation Magazine, Unity Magazine, Writer's Digest, The Writer,* and *Women on Writing*. She is also a volunteer judge of other writers' manuscripts for *Rate Your Story*.

Her children's book of original riddles, *Tyrannosaurus Wrecks: A Book of Dinosaur Riddles* (HarperCollins), was in print for eighteen years and has been widely excerpted in children's magazines, humor collections, and teacher education textbooks. The book was featured on the first dinosaur show of the ongoing PBS television children's series, *Reading Rainbow*.

In Dr. Sterne's book *Trust Your Life: Forgive Yourself and Go After Your Dreams* (Unity Books), she helps readers release regrets, relabel their past, and reach lifelong yearnings. *Challenges in Writing Your Dissertation* follows in this tradition. This pragmatic and spiritual guidebook, a distillation of her years of practice, helps.

Visit Dr. Noelle Sterne at www.trustyourlifenow.com.